"Tearin' Up the Pea P...

15.
SP

EDITED BY ANDREW PAUL MELE

A Brooklyn Dodgers Reader
(McFarland, 2005; paperback 2010)

"Tearin' Up the Pea Patch"

The Brooklyn Dodgers, 1953

Andrew Paul Mele

McFarland & Company, Inc., Publishers
Jefferson, North Carolina

ISBN 978-0-7864-9620-4 (softcover : acid free paper) ∞
ISBN 978-1-4766-1926-2 (ebook)

LIBRARY OF CONGRESS CATALOGUING DATA ARE AVAILABLE

BRITISH LIBRARY CATALOGUING DATA ARE AVAILABLE

Front cover: 1953 Brooklyn Dodgers team (National Baseball
Hall of Fame Library, Cooperstown, New York)

Printed in the United States of America

*McFarland & Company, Inc., Publishers
Box 611, Jefferson, North Carolina 28640
www.mcfarlandpub.com*

Acknowledgments

It has been said that baseball is a team game played by individuals, and so it is with writing a book. The contributions vary in magnitude and intensity, but each leaves a mark that in the end proves to be a valuable addition to the result. A sacrifice bunt, a stolen base, a home run all show up in the box score. This game opened with some sterling advice from Donald Honig, arguably the most prolific writer of baseball books. I am most grateful for his kindness, encouragement and willingness to talk baseball and writing, two subjects in which his expertise is second to none.

I am equally grateful to Dave Anderson for his friendship and guidance. In 1953, before winning a Pulitzer Prize while writing for the *New York Times*, he covered the Brooklyn Dodgers for his hometown newspaper, the *Brooklyn Eagle*.

I appreciate the sharing of memories by those such as Joe Pignatano, a Brooklyn kid who got to play in Ebbets Field, and the sons of former players, Ernest Lavagetto, son of "Cookie," and Carl Furillo, Jr. Talking with these fellows provided more than material for the book; they stimulated a willing mind with fond memories of youthful adoration for this magnificent ball club. Of the 1953 Dodgers regulars, only one remains, and he is a Brooklyn icon. Carl Erskine pitched two no-hitters and set a World Series strikeout record in his Brooklyn years from 1948 to 1957.

On October 2, 1953, my dad and I sat in the center field bleachers at Ebbets Field and watched as "Oisk" sent 14 Yankee hitters back to the bench shaking their heads. To be able to speak of that great season with Carl and get the benefit of his exuberance, opinions and reminiscences was the single most essential ingredient in the making of a chronicle of this, his finest season.

I am indebted to Mark Levine of the Brooklyn Public Library for his constant vigilance of my work and Ben Gocker of the library's Brooklyn collection for allowing the use of marvelous photographs of the Dodgers of 1953. These were an essential source of information through the material contained in the old *Brooklyn Eagle*, once the "voice of the borough" and like the great ball club, eventually doomed to oblivion. My thanks to friends John Famulari, Victor Arroyo and Jim LoNano, who searched the internet for statistics and viable information. They all have my gratitude.

And always there is family, my wife, Mildred, for remembering Brooklyn with me, and my children and grandchild. Their support was far more than emotional, as valuable as that is. They were my conduit to the computer, advising which buttons to press and when to press them, saving me countless hours of guessing and criticizing the inanimate object on the desk in front of me.

This publication is blessed with the work of two great artists. One is the cartoon by Willard Mullin, the man who created Brooklyn's beloved "Bum," an enduring symbol since the thirties. I wish to thank Mullin's daughter, Shirley Mullin Rhodes, for the use of her dad's work.

Gabe Perillo, Jr., was kind enough to provide a portrait of Jackie Robinson by his dad, the brilliant artist Gabe Perillo, Sr. It is fitting that such accomplished artwork should complement the majesty of this brilliant 1953 Brooklyn Dodgers team.

Table of Contents

"The best thing about baseball today is its yesterdays"
—Lawrence Ritter

*"This game is starting out slow, but I guarantee you
before long they'll be tearin' up the pea patch"*
—Red Barber

Preface

The Gold in the Golden Age

"The 1953 Brooklyn team was the greatest Dodger team I played on."
—Carl Erskine, 1948–1957

Some called it baseball's golden age; it certainly was true in New York City. There were three major league teams that played there, and in the 11 seasons from 1947 to 1957, at least one of the three was in the World Series at the end of 10 campaigns. On seven occasions both combatants represented the Big Apple. There were 13 Most Valuable Player Awards presented to New York players. Fifteen players and managers are enshrined in the Baseball Hall of Fame at Cooperstown, New York.

But that was only the half of it. If you made the trip to Yankee Stadium, the Polo Grounds or Ebbets Field, you were treated to the sheer joy of seeing opposing players like Stan Musial, Henry Aaron, Willie Mays, Nellie Fox or Ted Kluszewski. Among the pitching greats of the time who challenged the New Yorkers were Warren Spahn, Robin Roberts, Bob Feller and that ageless phenomenon, Satchel Paige. We saw them all!

You could never minimize the excitement that was experienced by fans of the Giants, Yankees and the Dodgers, who lived in New York during those golden years, and if you came from Brooklyn, the joy, the heartbreak, and the passion was maximized beyond explanation. There was the lady who sat on the steps of her home—in Brooklyn they called it a "stoop"—in the Borough Park section minutes after Bobby Thomson had lined one into the left field seats at the Polo Grounds on Brooklyn's second saddest day in baseball, only a touch behind the day O'Malley took the team to L.A. She was crying, real tears, streaming down her cheeks as she moaned, *"Those stinkin' Giants!"* Four years later as Brooklyn celebrated its happiest baseball day in euphoric splen-

1

dor, there on the same stoop, the same tears, the very same throbbing voice, the same lady moaned, "*Those stinkin' bums, they finally won it all!*" There was passion in rooting for the Dodgers.

Every street in Brooklyn had a corner candy store and every one of them had a radio and later a small screen black and white television set, ubiquitously tuned in to Brooklyn Dodger baseball during the spring, summer and nearly every fall. There were cheers and groans, and betting. "Bet ya a quarter he strikes da next guy out." This was done all the while slurping a seven-cent chocolate egg cream or a nickel Coke.

Of the 33 teams fielded during those 11 seasons, the best of them all was the 1953 Brooklyn Dodgers—a magnificent ball club with staggering offensive statistics, but numbers were only part of the story. There was a distinctly human side. Gil Hodges, the popular first baseman, suffered through a horrendous slump but was buttressed by enormous support from the "Flatbush faithful." Jackie Robinson was in his seventh year in the National League, having broken the color barrier in 1947, yet the ugly racial incidents persisted and remain a part of the 1953 story. Another part of the saga was the greatest rivalry in all of sports history between the Brooklyn club and the New York Giants. It was made all the more intense in the golden age when the stick-it-in-his-ear, no-holds-barred manager of the Giants was Leo Durocher, who had come over from Brooklyn in mid-season 1948. His orders to his pitchers to throw at hitters, especially Dodger hitters, led to incidents on the field that climaxed in September when an irate Carl Furillo dove into the Giants dugout and locked his nemesis in a stranglehold. The animosity between the clubs was so intense that the Brooklyn players did not want to see the fight broken up. "Let them fight," they screamed. "Let him kill him."[1]

The inordinate relationship between the team and their devoted and tenacious fans was never stronger than during this era of Brooklyn Dodgers superiority. Ebbets Field was a joyous place to be. There was Hilda Chester, a raspy, boisterous biddy wielding a cowbell and carrying a sign that read, "Hilda Is Here!" There were the boys from Williamsburg who fancied themselves musicians and played their hearts out for the fans. Red Barber dubbed them "The Brooklyn Dodgers' Sym-Phonies" and the name stuck until the team left town.

They didn't win the World Series in 1953, just as they didn't win it in '47, '49 or '52. As Peter Golenbock pointed out, "It wasn't just the Yankees they were fighting. It was the Yankee tradition, the Yankee reputation, the Yankee complex."[2] Brooklyn and its fans bore the stigma that carried with it a sense of futility and frustration. "It was a pent-up frustration," recalled Dodgers pitcher Carl Erskine. "We had a great team."[3] But they did build up an October rivalry with the Yankees that made the long-awaited victory in 1955 that much sweeter.

The fifties were anything but the tranquil, laid back period in history that has often been depicted, and 1953 was a watershed year in the decade. The war in Korea ended and the cold war began. The changes in the lifestyle in Brooklyn were to become evident over the next few years. The borough's voice and only newspaper, the *Brooklyn Eagle,* folded in January 1955. The trolley cars, the vehicles that gave birth to the team name, vanished by late 1956, and by the early sixties even Steeplechase Park in Coney Island was gone.

It was a period of transition. It was Erskine who put it in proper perspective. The right-hander, who played with Brooklyn from 1948 through the '57 season, said that during that time, "We went from day to night baseball, we integrated the game, planes replaced trains, radio gave way to TV, and we went from the East Coast to the West Coast."[4]

Brooklyn's own ball club, their "Beloved Bums," who reached the soaring heights of baseball Valhalla in '55, sunk into oblivion just two years later. The move hit the populace like the hammer of Thor and then it was over, leaving a nagging pain that would traumatize the faithful for decades to come. The '53 Dodgers were the best to come out of the era and their story is representative of a time and a place that can never be replicated.

Those old enough to have been there can still recall climbing a ramp at Ebbets Field and reveling at the sight of the players gliding over an emerald sea. They remember coming early to watch batting and infield practice and the anticipation they felt when the big cage was rolled away. And of course, a baseball dinosaur, the pepper game; it was here that a fan could call out to Pee Wee Reese and the Dodger captain would respond without missing a swing. It was also at this place and about these players that Roger Kahn would pen his gem. At the conclusion of *The Boys of Summer*, Kahn asked rhetorically, "Who will remember? Is that the mind's last, soundless, dying cry? Who will remember?"

The answer is simple. Who can *ever* forget?

ONE

There Used to Be a Ball Club

"The Dodgers of 1953—the eight men in the field—can be put forth as the most gifted baseball team that has yet played in the tide of times."
—Roger Kahn, *The Boys of Summer*

There was once a ballpark in Brooklyn, New York, where a certain ball club played, and for a time it was one helluva club at that. In an era that spanned 11 seasons and was thought of as a golden age in baseball, this club was as good as any that ever played the game. The men of Brooklyn parlayed their abilities as a team with a social manifestation that at times threatened to tear the foundation asunder, both from within and from without, yet with a perseverance that triumphed, they willed themselves to near perfection.

The age and arduous journey began on Opening Day, April 15, 1947. On that clear, sunny, chilly afternoon at Ebbets Field in Brooklyn, the first African American to set foot on a major league diamond since the 1880s took the field with his mates. Amid rumors of unrest among the players, a possible petition against Jackie Robinson by his teammates, and ruthless goading and taunting by the opposition, this team won the National League pennant and Robinson led the way.

By the time the 1953 season began, the Brooklyn Dodgers had won two more pennants and lost on two other occasions in the last inning of the last game of the year, both times as victims of explosive home runs. Yet racial tensions had not subsided by much even as Jack Robinson entered his seventh season in the majors, and the '53 season would fulminate with even more episodes on the field.

Great ball clubs are usually measured by a World Series victory, but the true value comes over the long season; 154 games (162 today) are the determining factors in evaluating a team's worth, not the short series in the fall. Writer Donald Honig knew this when he included the Dodgers of 1953 among his 10 greatest teams of all-time (published in 1982). Honig went so far as to suggest, "One might say, arguably, the 1953 Dodgers were the strongest team in National League history."[1] More than 30 years later, Honig still holds to the same opinion.

"What a great ball club," he said. "They led the league in so many capacities. They even led in stolen bases. And you couldn't beat them in fielding. You never saw so many great gloves on one team."[2]

This club batted .285 collectively, 20 points higher than the league average. They stole nearly double the number of bases as the second-highest team, and compiled a .474 slugging percentage, which was one of the highest recorded in baseball history. Their 208 home runs was at the time the second-greatest total ever. The Dodgers scored 955 runs, the fourth-highest total in history. The other three did it in 1930, that year of the hitter when the league as a whole batted .308. The eight starting regulars hit .308 collectively. Snider, Campanella and Hodges combined for 114 home runs. The entire Yankee team

The Ebbets Field grounds crew readies the old ballpark for play (Brooklyn Public Library—Brooklyn Collection).

hit 113. Five players drove in 90 or more runs. The Dodgers set a record by hitting homers in 24 consecutive games. They made 118 errors, the fewest in the league; the next best club had 129.

They went on a tear late in the season by winning 46 while losing only 11 games from the All-Star break to Labor Day. In winning 105 games, they overwhelmed the second-place Milwaukee Braves by finishing 13 games ahead of them. This remarkable team led the league in runs scored and runs batted in for the fifth consecutive time, home runs and slugging average for the fifth consecutive time, stolen bases for the eighth year in succession, and fielding average for the third consecutive time. For the sixth year in a row their pitchers led the league in strikeouts.

They had the National League batting champion in Carl Furillo, who hit .344. The league RBI leader was Roy Campanella at 142, and Duke Snider topped the senior circuit in runs scored with 132 and slugging at .627. Campy hit 42 home runs, Duke 41, and Gil Hodges, after struggling through a horrendous slump, wound up with 31. There were five .300 hitters in the regular lineup. They led the league as a team in home runs, hits, runs, stolen bases, batting average, and slugging percentage. If they weren't the best the National League ever saw, they were certainly among the most potent.

Always a little short in the pitching department, the 1952 staff was led by Erskine with a 14–6 record and Billy Loes at 13–8. Joe Black had the most wins with 15, but all but one came in relief.

Going into the new season the starting pitching was uncertain. The hard-throwing right-hander, Don Newcombe, who had won 56 games from 1949 to 1951, had been drafted into the army and was lost for the '52 and '53 seasons. The Korean War had broken out in June 1950 and took its toll on many Americans. Don Newcombe was one of the major stars who was drafted during the conflict. Inducted into service after the '51 season, Newcombe lost two seasons to the army. So did Yankees pitcher Whitey Ford and second baseman Jerry Coleman as well as Boston outfielder Ted Williams. The big right-hander was a major loss to Brooklyn. He had won 56 games and lost 28 during the three previous seasons, going 20–9 in 1951. After his return he struggled through '54 with a 9–8 record, but went 20–5 in the world championship year of '55 and won a whopping 27 games in 1956 while losing only seven.

The Dodgers had won the pennant the previous year and reached the seventh game of the World Series before losing to the Yankees. The Brooklyn club shed the image of "lovable losers" garnered during the era of the Daffiness Boys and "Uncle" Wilbert Robinson with a pennant victory in 1941. They would, however, retain some vestige of being a team that could drop the big one when it hurt the most.

In 1942 the Dodgers won 104 games but finished two behind the St. Louis Cardinals. In the first full season after the war they wound up in a tie with St. Louis and lost the first two of the best-of-three playoff. They won pennants in '47 and '49, but lost to the Yankees in seven and five games, respectively, in the World Series. The next two years had disastrous finales. In 1950 the Phils and Dodgers battled to the last day of the season. Philadelphia led by two games going into the final weekend at Ebbets Field. The Dodgers won on Saturday behind Erv Palica, 7–3. It was their ninth straight victory. On Sunday Don Newcombe was opposed by Robin Roberts. After five scoreless innings, the Phillies got a run in the top of the sixth. In the bottom of the inning, Pee Wee Reese tied it with a home run that would be declared bizarre any place else but Brooklyn. His fly ball stuck in the screen in right field, then dropped to the wall above the Esquire Boot Polish sign just inside the foul line. The ball just sat there as Reese scampered around the bases for an inside-the-park home run.

With the game tied at one, Cal Abrams led off the ninth with a walk and went to second on Reese's single. When Duke Snider followed up with a single up the middle, Richie Ashburn, playing shallow, took the ball on one hop and threw home. The Dodgers' third base coach was Milton Stock, and knowing that Asburn had a weak throwing arm, waved Abrams home. The throw had him by a wide margin. With runners on second and third, Robinson was walked intentionally, but Furillo fouled out and Hodges flied deep to right for the third out.

In the tenth, Philadelphia outfielder Dick Sisler hit a Newcombe fastball into the left field seats with two on, giving the Phillies a 4–1 victory and the National League pennant. The very next year it was game three of the playoff against the Giants when Bobby Thomson's three-run "shot heard 'round the world" ended Brooklyn's hopes with a crushing finality.

In that torrid pennant race the Giants came from 13½ games back in August to tie Brooklyn on the last day of the season and force a three game playoff. Dodgers ace Don Newcombe had thrown 32 innings in the final eight days, including 20⅔ scoreless innings over the previous five days. After going eight and two-thirds innings in game three, the big man was spent, so manager Dressen summoned Ralph Branca from the bullpen with two runners on base and the score 4–2. In the dugout at the end of the seventh the exhausted pitcher wondered whether he had anything left. Robinson and Reese pushed him. "Give us one more inning," the captain said.[3]

Newcombe credited Robinson with the prodding that always drove him onward. "One of the reasons I was as successful as I was had to be Jackie," he said. Robinson yelled at him, "Go out there and pitch!"[4] He went back out for the eighth and got Rigney swinging at strike three. Stanky, meanwhile, was saying on the Giants' bench that the big guy was losing it. Rigney saw the last strike as a pea. "Yeah, Eddie," he mumbled to Stanky. "He's really losing it."[5] Hank Thompson then hit a ground ball to the first baseman and Stanky popped to short; one, two, three.

Newcombe described how he felt in the ninth inning. "I was pretty tired," he said. "I pitched three times in five days. I didn't want to go out; but I didn't want to stay in and hurt the team either."[6] As he was leaving after being relieved, he stopped just beyond the infield to exchange a few words with Branca. Don was in the shower when Thomson's drive settled just above the head of left fielder Andy Pafko and into the lower deck for the game and the pennant. The crowd, of course, went wild. "I heard this yell," Newcombe remembered. "It was like an explosion. I stuck my head out and said, 'What happened?' Somebody said, 'Thomson hit a home run.' From there on it's history."[7]

It was Ralph Branca who took the brunt of the blame for the Dodgers' loss. By serving up the gopher pitch, he was christened with the goat horns that would stay with him for good. Branca, however, toted his burden with dignity and grace. More than 50 years later he would earn some degree of redemption when it was revealed the Giants had been stealing signs over the past month with an elaborate ruse that involved a telescope set up in the Giants' center field clubhouse. Initially indignant when the story unfolded, Branca told a photographer from *Sports Illustrated*, "If you want a picture take one of the guy with the binoculars."[8]

"Uncomfortable," said Thomson when the question of the scheme was put to him. "Uncomfortable."[9]

Elbie Fletcher was with the Boston Braves in 1938. Although not involved in the pennant race between Chicago and Pittsburgh, Fletcher made an acute observation the following season when he joined the Pirates. Gabby Hartnett of the Cubs had hit a home run to knock Pittsburgh out of the race. With darkness descending at Wrigley Field and the Cubs and Pirates deadlocked at 6–6 on September 28, Hartnett hit his famous "Homer in the Gloaming," effectively eliminating the Pirates from the race.

Fletcher recalled how the next season "was sad, because that's all they talked about on that Pirate club that year; Hartnett's home run. I knew we weren't going to win it. That home run was on everybody's mind, haunting them, like a ghost."[10]

The fans in Brooklyn clung tenaciously with seemingly eternal optimism to the dictum "Wait 'til next year!" Roger Kahn wrote, "You may glory in a team triumphant, but you fall in love with a team in defeat."[11] But the character and the courage of this club was not to be denied. The fans' loyalty, devotion, and fanaticism was rewarded. The team won four pennants in the next five years and the one and only world championship the old borough would ever see.

There was a trivia moment that occurred at Ebbets Field on May 1, 1949. As the Dodgers trailed the Phillies, 4–2, in the ninth, manager Burt Shotton sent Chuck Connors in to pinch-hit for Carl Furillo with a runner on first. There was one out and the Phils pitcher was Russ Meyer. On a belt-high fastball on the outside corner, Connors swung. "I creamed it," he recalled. " A one-hopper back to the mound and he turned it into a double play. I can still see that pitch in my dreams. It's as big as a zeppelin. If I waited a little longer, I might still be playing."[12]

Of course, had the big first baseman creamed it, he probably would not have starred on television's *The Rifleman*, might not have had his star imprinted in Hollywood's Walk of Fame, not have gotten to the Cowboy Hall of Fame. He's probably the only cowboy in there from Bay Ridge, Brooklyn.

The Dodgers' field general was a cocky, egotistical little rooster named Charlie Dressen. It was said of him that his three favorite words were "I," "I'm" and "I'll."[13] Noted as a proficient sign stealer, he suffered from a glaring fault among managers: the inability to communicate well consistently with his players. Pitcher Clem Labine said, "When you talked to Charlie, he wouldn't be thinking about what you were saying to him, but rather what he was going to say to you. So you never really got it in."[14] Charley took over the club for the '51 season. He had that play-off loss to the Giants, then won two pennants, but was gone before the '54 season began.

Dressen, of whom writer Donald Honig wrote "was a chipper character whose egomania charmed rather than offended," was born September 2, 1898, in Decatur, Illinois.[15] Charlie played baseball and football in high school and was quarterback for the Decatur Staleys, the team that would evolve into the Chicago Bears. His major league playing career began in 1925 with Cincinnati and lasted for eight years. He hit .272 in a little more than 600 games. Dressen coached and managed in the minors until he took over the helm of the Reds in 1934. The only pennants his teams won in his 16 years were in 1952 and '53 with the Dodgers, though he also had a first-place finish in 1951 in Brooklyn before losing to the Giants in that fabled playoff.

Charlie coached under Leo Durocher. It was generally considered among baseball people that Dressen's greatest challenge as he saw it was to out-manage his former boss. He had his assets. Always considered a great sign stealer, Roy Campanella said of his manager, "Charlie was one of the best at reading pitchers' signs. He could tell what a pitcher would throw just by watching his hands."[16] Erskine gave Charlie a lot of credit for his strong finish in 1953. The pitcher was just 5–4 at the All-Star break, but Dressen expressed his confidence and told him to relax. "'You're having a bad stretch,'" Erskine recalls the manger telling him. "'I'm going to change your luck. I'm going to take you fishing.' We went to a place owned by a friend of Charlie's in upstate New York. We fished and then we came back and I went 15–2 the rest of the way."[17]

After three successful years in Brooklyn, Charlie lost the handle. He asked for a multi-year contract, which was against the "one year at a time" policy of owner Walter O'Malley. Dressen stuck to his guns; so did the Dodger boss, and Charlie found himself out of a job. Apparently Dressen's wife, Ruth, had written to O'Malley demanding three years and $50,000 for Charlie. O'Malley reiterated that Dressen could sign a one-year deal but anything more was out of the question. While Dressen thought the question of his acceptance of a one-year deal was open for the next 24 hours, the Dodgers owner had already taken the necessary steps to hire another manager. He signed to manage Oakland in the PCL and resurfaced in the majors a year later as the manager of the Washington Senators. Charlie Dressen never won another pennant.

Although no longer with the ball club, the architect of this great Dodgers dynasty was baseball's resident genius, Branch Rickey. Rickey came to Brooklyn in September 1942 and left after the 1950 season. But the '53 club was essentially his. Only Pee Wee Reese had preceded him to Brooklyn, and under "The Mahatma," the Dodgers signed Carl Furillo, Duke Snider, Gil Hodges, Roy Campanella, Jackie Robinson, Carl Erskine and Johnny Podres. Rickey's great 1948 trade with Pittsburgh put Preacher Roe and Billy Cox in Dodger uniforms.

Duke Snider had broken in with the Dodgers with a pinch-hit appearance on Opening Day, April 15, 1947, the same day Jackie Robinson made his major league debut. Snider was a tremendous natural talent, but the question constantly being asked was, When will Snider reach his potential? Signed off a Montebello, California, sandlot, he carried the stigma of being described as temperamental and a sulker. A National League manager in 1952 declared of Snider, "The worst waste of talent I've seen in a long while."[18] Al Stump in a spring article in *Sport* suggested that the 1952 World Series might be the breakthrough for Duke. The 26-year-old left-handed hitter batted .345 and hit four home runs, tying the all-time Fall Classic mark set by Babe Ruth and Lou

Gehrig. He led both teams with eight runs batted in and set an all-time record with 24 total bases. It seemed the "Dook of Flatbush" was ready to explode in 1953.

Despite having gone hitless in the '52 Series, Gil Hodges was a fixture at first base. He had two at-bats in 1943 before the war, and after playing third base and catching, Leo Durocher moved him to first base in 1948 to make room for Roy Campanella. Hodges became the best of his time at the initial sack, bar none.

Carl Furillo had been a Dodger since 1946, a solid defensive player with an arm so powerful they called him "The Reading Rifle." But Furillo could hit, always around .300, always around 20 homers, and usually about 80–90 RBIs. He could hit in the clutch, was aggressive on the field, and was tough as nails. Roy Campanella was as good as anybody behind the plate. He had a great throwing arm and could block pitches in the dirt. Campy was a slugger and as fine a hitter as there was among major league catchers.

Jackie Robinson was in his seventh season and was 34 years old and in the midst of the early spring controversy regarding the promotion of Jim Gilliam from Montreal to the Dodgers' roster. The problem with playing Gilliam at second was that nobody was going to put Jack on the bench. "If Gilliam pushes me off second base, I know I'll play someplace on this team, " he said.[19] He would ultimately play both third base and left field and have another fine season, hitting .329 and driving in 95 runs. There were other candidates for the left field position; George Shuba could hit and Sandy Amoros could run, but in the end Robinson would play more games in left field than anyone else. Amoros, however, was wielding a hot bat at Montreal early in the season, highlighted by a six-for-six performance against Rochester, and was in Dressen's scope as a possible candidate for the open spot.

In the spring the starting pitching was suspect. Preacher Roe, the skinny southpaw, was on the downside. After 200 innings pitched for the previous three seasons and an overall record of 79–30 since joining the Dodgers in 1948, he had fallen to 158⅔ innings in 1952, though he recorded an 11–2 mark for the season. Billy Loes had gone 13–8 but was considered a bit of a flake. Loes said he didn't want to win 20 games because they would expect it every year. Charlie Dressen said, "You gotta take care of yourself, Billy. You'll be a terrific pitcher. You'll go for 15 years." Billy responded, "I don't have to go for 15 years. I'll have enough money in five."[20]

The Dodgers gave Loes a bonus of $21,000 to sign, but Branch Rickey expressed some pessimism over the deal, believing Billy lacked a good fastball. The pitcher from Queens, however, had his backers in Dressen and catcher

Campanella. "He's got a fastball," Campy insisted. "Much faster than anybody thinks."[21]

Loes was born on December 13, 1929, in Long Island City, and signed out of Bryant High School. He stayed in the majors for 11 years. It seems that his attitude prevented him from being a better pitcher as he never won more than 14 games in a season and ended up with a record of 80–63. Noted more for his eccentricities than his pitching, it was in the 1952 World Series that a ball hit by the Yankees' Vic Raschi bounced off his leg and went for a single. Loes remarked to newsmen that he lost the ball in the sun. Prior to the series, Billy picked the Yankees to win in six, then said he was misquoted; he meant they would win in seven.

An interesting trivia tidbit on Loes involved hitters who had four home runs in a game. Billy was a rookie in 1950 when Gil Hodges hit four round-trippers in a single game. He was there in '54 when the Braves' Joe Adcock did it against Brooklyn, and he was with Baltimore when Cleveland's Rocky Colav-

Captain Pee Wee Reese poses for fans at friendly Ebbets Field.

ito went deep four times. Then in 1961, Loes was a teammate of Willie Mays when the "Say-Hey Kid" hit four against the Braves.

Loes was befriended by Jackie Robinson, a bit of an odd couple pairing but both loved to play cards, which created a common bond between the teammates. Billy had his winningest year in '53, going 14–6. Traded to Baltimore in 1956, Loes closed out his career with the Giants in San Francisco in '61.

Carl Erskine loomed as the ace of the staff, having won 16 and 14 games in the last two seasons. He had been a dependable commodity for the Dodgers since arriving from Fort Worth in 1948, but Erskine, lovingly known as "Oisk" in Brooklyn, pitched with a perennial sore arm he suffered his first year in the majors, and there was the air of uncertainty surrounding the gentleman from Indiana. The Dodgers need not have worried, however. The gutsy little right-hander would have his only 20-win season in '53, going 20–6 and leading the National League in winning percentage at .769. He started 33 games, completed 16, and struck out 187 in 246⅔ innings.

The leader among a clubhouse full of leaders was the team captain, a guy they all called "Pee Wee." Harold Henry Reese was born July 23, 1918, on a farm between Ekron and Brandenburg, Kentucky, and grew up in and around the city of Louisville. He recalled for writer Peter Golenbock the attitude towards race in his part of the world. "There were a few blacks that lived not far from us, but they were not allowed in the parks. And they rode in the back of the buses. You just thought, 'That's the way of life. That's where they should be.' They had their own schools. All the schools were segregated. I can't say that we really looked down on the blacks. We just thought that that was the way it was supposed to be."[22]

Considering the climate in his environment, at a glance it seemed that the relationship between Reese and Jackie Robinson that developed would be an unlikely alliance and even a less likely friendship. Yet with his great career in baseball and Hall-of-Fame status, the southerner, whose father once pointed out to him a "hanging tree" near his home outside Ekron, 40 miles or so from Louisville, would be remembered for his humane and courageous stance regarding the treatment of Jackie Robinson and for a singular event that would symbolize the man.

Brought together by fate or chance, the southern player and the Negro pioneer fighting for his right to simply play baseball, facing every slur and barbaric insult hurled at him, including death threats and the antagonism of his peers, the two came to stand for an era and the dissolving of a regrettable period in American history.

Reese first heard of Robinson while on a troop ship returning from the Pacific in the final stages of World War II. A major league shortstop with the Brooklyn Dodgers, Reese had lost three years of playing ball while serving in the navy. He was anxious to resume his career, and like millions of others, return to a normal life.

"Hey," someone said, "the Dodgers signed a colored guy. It's on the short-wave."

"Is that a fact?" Reese said.

"And hey, Pee Wee, he's a shortstop."[23]

And yet one day Jack Robinson would say of the southerner from Kentucky, "I was helped over these crises by the courage and decency of a teammate who could easily have been my enemy rather than my friend."[24] The tale of the two Dodgers is as interwoven within the mélange of this "Great Experiment" as any other part of this fascinating and historical epic.

Carl Reese worked as a railroad detective for the Louisville and Nashville Railroad. The times when he worked the night shift, he had free afternoons to pass along to his son the rudiments of the game of baseball. This came after the elder Reese had given up the farm and moved his family to Louisville. Although a runt of a kid, Reese did not get his nickname because of his size. He became a top-notch marble player and his favorite shooter was called a "pee wee," so in 1932 when he was runner-up in a national marbles tournament, he was known to one and all as "Pee Wee." The name stuck.

Pee Wee attended DuPont Manual Training High School and played American Legion ball as well as with the New Covenant Presbyterian Church team. Too embarrassed to try out for the high school varsity team his first year because of his size, he went back the next spring and made the team. After graduating Reese went to work as a cable splicer for the Southern Bell Telephone Company. That summer while working and still playing for the New Covenant team, he grew four inches and weighed 140 pounds. The team's manager, Keith Sparks, switched the young outfielder to shortstop because of his strong throwing arm.

Sparks thought enough of Pee Wee to pass the word to Cap Neal, owner and manager of the Louisville Colonels in the American Association, and negotiated a deal that had Reese signing a contract for $100 a month. The little guy was a professional, although he was advised against leaving a secure job with the phone company. Reese took the chance and in 1938 hit .279 for the Colonels. He excelled as a defensive shortstop and was being watched closely by scouts from the Red Sox, Cubs and Dodgers. As it turned out, 1939 would be a significant year for the young ballplayer.

He re-signed with Louisville and was given a raise to $400 a month. During that summer Pee Wee often visited his married sisters when the team was at home. On one such occasion he met a neighbor, Dorothy Walton, and the shy, boyish youth soon was rocked with early love. The couple began to date and were married in 1942. It was also the year that Neal decided to sell his ball club and retire. He knew Pee Wee was his most valuable commodity so he managed to convince the Red Sox to purchase the franchise in order to land Reese. However, the Boston manager and shortstop, Joe Cronin, still had a couple of years in him and didn't want the promising youngster breathing down his neck.

It was also in '39 that Reese started to show that he could hit in the clutch, an asset that would be one of the hallmarks of his major league career. He hit .272 with 22 doubles and led the American Association with 18 triples. The fleet-footed young man also stole 35 bases and was caught only once. The Colonels were the victors in the Little World Series that year. It was the enthusiasm of Dodgers scout Ted McGrew that got Larry MacPhail to shell out $40,000 and four players for Reese before the end of the '39 campaign. When Reese heard the news, he was stunned. His gaping reaction was, "Oh, no! Not Brooklyn!"[25]

There were questions when Reese reported to the Dodgers' spring camp in Clearwater, Florida, since the shortstop was also the manager, Leo Durocher. Leo knew he couldn't cover the ground like he once did and inserted Pee Wee into the spot almost immediately. Reese had a great spring but struggled once the season opened. In the typical MacPhail-Durocher pattern, the two clashed over the shortstop position. MacPhail ordered Leo to put himself back into the lineup and bench the kid. Durocher refused, and MacPhail fired him. As usual, the next day life went on and the firing was not mentioned. Leo went back to short but gradually moved Pee Wee in by mid–May and he began to hit. His first major league home run came on May 26 in the 10th inning to defeat Philadelphia, 2–1.

Then on June 1 on an 0–1 pitch from the Cubs' Jake Mooty, Reese was hit in the head with a fastball. He spent a week at Chicago's Masonic Hospital with a brain concussion. Once it was determined that there would be no physical damage, the concern turned in another direction. Would the young player be "gun-shy," often the result of a beaning? He returned to the lineup on June 21 against Pittsburgh and hit in the leadoff spot. In the Dodgers' 10–8 win, Pee Wee had three hits in four trips—a single, double and triple. He went on to have a fine year until mid–August when he broke a bone in his heel sliding and was out for the rest of the season. Brooklyn finished second to the Reds.

The MacPhail-Durocher train was barreling towards a pennant and Pee Wee Reese was on board.

In the spring of 1940 the Dodgers exhibited two of the most promising young players in baseball—Reese and a kid from St. Louis, "Pistol" Pete Reiser. During the season the press would label them "the gold dust twins." There were similarities. Both had the given name of Harold, both were about the same age, both were hitting the majors at about the same time, and both were so highly regarded that Brooklyn was already counting the pennants these two would help to generate. They shared an apartment in Brooklyn and soon were inseparable companions off the field. Although their personalities differed (Pee Wee was more outgoing and Pete sort of moody), they had no trouble being close friends. In the spring of 1942 when both Dotty Walton and Ruth Hurst, Pete's girl, visited the boys at Daytona Beach, they immediately hit it off.

In 1941 the Dodgers won the pennant, their first since 1920, and Pete had a tremendous year. He led the league in nearly every offensive category, including batting, while Pee Wee had a tough year, hitting just .229 and making far too many errors at short. But he played 152 games. That winter Pearl Harbor was attacked and the United States was at war. Reese knew it was just a matter of time before he would be in the military but he played 151 games, hit .255, and was named to the All-Star squad. Brooklyn and St. Louis battled down to the wire, the Dodgers winning 104 games but the Cardinals' 106 won them the pennant. On March 29, Pee Wee and Dotty were married in Florida and the next day Pete and Ruth were wed. The two couples stood up for each other and their friendship was further secured.

On January 23, 1943, Reese enlisted in the navy. A year later he was shipped to the Pacific. He played some ball in Hawaii, and when he came home it was in time for the 1946 season. Again the Dodgers fought to the wire against the Cardinals, this time to a dead heat. Then they lost the first two of the best two-of-three playoff, the first in National League history. Without missing a beat the Dodgers took part in another of baseball's historic moments. On April 15, 1947, Jackie Robinson played his first regular season game as a Dodger. Pee Wee hit in the eighth slot that day and had one hit in three at-bats as the Dodgers beat the Braves, 5–3, before a crowd of 26,623 at Ebbets Field.

But it wasn't just Reese's friendship with Jackie that solidified his place in the Rickey experiment. No incident was more symbolic of the acceptance of the African American to the big leagues than the scene of Reese putting his arm around Robinson's shoulder in front of jeering fans and the opposing dugout. In 2005 a statue commemorating the gesture was dedicated outside the stadium of the first professional club in Brooklyn since 1957, the short-season Class A Brooklyn Cyclones, an affiliate of the New York Mets.

The details are a bit unclear. Even Jackie wrote that it happened in Boston, but the consensus seems to point to Cincinnati during a series with the Reds. The year is equally unclear as to whether it occurred in 1947 or '48, but no one doubts that it actually happened. There is complete agreement by all accounts that the shortstop walked over to the first baseman and put his arm over his shoulder as though to whisper something in his ear. Rex Barney recalled that it was in Cincinnati. He could hear the screams from the Reds' bench. "And then they started on Pee Wee, 'How can you play with this nigger bastard?' and all that stuff. While Jackie was standing near first base, Pee Wee went over to him and put his arm around him as if to say, 'This is my guy. This is the guy.'"[26] Roger Kahn said it happened in 1947, and he quotes Jackie as saying, "After Pee Wee came over like that, I never felt alone on a baseball field again."[27] Of course, both players were still teammates and friends in 1953 and both made valuable contributions to yet another Brooklyn Dodgers pennant.

The last pennant in Brooklyn came in 1956 as the aging ball club hung on to outpace the Milwaukee Braves by a single game. For the first time Brooklyn was a defending World Series champion and they took that into another World Series with their Bronx rivals. The Dodgers won the first two games at Ebbets Field and the Yankees evened it up at the Stadium. In the fifth game Yankees right-hander Don Larsen threw the only perfect game in Series history. When Clem Labine outdueled Bob Turley, 1–0, in 10 innings, another series went to seven games. But Brooklyn was not destined to celebrate another world's championship. Johnny Kucks defeated Don Newcombe, 9–0, in the finale and Brooklyn's World Series history was done.

It was the end. It was completely over. The last chapter had been written. There could never be any more to add or subtract. It was locked in the vault. No one could eclipse Duke Snider's franchise-leading 316 home runs. Brooklyn's Babe, Herman, would forever lead the Dodgers in batting with his .393 average in 1930, and Dazzy Vance's 28 victories in a single season can never be matched nor topped. And there would never be another Dodgers team to equal that superlative squad of 1953.

Erskine gave tribute to that club when he said, "I still get chills up my back when I think of looking around me at the infield and outfield. I could not in my wildest dreams have ever placed myself on a team that gave any greater advantage to a pitcher."[28] Johnny Podres, two years short of being the hero in Brooklyn's only World Series victory, echoed Erskine's view when he said of the '53 club, "That was the best Dodger team I ever played on, the best. All those great players were at their peak."[29]

If there was one commodity missing in the spring of '53 it was another starting pitcher and the Dodgers found him in Russ Meyer, who came from the Phillies. Delighted to be with the Dodgers and having that great team behind him, Meyer was 15–5 in '53. He won 11 and lost six the next year and was 6–2 in 1955 before being traded to the Cubs. After he left Brooklyn, Russ Meyer made a comment that said it all. "To me it was a joy to be on a ball club like that, because in my mind that ball club was as good a ball club that ever walked onto a ball field."[30]

Two

Brooklyn: The Time and the Place

"I like the mix of neighborhoods. To my mind it is a microcosm of America at large."—Branch Rickey

Brooklyn is 70.61 square miles and one of the five boroughs that make up the city of New York, the result of a consolidation that took place in 1898. Still rued by many Brooklynites, the move relegated the residents to a role subservient to the borough of Manhattan in just about all aspects of everyday life. Manhattan, or "the city" as it is referred to in Brooklyn, was superior in arts and entertainment, work places, shopping, restaurants and nightlife. Brooklyn became the stepchild to the big city, the "bedroom" community to the place where they went to earn their living every day. Robert Creamer called it "Manhattan's Sancho Panza."[1]

Although the folks of Brooklyn can make a hefty argument for rivaling Manhattan in just about every one of the aforementioned categories, there was never an argument about the one thing that Brooklyn had over its counterparts: a ball club! For 59 years it was the only borough that identified directly with a big league team. The Brooklyn Dodgers. New York's other two clubs were just that; it wasn't the Bronx Yankees or the Manhattan Giants. They belonged to New York and the Dodgers belonged to Brooklyn.

The area that would become Brooklyn was at one time inhabited by Native Americans who are known to history as the Canarsees. They spoke their own language, of course, but it wasn't Brooklynese, and so far as anyone knows, they never played baseball. They first became known to Europeans in 1609 when English explorer Henry Hudson, sailing for the Dutch East India Company, anchored his ship, *Half Moon*, on a piece of land just inside New York Harbor. Within 24 hours of landfall the crew was attacked by a band of these same Canarsee tribesmen. Strangely, the next morning the Canarsees once more approached the ship, this time in friendship and bearing gifts, and so ultimately the Dutch were able to settle in North America.

The place on which the explorers set foot was the Indians' sacred land called *konjin*, a word that meant rabbit, for thousands of the critters roamed the land and were considered by the natives to be the gifts of the gods for providing them with fur and food. Lady Deborah Moody was the leader of a group of religious dissenters who established a settlement in Gravesend. Over a few years there were alternately attacks and periods of calm between the two groups and by the second half of the seventeenth century, friendly relations had been achieved and trading was commonplace. In line with the profitable exchange of goods, the Canarsee chief allowed Moody and her people to occupy the Konjin land, the name of which she anglicized to Conyne Island or Coney Island.

By 1664 the British had arrived and forced the Dutch to cede the island of Manhattan to them. In 1683 the British divided New York into five counties, Brooklyn, or Kings County, being one of them. The first beach resort was built by John Terhune in 1823, who called it the Coney Island House. By the middle of the nineteenth century the area became extremely popular and was visited by famous names of the era—Washington Irving, Herman Melville and P.T. Barnum among them. It was in 1865 that Peter Tilyou opened a hotel and restaurant called Surf House.

Soon after Charles Feltman brought his version of the old German wiener, the hot dog. After just three years he built the Ocean Pavilion Hotel and then a 100-foot-long pier that was the precursor to the famous Coney Island boardwalk. It was in 1915 that Nathan Handwerker came to the Island and took a job slicing hot dog rolls at Feltman's restaurant. Eventually he rented some space of his own and offered the frankfurter for five cents, half of Feltman's price. At Nathan's it was frankfurters and French fries and chow mein on a bun, and by July 6, 1955, Nathan's had sold its one millionth hot dog.

In 1897 Peter's son, George C. Tilyou, opened his amusement park in Coney Island and called it "Steeplechase Park" for the iron horse ride. He introduced the Great Ferris Wheel, which he had purchased at the Chicago Midway, and called it the Wonder Wheel at Coney. Luna Park opened in 1903 and a third park, Dreamland, was added in '04. There was nothing in the world to rival Coney Island in the early years of the twentieth century.

A series of disasters kept changing the configuration of the Island. Dreamland was destroyed by fire in 1911 and never rebuilt. Although Steeplechase was also destroyed in the same way, Tilyou rebuilt immediately and added the

Parachute Jump in 1941 to add to the Cyclone ride and the Carousel. The Cyclone was a wooden roller coaster built in 1927 and its 2,640 feet of track contained 12 drops and six hairpin turns. All of these were still flourishing in the early 1950s, when Coney Island was a stunning and exciting place to see and be.

Although the "stepchild" label seemed to persist, Brooklynites needn't go to Manhattan for culture and entertainment. There was plenty of nightlife at home. The Elegante was a lavish nightclub on Ocean Parkway, and at The Airport on Flatbush Avenue near Floyd Bennett Field, there was continuous music from two bands, one American and one Latin. The Latin band was usually Tito Puente and his orchestra. Ben Maksik's Town and Country Club was a jumping off point for performers like Buddy Hackett, Milton Berle, Martin and Lewis, and Eddie Fisher. The next stop for these entertainers was often Manhattan's Copacabana or the Latin Quarter.

The Brooklyn Academy of Music was opened in 1912 and it was here that the great tenor Enrico Caruso collapsed on stage in his next-to-last public appearance. The great Civil War memorial at Grand Army Plaza was built in 1870 and styled after the Arc de Triomphe in Paris. Just up the street from the Great Arch on Eastern Parkway the Brooklyn Museum boasted one of the world's finest collections of Egyptian art, and at Eastern Parkway and Flatbush Avenues stood the main branch of the Brooklyn Public Library. When compared to those at Harvard, Yale, the Congressional and New York, *The New Yorker* critic Lewis Mumford wrote, "Brooklyn's new one is tops."[2]

Continuing along Flatbush Avenue to Empire Boulevard, one encountered the beautiful Brooklyn Botanical Gardens directly across the street from Prospect Park, Brooklyn's only zoo, and a 60-acre lake with paddle boats. A creation of designers Frederick Lew Olmsted and Calvert Vaux, who considered it their masterpiece even over Central Park in Manhattan, the park and its 526 acres contained the zoo and a carousel with 51 animals carved in 1912 by Charles Carmel. Just a block-and-a-half past the Gardens stood Brooklyn's crown jewel, the little ballpark named for its club's president, Charles Ebbets, who in 1902 used whatever influence he could muster to block a move by Ned Hanlon to take the club out of Brooklyn. "I still have faith in Brooklyn," Ebbets famously stated.[3]

Fulton Street was the main drag in the area that was called simply "downtown." It had department stores, the kind where parents took the kids to buy communion outfits or Easter clothes. Abraham and Strauss (A&S), Namn's, Loesseur's, and Mays were the major department stores. There was the Horn and Hardart cafeteria, nickel heaven, and theaters like the Fox, the Albee and the Brooklyn Paramount, where the live rock 'n' roll shows helped to usher in a sea change in music.

A day or evening out was not complete without a good meal at a fine restaurant, and Brooklyn had enough of them to satisfy any pallet. One could eat at the Nom Tong Chinese restaurant on Church Avenue and get a combination dinner for 60 cents. There were Italian restaurants on almost every block, especially in those neighborhoods that were predominantly Italian populated. There were Jewish delicatessens, an epicurean mecca for hot dogs and potato knishes, corned beef or pastrami on rye or club, the only bread choices, and a cold Dr. Brown's cream soda or Cel-Ray tonic. Juniors on Flatbush Extension is still renowned for its corned beef and pastrami sandwiches as well as its out-of-this-world cheesecake. Peter Luger's Steakhouse in Williamsburg is considered by many to offer the best steak in New York City. Located at Broadway and Driggs Avenue, the establishment was opened in 1876 as Charles Luger's Cafe, Billiards, and Bowling Alley. Later his son, Peter, took over, followed by grandson Frederick.

There was Michel's at 346 Flatbush Avenue and Patricia Murphy's Candlelight Restaurant on Henry Street. An immigrant from Newfoundland in the thirties, Patricia named the eatery after herself. Her delectable popovers became famous, and she later opened another Candlelight on Sixtieth Street in Manhattan. Gage & Tollner's on Fulton Street was often considered to be one of Brooklyn's finest dining establishments in Brooklyn. Cafeterias like Bickfords and Garfields were very popular, and at Nedick's a frank and an orange drink were heaven. Sheepshead Bay featured fishing boats and sea gulls and the smell of the sea air. Tappen's was located on Emmons Avenue, between East 26 and East 27 streets, from 1845 until it was sold to Lundy Brothers in 1948. After the place burned down in 1950, the name was sold to a restaurant on Ocean Avenue and Belt Parkway. The landmark eatery F.W.I.L. Lundy Brothers, or simply Lundy's, originally opened on a pier over the water in 1920. Later it moved to the corner of Emmons and Ocean avenues as a two-story mission-style stucco structure, with 2,800 seats in a huge cavernous interior with marble floors and stairways and a clam bar with access on Ocean Avenue. Lundy's could boast of serving up to 15,000 meals in a single day.

Brooklyn had its industry that lasted past the fifties. Domino Sugar and Joyva Halva, the "sweetmeat," were in Williamsburg, Fox's U-Bet in Brownsville, and for a time Brooklyn was the largest beer producing center in the United States. The F & M Schafer Brewing Company, whose "h" lit up to signify a hit and "e" for error on the big Schafer sign over the scoreboard in

Ebbets Field, was on Kent Avenue. Among Brooklyn's breweries, Schafer joined Piels, Reingold, and a number of others that were still flourishing in 1953.

In a loft at Busch Terminal, Topps Chewing Gum turned out delicious gum and beginning in 1951 their ever-popular baseball cards that in later decades would allow owners of mint condition cards to turn a dollar or two. Virginia Dare extracts was on Third Avenue.

The Brooklyn Navy Yard was built in 1781 and produced the USS *Maine*, the warship of the Spanish-American War, the USS *Arizona*, sunk at Pearl Harbor, and the USS *Missouri*, the ship upon which the Japanese surrender ceremonies took place in 1945. During the Second World War the Yard employed more than 70,000 workers in a 24-hour, seven-days-a-week operation.

Scores of poets and writers dwelt in Brooklyn neighborhoods. Marianne Moore lived at 260 Cumberland Street and turned out a memorable poem about her Dodgers in 1956, "Hometown Piece for Messrs. Alston and Reese."

But what defined Brooklyn in the fifties was its neighborhoods, the blocks. Each was autonomous, like Greek City States. Generally ethnically defined, each section bore the sign of the generations that followed the immigrants at the turn of the twentieth century. Writer Tommy Holmes wrote in 1953, "All the racial strains are embedded there, formed into neighborhoods of fierce pride. Brooklyn is a sprawling city of diverse peoples, different traditions, varied tongues and accents, smells and habits. There has been no ordinary planning in Brooklyn. The place has just grown."[4]

There were Irish in Park Slope, Windsor Terrace and Gerritson Beach; Germans in Bushwick, Ridgewood and East Williamsburg. The Jews were strong in Brownsville and East New York. There were Scandinavians in Sunset Park and along Fifth Avenue, all the way to Bay Ridge. Italians were predominant in places like Bensonhurst, Bath Beach, South Brooklyn and Borough Park.

After World War II African Americans swelled the population of Bedford-Stuyvesant and Puerto Ricans began to proliferate in sections like Williamsburg and South Brooklyn. But the neighborhoods mattered. In any one of them residents could be observed sitting on stoops or on the sidewalk on folding chairs. There was no air conditioning, of course, and neighbors visited while getting a breath of the cooler night air. They watched the stick ball games in the street and some played cards while portable radios were tuned to Dodger ball games.

Kids lived on the streets. They played their games like ring-o-livio, Johnny-on-the-pony, and kick-the-can. In the winter months it was roller

Stickball on a borough park street (author's collection).

hockey and touch football. All summer the games were anything that mimicked baseball—punch ball, slap ball, stoop ball, or stickball. They were played with a pink rubber ball that was made by the Spaulding company and known as a "spauldeen." Every block had its own version tailored to suit the terrain. Into the trees was two bases, or if it bounced off the garage roof, it was in play. Distances were measured not in feet but in sewers. Two sewers was a good shot, three was great. Blocks often had their own teams and played games against other blocks.

Billy Nigro made 35th Street history when he hit one nearly four sewers. "It was against 40th Street," he remembered, "and we played for a buck a man."[5] Fellows that played the infield did so with one foot on the curb and the other planted in the gutter, and they had to be adept at latching onto and squeezing the spauldeen that was egged from the speed and would spin out of the player's hands if he didn't squeeze it just right.

There was a fair amount of industry in Brooklyn during the World War

II years and early post-war era. Places like the Navy Yard and Bushwick Terminal were extremely productive for years. Williamsburg was a section that catered to many factories and warehouses, but for the most part communities were decidedly residential. There were brownstones in Park Slope and Brooklyn Heights, ranch homes in Midwood and Flatbush and more luxurious dwellings on Shore Road overlooking Bensonhurst and the Narrows.

Nearly every block had a meeting place, a corner candy store or a luncheonette where the locals hung out and indulged in nickel cokes, two-cent seltzers and conversation. During the baseball season a radio would be ubiquitously tuned to a Dodgers game, and by 1953 most places had a small black-and-white television set. The pitcher was at the top of the screen, the batter and catcher at the bottom. The central camera angle was the grass between the mound and the plate. When the reception got snowy, someone, usually a neighborhood kid, went on the roof and moved the antenna around while the proprietor yelled to someone outside the store who relayed the message to the kid on the roof. They did this until the picture cleared and repeated the process several times each day. The chocolate egg cream was the elixir in these Brooklyn shops in the fifties, an amalgamation of chocolate syrup; it had to be Fox's U-Bet, milk and seltzer.

There is a history behind the popular drink. In an article published in *Esquire* magazine some years ago, it was pointed out that the egg cream was invented in 1890 by Louis Auster, who owned a candy store in Brooklyn. The drink became so popular that there would often be lines two and three deep at the fountain. The great conundrum associated with the story is that no one has ever offered any explanation as to why or how it got its name since there are neither eggs nor cream in the mixture. In 1953 it sold for about seven cents.

Strolling just about any neighborhood meant snacks. Thirteenth Avenue in Borough Park was egg creams, charlotte russe, a dill pickle snatched from a barrel of brine and a slice of "ah-beetz." The subways were limited to the BMT (Brooklyn-Manhattan Transit), IRT (Interboro Rapid Transit) and the IND (Independent Subway System), but they took riders wherever they wished to go.

Brooklyn even had a holiday all its own. The creation of the Brooklyn Sunday School Union, a Protestant organization, in 1829, Brooklyn Day was celebrated the first Thursday in June each year until 1959. Brooklyn schools were closed and there was a big parade on Eastern Parkway. In 1940 Mrs. Edward C. Blum, the wife of the president of Abraham and Straus department store, convinced Borough president John Cashmore to designate the yellow forsythia as the official flower of Brooklyn.

One would be hard-pressed to find two words in the English language more synonymous than "Brooklyn" and "baseball." If the game wasn't born in the borough of churches, it certainly spent its formative years there. One of the game's early promoters was the editor of the *Brooklyn Eagle,* Walt Whitman, whose classic collection of poetry, *Leaves of Grass,* once graced the pages of the *Eagle.* Whitman, in a commentary on July 23, 1846, wrote in part, "We have observed several parties of youngsters playing "base," a game of ball. We wish such sights were more common among us."[6] In the June 20, 1857, issue of *Porter's Spirit of the Times,* a statement reads, "Verily Brooklyn is fast earning the title of the City of Baseball Clubs." As the game continued to grow, so did the number of ball clubs representing the area. In the 1850s some prominent clubs developed. There were the Excelsiors of South Brooklyn, the Putnams of Williamsburg, the Eckfords represented Greenpoint, and the Atlantics were of Bedford. In New York the Knickerbockers, Eagles, and Empires were the vaunted opposition, and great rivalries sprung up among them.

One of the first of its kind involved a series of matches in 1858 held at the Fashion Race Course in what is now Corona, Queens, between all-star teams representing Brooklyn and New York. It was the first time spectators paid to watch a game, spending the exorbitant sum of 50 cents for the privilege. Brooklyn lost two of the three games, but an intercity rivalry, perhaps a horse-and-buggy series, was initiated, to evolve eventually into New York's "subway series." Professionalism would soon replace the amateur ball clubs, and in March 1871 the formation of the National Association of Professional Baseball Players was created as the first pro baseball league.

After that it was the Brooklyn Grays, the Bridegrooms, Ned Hanlon's Superbas and Washington Park. The Trolley Dodgers, the Robins and Ebbets Field followed. But Brooklyn baseball was much more than that. One of the country's top semi-pro teams was the Brooklyn Bushwicks, playing at Dexter Park on the Brooklyn-Queens border from the early 1900s. The Bushwicks drew as many as 15,000 fans on weekends, often outdrawing the Dodgers. Many local names were represented at Dexter Park in the late forties and early fifties before semi-pro ball drifted into oblivion. A number of professionals played under assumed names, such as Gene Hermanski, who played as Gene Walsh. Ralph Branca, Whitey Ford, Phil Rizzuto, Cal Abrams, Tommy Holmes and a host of other local ballplayers were commonly seen in Bushwick games.

Negro League teams came into Dexter Park regularly to face the Bushwicks, which meant such future Dodgers as Jim Gilliam and Joe Black along with Willie Wells and a host of Negro League stars of the day. Additional pros like Sam Mele, Buddy Hassett and Al Lopez were a few more names added to the list.

Waite Hoyt was one of two hundred or so Brooklyn natives who eventually got to the big leagues. A graduate of Erasmus Hall High School, Hoyt had a 21-year Hall-of-Fame career, the most productive of those years, 1921–1930, were spent with the Yankees. Hoyt came home to Brooklyn in 1938 when he finished up with just 16⅓ innings before retiring. Not ready to give it all up, however, and still needing a paycheck, Hoyt signed on with the Bushwicks and was paid $150 a game. A true Brooklynite, Hoyt left his mark on Brooklyn folklore when he was injured and the word spread throughout the borough that "*Hert was Hoit!*"

The foundation of Brooklyn baseball life lay in the sandlots and a 40-acre facility, Parade Ground, a fungo drive from Ebbets Field. Thirteen diamonds spawned dozens of big leaguers. In the post–World War II years and until the mid-sixties, as many as 80 games involving 160 teams were played on summer Saturdays and Sundays. Following Hoyt were Tommy Holmes, Tommy Brown, and Hank Behrman, who preceded Sandy Koufax, the Torre brothers, Frank and Joe, the brothers Aspromonte, Ken and Bob, Rico Petrocelli, Tommy Davis, John Franco, and Willie Randolph.

The recreational facility opened in 1869 as an area for military drills and exercises and soon evolved into a playing ground for sports. In the 1890s the annual polo championships were held and the rapidly growing activity of baseball soon took over. Henry Chadwick, who introduced the box score in the *New York Clipper* in 1872, wrote of the Parade Ground, "It is a glorious sight to see the hundreds of young men and boys enjoying themselves to their heart's content as they do on the Prospect Park Parade Ground every fine afternoon during the summer."[7]

The Dodgers bonded with the youth of Brooklyn in a great many ways. There were free bleacher tickets to be had at local Police Precincts from the PAL (Police Athletic League). The team sponsored a program initially called "Brooklyn Against the World" and later changed to the "Dodger Rookies." At tryouts at Ebbets Field and the Parade Ground they selected a team and then played a schedule of 15 or 20 games in the tri-state area, usually signing a couple of kids to Dodger contracts. Steve Lembo was one who got a shot and made it all the way to Ebbets Field albeit for just a "cup of coffee"—seven games and 11 at-bats—but the experience set him up as a Dodgers scout who patrolled the Ground for the next thirty or so years. A dubious honor was Lembo's. He was in the Dodgers bullpen warming up Erskine and Branca on that October day in 1951 and watched Thomson's drive into the seats from that vantage point.

Brooklyn sandlot baseball flourished in this era with players like Cal Abrams, Bill Lohrman, and Jim Romano. Don McMahon came out of Erasmus Hall High School and had an 18-year career as a relief pitcher in the major leagues. There are four Brooklyn boys in the Baseball Hall of Fame: Wee Willie Keeler, Waite Hoyt, Sandy Koufax and Joe Torre.

In the spring of 1953 one of the local Brooklyn boys was on the Dodgers roster. Bill Antonello was scouted on the sandlots and signed by scout Arthur Dede. Dede hailed from Brooklyn and reached the Dodgers in 1916 for a single hitless at-bat. Like Lembo, Dede was another of the highly visible scouts at the Parade Ground as well as other local venues.

Antonello was a promising outfielder when he signed in 1946. An eight-year minor league career left him on the doorstep of the big club after a breakout season at Mobile in 1952. Bill played in 152 games and hit .290, but the promise of power seemed to materialize in a big way when he hit 28 home runs and drove in 130. It is difficult for a young player to get into a game once a week or so and still prove himself. Antonello appeared in just 40 games with Brooklyn. His 43 at-bats produced one double, one triple, one home run and four RBIs. He struck out eleven times and hit just .163. The '53 season was the only one Bill Antonello would see in the majors.

Brooklyn had its Dodgers and one of the things that made the relationship between the fans and the team so secure was the fact that the players lived in the borough. They lived, they worked, they shopped, they entertained in Brooklyn during the season. The Reeses, the Erskines, the Sniders, the Walkers and the Roes all rented homes in Bay Ridge. Jackie and Rachel Robinson lived with their infant son in an apartment on MacDonough Street in Bedford Stuyvesant, later buying a home in Saint Albans, Queens. One Dodger stayed for good. Gil and Joan Hodges lived on East 32nd Street between Avenues K and L. While Gil Hodges was born in Princeton, Indiana, and grew up in Petersburg, unlike his fellow Hoosier, Carl Erskine, Gil stayed in Brooklyn each winter as well as once his playing days had ended. Hodges married a Brooklyn girl named Joan Lombardi and lived in the borough for the next 25 years, although as Joan said, "Indiana was his home."[8]

Gilbert Ray Hodges was the middle child of Charles and Irene, born on April 4, 1924, in Princeton. When Gil, called "Bud" as a boy, was eight years old, the family moved to Petersburg and Gil, brother Bob and sister Margaret all grew up in that town in the southwest corner of the state. Another sibling, Kenneth, was born in 1926 but died at three months of whooping cough. Both

Princeton and Petersburg were mining towns about 25 miles apart and Charles Hodges worked in the bowels of the earth. Inhaling coal dust left him with a persistent cough, he lost the sight of one eye in a mining accident, and in another had two toes amputated. Charlie also broke his back and his legs. If he had one goal in life, it was, "Charlie's boys will never work the shafts."[9]

Gil and Bob, who was older by one year, were inseparable in youth and both were good athletes. They played five-man football and basketball at Petersburg High School, but since the school did not have a baseball team, they stuck to the sandlots. Gil, being a big, strong kid, was also recruited by the track team to throw the shot put. A fair amount of their baseball came by throwing the ball around with their dad; Charlie had played some semi-pro ball and was always encouraging his boys in the game. Bob became a fairly good pitcher, while Gil played mostly at shortstop.

Irene and Charles were devout Catholics and brought up their children the same way. Bob and Gil served as altar boys at Sts. Peter and Paul parish and attended daily mass. Gil's favorite sport was basketball, and he planned to become a high school coach. Not a particular lover of the game of baseball, Gil was often flippant about it. That attitude got him kicked off the Petersburg Legion team by coach Lonnie Spade. "Bud wasn't even upset by it," recalled a friend. "He just went and played for someone else."[10]

Both Hodges boys received athletic scholarships to St. Joseph College in Rensselaer, about 200 miles away, and they began in September 1941, just three months before the Japanese attacked Pearl Harbor. Gil and Bob joined the Marines ROTC and it was not a question of if but when they would be called to military service. Bob enlisted first, joining the army on March 30, 1943. The two summers that Gil was a college student he played baseball for an industrial team, which is where Stan Freezle got a look at the strapping young ballplayer. Freezle ran a wholesale sporting goods store in Indianapolis and scouted the area for the Brooklyn Dodgers. In addition to Gil, he would sign Carl Erskine and Bob Friend of Lafayette, Indiana.

Freezle invited Hodges to a Dodger tryout camp at Orlean, New York. Brooklyn's Branch Rickey knew that young men like Hodges would soon be in the military, but his game plan was to sign as many players with potential as possible so that when the war ended he would have a wealth of talent to choose from. Highly regarded by Olean manger Jake Pitler and Branch Rickey, Jr., Gil was sent to Ebbets Field so that Rickey could get a look. The boss liked what he saw and signed Hodges with a $1,000 bonus, but it came with a clause.

"I only got half of it," Hodges said. "If I came back from military service I got the other half. Mr. Rickey was not taking any chances."[11]

Hodges slipped into a Dodgers uniform at the end of the '43 season and spent a month learning how to catch. He did not play until the final game of the year, in Cincinnati, at third base. He was hitless in two official trips and made two errors, but he also walked and stole a base. On September 27, 1943, Gil Hodges, 19 and a half years old, enlisted in the United States Marine Corp. After basic training in San Diego, he shipped out to the Pacific aboard the USS *Santa Monica* and by March 1945 was a part of the greatest naval armada ever assembled in preparation for the invasion of Okinawa.

The island lies just 400 miles south of Japan, and as the last line of defense, the Japanese were dedicated to defending the island to the last man. They assigned 85,000 to 100,000 troops to Okinawa's defense. Dubbed Operation Iceberg, the battle began on April 1 and lasted for 82 days. Americans suffered 12,000 casualties; one in five were Marines. Hodges landed with the invasion force at Hagushi Beach. His Sixteenth Antiaircraft Artillery Battalion fought off 108 air raids.

In August two atomic bombs were dropped on Japanese cities and the surrender took place aboard the USS *Missouri* on August 15, 1945. Gil arrived back in California on November 8 and was honorably discharged on February 3, 1946. The Hodges family reunion included brother Bob, who escaped with his life when he was blown out of a Jeep in Germany while serving with the Ninth Army. Hodges never spoke of his war experiences nor of his medals, only that he learned to chain smoke in the foxholes. Several years later when writer Roscoe McGowen called and spoke with Joan Hodges, he asked about the Bronze Star that Gil had been awarded. "I was married three years and I never knew that my husband was awarded a Bronze Star! And when I later told Gil about the call, he still wouldn't talk about it."[12]

Gil joined the Dodgers for spring training and was sent to Class B Newport News where he had a good year in '46, hitting .278 as a catcher. In 1947 Hodges joined the Dodgers amid a tumultuous setting as Jackie Robinson came to Brooklyn. Some teammates tried to prevent Robinson from playing with the club; Hodges was not one of them. Then manager Leo Durocher was suspended for the entire season, and after two regular season games, Burt Shotton took over as the skipper. Hodges got into 28 games that season, but it was the next campaign that Brooklyn's game plan for the next ten years was laid out. They traded second baseman Eddie Stanky to the Braves to allow Jackie Robinson to take over his best position, leaving an opening at first base. It was Durocher who was responsible for putting Gil on first base. He knew that the team's future behind the plate belonged to Roy Campanella and was anxious to bring him to Brooklyn. He also knew that

Hodges, great athlete that he was, could excel defensively at just about any position on the field.

Beginning in 1949 when Gil played 156 games and hit 23 home runs, he would embark on a string of 11 consecutive seasons with 22 or more home runs. His 115 RBIs represented the first of seven straight 100-RBI seasons. He topped out at 130 in 1954. His best homer season was also '54 when he belted 42. He finished with 370 lifetime and 1,274 runs batted in. Over 18 seasons he hit a collective .273, while becoming one of the most feared sluggers in baseball. During the decade of the 1950s Duke Snider hit more home runs and had more RBIs than anyone in baseball. Gil Hodges was second in both categories.

Hodges hit 14 grand slam home runs in his career, and on August 30, 1950, hit four homers in one game. He became the premier defensive first baseman of his era, and rated among the best of all-time. A sample of his prowess came on September 5, 1950, in a game against the Giants. With a runner on first, Gil charged the plate on a bunt, picked it off and tagged the hitter who was barely out of the box, then wheeled and threw to second for the double play. Teammate Carl Erskine remarked, "I've never even heard of anyone else ever doing that."[13]

Hodges developed the reputation of being one of the strongest men in baseball, and it did not come merely from hitting home runs. He was also one of the gentlest and nicest men, but never was he a pushover. In a series at the Polo Grounds in 1952 during the heyday of the great Giants-Dodgers beanball rivalry, Gil was hit by a pitch. He spiked Giants second baseman Bill Rigney, which put him out of the game. The day before he had knocked Davy Williams for a loop with a hard slide at second, putting two Giants keystone sackers out of action in two days.

No stranger to on-the-field chaos when playing for the Dodgers, Hodges was usually a peacemaker. He pulled the Braves' Eddie Mathews away from a brawl by lifting him off the ground, and did the same to shortstop Johnny Logan during a typical Dodgers melee. In a game at Fort Worth, Dee Fondy went after Pee Wee Reese. Hodges lifted the 6'3" 190-pound Fondy off his feet and removed him from Pee Wee's vicinity. His hands were enormous. They said he didn't need a mitt. Gabe Verde, a Brooklyn lab technician, once had to do an X-ray of Hodges' hand. "It was so big," Verde said, "I had to use two plates."[14]

Coming into the 1953 season, however, Gil had a problem. His 0-for–10 performance of the plate at the end of '52 had led into the 0-for–21 World Series showing and the new season began with Hodges still mired in a slump.

By mid–May the slugger remained helpless at the plate. He was benched with a .187 average. It was during this period that the story takes on the aura of legend. On a sultry Sunday morning, May 17, at the 10 o'clock Mass at St. Francis Xavier Roman Catholic church, Father Herbert Redmond addressed the congregation with the words, "It's too hot for a sermon today. Go home, keep the commandments, and say a prayer for Gil Hodges."[15] The first baseman broke out of his slump a few days later and went on to have one of his best years.

Gil's last home run as a Brooklyn Dodger came on September 20, 1957, against Phillies pitcher Warren Hacker. It was his 298th. The next year the Dodgers were in Los Angeles and Gil played for them through the '61 season. He then returned to New York as a member of the expansion Mets. After 11 games in '63 he was traded to the Washington Senators to become their manager. The decision took some of his teammates by surprise. "I didn't think he

Gil and Joan Hodges and family (Brooklyn Public Library—Brooklyn Collection).

had the right kind of personality to become a manager," said roomie Carl Furillo. "Once he took the job, though, I knew he'd be successful."[16]

Hodges managed the Senators through the '67 season and then joined the Mets in '68 when they finished in ninth place. Seldom has a manager received more plaudits from his players than Hodges did from the '69 Mets. The media called them a "Miracle" team, but the players knew better. "We had 25 players and we had 25 heroes in the final six weeks of the '69 season," said ace right-hander Tom Seaver, "and the biggest hero of all was Gil Hodges."[17]

"Gil was always in complete control of himself," Ed Charles said. "No matter what the situation he just never wavered. He steadied the ball club."[18]

Right from spring training, Gil believed that the talent was there and he never lost faith in his players. A disciplinarian yet popular with them, Gil kept things bottled up inside. Art Shamsky, an outfielder with the club, recalled how often when Gil would be bothered about something, he would not say anything but "the veins in his neck would bulge and you knew you were in trouble."[19]

Hodges took the underdog Mets to a pennant and an improbable World Series victory over the Baltimore Orioles. But the smoking and the pent up stress seemed to take its toll. "Most of us blow up," Mets coach Joe Pignatano said. "Gil just sits there and lets it grind away at him."[20] In September 1968, his first year as Mets manager, Hodges experienced sharp pains in his chest. On the 24th during a game against the Braves, he went to lie down in the clubhouse and then was taken to the hospital. He was diagnosed with a heart attack. Hodges took the winter to convalesce and went into the '69 season feeling much better. The Mets finished third in '70 and '71 with identical records of 83–79. In the spring of 1972, on April 2, only two days before his 48th birthday, Gil Hodges suffered a fatal heart attack. He had just completed a round of golf with his coaches, Rube Walker, Eddie Yost and Joe Pignatano. "He was walking with me when he fell," said Pignatano. "His head hit the sidewalk and he was bleeding and I cradled him in my arms."[21]

Gil's death was a shock to his friends, his team, all of baseball and Brooklyn's fans. His family was devastated. A wake was held on April 4, his birthday, at Our Lady Help of Christians Roman Catholic Church on East 28th Street in Brooklyn. It was estimated that more than 10,000 mourners viewed the casket. It was a last goodbye to a man that it is said was never booed in Brooklyn. In spite of slumps, Carl Erskine pointed out, "He never got booed. The Brooklyn fans booed every one of us at one time or another—if we played bad, they'd let us know. But never Gil. It was partly that he married a Brooklyn girl and lived there year round, but it was mostly because they recognized that he was so genuine."[22]

Gil Hodges is not in the Baseball Hall of Fame, a disgraceful omission; suffice to say, he belongs. There is a stone monument in Princeton, Indiana, that stands next to the Gil Hodges Bridge. There is a space at the bottom of the slab meant to house the words on Gil's Hall of Fame plaque. The space remains empty, as empty as the space on the Wall of Plaques in Cooperstown.

Hodges opened a 48-lane bowling alley near his home, another way of bonding with the community. There were other ballplayers over the years who had businesses in Brooklyn. Relief pitcher Hugh Casey had a popular bar and pitcher Freddie Fitzsimmons had a bowling alley on Empire Boulevard, near Ebbets Field.

Bowling, dancing, going to nightclubs or the movies, this is how Brooklynites spent their free time in the fifties. Brooklyn at that time was chocolate layer cake at Ebingers bakery, a "kitchen sink" at Jahn's ice cream parlor, nickel Cokes at the corner candy store and seven-cent egg creams at Walter Dahl's luncheonette on Church Avenue. It was double features at the Loew's Kings on Flatbush Avenue and a new baseball glove bought at Friedman's Sporting Goods. It was confraternity dances, sandlot baseball, street games, touch football, roller hockey and stickball. It was a language where "*erl*" meant "oil," and "*oil*" meant "Earl."

It was neighborhood block parties and it was diversity; ethnic, racial, customs, mores—with all of that this working class culture sought one thing to bring it all together. Albert Einstein sought a unifying force for all the matter in the universe. In Brooklyn they found it ... and they called that force the Brooklyn Dodgers!

Three

A Dubious Spring

"Trouble on the Dodgers"—Milton Gross, *New York Post*

The year 1953 opened on a high note for the reigning National League champs. On January 12 at the Hawaiian Room of the Lexington Hotel in Manhattan, Dodger president Walter O'Malley threw a party, ostensibly to announce the signing of his "Big Three" to 1953 contracts. Jackie Robinson would receive $38,000 for the upcoming year of play, Captain Pee Wee Reese $33,500, and catcher Roy Campanella put his signature on a contract calling for $25,000. By February 3 it was reported that all the Dodgers had signed their contracts, making them the first major league club to lock up a full roster for the upcoming campaign.

On February 1 the New York Chapter of the Baseball Writers Association held their annual dinner at the Waldorf-Astoria Hotel. They presented Dodgers shortstop Pee Wee Reese with the "Sid Mercer Player of the Year" award, only the second Dodger to be named the recipient of this prestigious honor, joining Dixie Walker in 1945.

Baseball's "Mahatma," Branch Rickey, the man who said, "Luck is the residue of design," had his imprint all over this '53 club. With the exception of Reese, who preceded Branch to Brooklyn, Jim Gilliam, a rookie, and Russ Meyer, who came in a trade, this was Rickey's ball club. In the same way, Vero Beach was the Dodgers' spring home, and its facilities were the offspring of the man who was the Dodgers' boss from 1942 to 1950. Opened on March 1, 1949, the new facility had everyone in awe; only Walter O'Malley claimed it was too expensive. Rickey called it "Dodgertown," and he could now implement his plan of creating a baseball college where all members of the organization could be taught the nuances of the game by a bevy of astute baseball men under the supervision of the great man himself.

All of the players in the organization, both major and minor leaguers,

36

were housed at the complex. They ate together in a huge cafeteria and worked out together. It was fitting that the land had once been a United States Naval base since Rickey ran it like a military establishment. The day began with reveille, breakfast and the Pledge of Allegiance to the American flag. Calisthenics were followed by work using an assortment of training techniques Rickey had developed. Rickey believed that spring was the time for instruction and he devised all sorts of instructional gizmos, most of which had not been used by any other clubs. Rickey was the first to use the pitching machine. "I introduced the pitching machine as a feature of spring training," he explained in a '53 article. "I also introduced the use of strings to define the strike zone at the plate, a device which theoretically should help the pitcher gain control."[1]

There were sliding pits in Rickey's camps that everyone, even the pitchers used to learn to slide properly. Hitters hit off batting tees and pitching machines. Players worked on defensive skills and took part in infield and outfield practice. The end of the day usually came with a lecture by Rickey about some aspect of the inside game, sprinkled with some of his motivational discoursing.

Wesley Branch Rickey was born on December 20, 1881, in Madison Township, Ohio. His parents, Emily and Frank, were devout and pious Christians and instilled principles in their children that remained with Branch throughout his life. Young Branch's famous vow never to play ball on Sundays was made to his mother during these years, and it would be a vow he kept all of his years in baseball.

Rickey attended a neighborhood school in Lucasville. Since there were not enough courses to achieve a high school diploma, he left without one but got a teaching job at a schoolhouse 18 miles from his home. He made the trip by bicycle each day. He taught himself Latin, higher mathematics and rhetoric and passed the entrance exams for Ohio Wesleyan University. Branch did two years of prep work and four years of college in three and one-third years. Rickey loved baseball and had grown up playing the game with his brothers. He played football and semi-pro baseball. In 1903 he caught for the Laramie, Wyoming, team, then with Dallas, and late that year joined the Cincinnati Reds. When he refused to play Sunday ball, he was sent back to Dallas. After that he always insisted on a contract clause excusing him from Sunday games.

Rickey earned a law degree and became a member of the St. Louis Browns while still a student. With school and a coaching job at Ohio Wesleyan in addition to playing with the New York Highlanders after the Browns traded him, he may have, as Harvey Frommer suggests, spread himself too thin. "He missed spring training because of commitments at OWU, and that season batted just .182."[2] He once made nine errors in an 11-game stretch and set a record for catchers by allowing thirteen stolen bases in one nine-inning game. In the spring of 1909 he suffered the symptoms that led to tuberculosis and spent six months recuperating at Saranac Lake in upstate New York. He tried studying law but his heart was in baseball. Clearly, his future was not as a player.

It was Rickey's farm system that turned the St. Louis Cardinals of the 1930s and '40s into winners. He received the approval of Cardinals owner Sam Breadon, because it was far less expensive to grow your own players. The first successful product was a first baseman, "Sunny" Jim Bottomly, who hit .310 over 16 major league seasons and was elected to the Baseball Hall of Fame in 1974. The last was a pitcher-turned-outfielder from Donora, Pennsylvania, that everybody called "The Man," the nickname incidentally given to Stan Musial by the fans in Brooklyn.

Described as frugal and given the name "El Cheapo" by New York columnist Jimmy Powers, Rickey was better known as "Mahatma," and his office was "The Cave of the Winds." Sportswriter Tom Meany, after reading John Gunther's book *Inside Asia,* in which he described Gandhi as a combination of Jesus Christ, Tammany Hall and your father, thought it was an apt description of Rickey; it stayed with him throughout his career. Rickey came to Brooklyn in the offseason of 1942 and began to apply his magic to the Dodgers.

Of all of his contributions to baseball, Rickey's everlasting legacy would be bringing Jackie Robinson to the major leagues, although there was more depth to his actions than ordinarily meets the eye. He brought Roy Campanella and Don Newcombe to Brooklyn soon enough, but baseball's Moses also had a young outfielder named Larry Doby in his sights. Rickey did not compete with Bill Veeck for the services of the 22-year-old Doby, however. He joined Cleveland six weeks after Robinson began with the Dodgers. Carl Erskine said, "Mr. Rickey had the wisdom to know the importance of having both leagues integrate at about the same time. " The Dodger right-hander believes that Rickey could have had Doby, and if the future Hall-of-Fame player had joined Snider and Furillo in the Dodgers outfield, "I would have had all those World Series rings instead of Yogi."[3]

The Rickey legacy had been further enhanced by a slew of exciting young minor league prospects invited to spring camp with the big club. Players like infielders Don Hoak, Don Zimmer and Wayne Belardi had successful seasons in the high minors and were ready. The same was true for outfield prospects Dick Williams, Bill Antonello, and Don Thompson. There was, however, a barrier that prevented these fine young players from realizing their dreams:

Brooklyn native Bill Antonello made it to the Dodgers in 1953 (Brooklyn Public Library—Brooklyn Collection).

the virtually impenetrable wall of Dodger regulars. At shortstop, Pee Wee Reese was the team captain and the oldest Dodger in point of service, having come up in 1940. The third baseman was Billy Cox, arguably the finest glove man at his position, and at first base the fixture was Gil Hodges. The big slugger had four consecutive 100-RBI seasons behind him and would add three more.

The outfield offered better opportunity. Furillo in right and Snider in center were solid fixtures, but the Dodgers had traded their left fielder, Andy Pafko, to the Braves. It remains a mystery why the Dodgers would send away the man who solved their perennial left field problem. A solid ballplayer both defensively and offensively, Pafko hit 30 home runs in '51. In his only full year in Brooklyn, he hit 19 of round-trippers, drove in 85 runs, and hit for a .287 average. For a time, with Furillo, Snider and Pafko, the Dodgers had the best outfield in baseball. The front office mentioned something about young out-fielders, but Andy was 31 and would have another seven productive years with Milwaukee, which included two more World Series appearances.

In any case, the trade opened up the left field spot and among those considered to have a chance was George Shuba. George Thomas Shuba, the second player who had a pinch-hit home run in the World Series, was born in Youngstown, Ohio, one of 11 children. His father, John, left his farm in Czechoslovakia in 1912 and came to America, settling in Youngstown. The area had other Slovak Catholics. George played his youth baseball at Borts Park in his neighborhood. In 1943 the Dodgers held a tryout that George attended as a third baseman. Nothing seemed to come of it, but that winter a Dodgers representative, Harold Roettger, came to the Shuba home to offer George a contract. A $150 bonus got him to New Orleans in 1944. At Mobile in 1947, Shuba hit .288 with 21 home runs and 108 RBIs.

Contract negotiations being what they were at the time, the next spring Branch Rickey informed Shuba that he was being sent back to Mobile. Fine power but not enough average, he was told. "I shorten up. It's '48," Shuba said. "I bat .389. The next spring it's back to Mobile again. 'Nice batting,' Rickey says, 'but your power fell off. We need someone who can hit them over that short right field wall in Ebbets Field.'"[4] Although not highly regarded as a defensive outfielder, Shuba had a quick left-handed bat and after 34 games in Brooklyn in 1950, he was back in '52 for 94 games and a .305 batting average. Though never getting the chance to play regularly, Shuba stayed in the majors for seven years, all of them spent with the Dodgers, and hit .259. In 1953 he appeared in 74 games, had 169 at-bats, and hit .254.

Another who came under front office consideration for the left field spot was the Cuban-born Edmundo "Sandy" Amoros. Sandy could run, and it was thought may be able to hit big league pitching. Sandy was born in Havana, Cuba, in 1930 and threw and batted left-handed.

The gap, however, would soon be filled from within, and the rookies, those who made the roster, would spend most of the season on the bench. With the departure of Pafko, it was rumored that the Dodgers might be interested in a trade with the Pirates for their great home run hitter, Ralph Kiner, said to be available. But O'Malley and Dodgers GM Buzzy Bavasi turned thumbs down on the idea citing the number of good young players in camp. "One of the things we need," said Bavasi, "is a pitcher who can start every four days, even if he doesn't finish."[5]

Russell Charles Meyer was born in Peru, Illinois, on October 25, 1923, and signed by Chicago in 1942. He made his major league debut on September 13, 1946, for the Cubs and put together a 13 year career in the majors, winning 94 games and losing 73. The right-hander was 9–11 with the pennant-winning "Whiz Kids" of Philadelphia in 1950 before the trade that brought him to Brooklyn prior to the '53 season.

Traded to the Phillies in 1949, Meyer had his best year to date that season when he went 17–8, though he was known more for his explosive and unpredictable temper. He was nicknamed "Monk" as a high school football player and it was later extended to "The Mad Monk" when examples of his tempestuous outbursts became legend. In a telling episode in 1948 while pitching for the Cubs at Ebbets Field, Meyer watched from the mound as Jackie Robinson stole home. Called safe by plate umpire Frank Dascoli, Meyer stormed to the plate, grabbed the ump by the lapels and ripped off some buttons while verbally abusing the arbiter in the exchange. As it turned out, a TV microphone caught his verbal denunciation of Dascoli and it was made available to the public. A fine and a week's suspension were handed to the pitcher.

The deal that brought Meyer to the Dodgers was a bit complicated. He had gone 13–14 in '52 with an ERA of 3.14 and threw 232⅓ innings, second only to Robin Roberts on the Phillies' staff. Refused a raise from $11,500 to $14,000 by Philadelphia owner Bob Carpenter, Meyer asked to be traded. Sent by the Phils to the Braves in exchange for Earl Torgeson and $100,000, six hours later the Braves shipped him to Brooklyn for Rocky Bridges and Jim Pendleton. Not particularly happy about going to the Braves, Meyer kept a dental appointment the morning he received the news. When he returned home, his wife informed him that he had wound up with the Dodgers. He was elated. "What started out to be the worst break of my life turned out to be the best," he said. "With that ball club behind me, if I don't win 18 or 20 games, I'll hang up my glove."[6] The clincher regarding the joy the Mad Monk felt about going to the Dodgers came when Buzzy Bavasi asked him how much he wanted. Meyer said $16,000, Bavasi said, "You got it."[7]

Intent upon making the new addition to the club happy, the Dodgers even picked up his moving expenses, something they were not obligated to do. Meyer didn't win 18 or 20 and didn't hang up his glove, but he did go 15–5 in 1953 and was a monumental acquisition for Brooklyn. In three seasons before he was traded to the Cubs, he won 32 and lost 13.

If there was any uncertainty on the part of the Dodgers' front office in making the deal, it most likely stemmed from a previous confrontation between Meyer and Jackie Robinson. Meyer would throw at Jackie and the Dodger would steal him blind. In an incident at Ebbets Field, Robinson was caught in a run-down between third base and home. When Meyer covered the plate, Jackie slammed into him, dislodging the ball. The irate Monk challenged Robinson to meet him under the stands. Jack came out of the dugout ready to fight but cooler heads prevailed. After the game, Meyer apologized to Robinson and Jackie accepted some of the blame and the incident was for-

Manager Charlie Dressen (right) instructs his new pitcher, Russ "Mad Monk" Meyer, on how to behave in Brooklyn (Brooklyn Public Library—Brooklyn Collection).

gotten. When Russ reported to the Dodgers, neither he nor Robinson showed anything but elation.

Meyer remembered entering the locker room for the first time. "When I walked in, Jackie got up, and he walked right up to me. He held out his hand, and he said, 'We've been fighting one another. Now let's fight them together.' I said, 'OK, pal.'"[8]

There were events in baseball that spring that to the observer seemed to have little bearing on the Dodgers, yet the tremors were substantial. On March 18, the National League unanimously approved the relocation of Lou Perini's Boston Braves to Milwaukee. It was the first time in 50 years that such a move had occurred, and it proved to be the onset of a new era of bouncing franchises. The next year the Browns would leave St. Louis for Baltimore, and in '55 the Philadelphia Athletics left their home for Kansas City. The Braves drew just 281,278 fans in Boston in 1952 and spent the next nine years attracting more than one million in the beer capital. After that attendance began to fall off until 1965, when the team packed up again and settled in Atlanta.

The initial move was made with the full support and aid of Walter O'Malley, the Dodgers' president, as he exercised his considerable influence among the National League owners. It was in O'Malley's best interest that the Braves succeed. By this time Los Angeles had become a no-brainer for expansion, having been on the drawing board since 1941. It remained to be seen who would get there first. It seems apparent in retrospect that the Dodger boss had the West Coast city in his sights since at least the late forties and 1953 may well have been the kick-off point for serious negotiations. O'Malley was sure to take notice of the 43,000 seats at the new Milwaukee County Stadium and the 10,000 parking spots.

The Dodgers head man knew that Ebbets Field had to be replaced; he would get no argument about that. But as writer Peter Golenbock pointed out, O'Malley's approach was, "Give me a bigger and newer stadium, he was saying. Give me. Not build me. Give me."[9]

Brooklyn's fans, however, unaware of the scheming in the O'Malley mind, were more concerned with the spring uncertainties in the Dodgers camp. Catcher Roy Campanella, the National League MVP in 1951, had suffered an injury to his right thumb and chipped a bone in his left elbow in '52. His average dipped to .269 and was accompanied by drop-offs in both his home run and RBI production. His 22 home runs were down from 30-plus the previous two years, although he did drive in 97 runs. It remained to be seen whether the powerful backstop would regain his health 100 percent.

During a routine eye examination early in the '52 season, right fielder

Carl Furillo was diagnosed with cataracts. He passed it off as some grit in the eyes and refused to have an operation. The result was a .247 average, some 50 points below his ultimate lifetime mark. On January 7, 1953, Furillo underwent surgery on both eyes at the eye, ear, nose and throat branch of St. Clare's Hospital in Manhattan. The Dodgers could only hope that Furillo's bat would be back to normal.

There was nothing physical about Gil Hodges' problems that spring. In his last 10 at-bats of the previous season, the first baseman had been hitless. Then followed that horrendous World Series that saw Hodges go hitless in 21 official times at the plate. He went 0-for-6 in the spring before connecting for a two-run home run on March 10 against the Phillies. A couple of days later he hit another two-run blast, but these bursts of power were nothing but fool's gold. There was real cause for worry as the slump continued into the new season. Going back to the onset of the trouble in '52, Gil would hit .132 in his last 106 at-bats. After being benched in late May, the slump broke and Hodges had one of his best seasons. But in the spring, the Dodgers could not know that, resulting in grave cause for concern.

All was not orange juice and sunshine for the club that spring, and when Dick Young's column in the *New York Daily News* hit the street early in the spring, ruminations of 1947 hovered over the ball club. Billy Cox was a sensitive, introspective man who still suffered from the effects of World War II. There were apparently psychological traumas from combat. When the press reported that Cox may be relegated to a utility role for the new season, manager Dressen's announcement came without informing the player, and Cox was upset. It was thought that the best third baseman in baseball could not play 154 games, and so it seemed the utility role was appropriate.

At a press conference in Vero Beach on February 21, Dressen expressed the idea of relegating Cox to a utility role, allowing either Bobby Morgan, Don Hoak or Jim Baxes to take over at third base. Dressen failed to mention the plan to Cox in advance and Billy heard the rumors from reporters. The introverted Cox was put in a difficult situation, and he was confused and distressed. His wife, Anne, expressed his disillusion when she said, "This was one spring when we thought Billy's job was all set at last. Every other year we came down here and we had to battle 10 others for it."[10]

There was some grumbling among other players—particularly the pitchers—about not having Cox's magnificent glove out there behind them every day. However, it was a managerial decision and they would live with it. That's where it seemed to end until the other shoe dropped. Dressen had never been sold on the other three infielders, and the next announcement was that Robinson would shift to third base, relegating Morgan and Hoak to the bench. Baxes was optioned to Fort Worth.

The Dodgers had a 24-year-old switch-hitting second baseman at Montreal who hit .301 and was the International League MVP in 1952. Young wrote that Jim Gilliam would take over at second base, moving Robinson to third and Cox to the bench. Young's analysis was correct, apparently having gotten his inside dope from Buzzy Bavasi. The trouble arose primarily because Cox was not informed about any of this, the sensitive player first heard about it through a reporter ... and Gilliam was black.

Jim Gilliam was born in Nashville, Tennessee, on October 17, 1928, and acquired the nickname "Junior" as a youthful member of the Negro League Baltimore Elite Giants. A member of Baltimore's championship season in 1949, the Chicago Cubs were interested in purchasing his contract, and along with a teammate, Stubs Ferrell, they were invited to the Cubs' Springfield, Massachusetts, club and then spring training in Haines City, Florida. This was in March 1950. Both players were released three weeks later. Gilliam was surprised. "I hit over .300 during spring training and fielded well," he said. "To this day, I don't know what it was all about."[11] Gilliam stayed with the Elite Giants through the 1950 season.

In December the Dodgers offered options on Gilliam and Joe Black and after spring training paid $10,000 for the two players to Richard Powell, the Elite's owner. The Baltimore Negro League club sent three players to Brooklyn and to the majors; Roy Campanella was the other. Joe Black was the 1952 Rookie of the Year and Jim Gilliam won that award in '53. But Gilliam's introduction to the team was a bit rocky.

The headline on the front page of the March 23 issue of the *New York Post* read "Ike Maps Action on McCarthy." Above the bold letters in a green banner the paper announced, "The Inside Story: Trouble on the Dodgers." The story written by Milton Gross said in part, "Negro baiting remarks were made, not all in jest." Gross blamed manager Chuck Dressen and vice president Buzzy Bavasi who, in failing to discuss the issue with Cox, "unwittingly began the movement of the clock back to 1947."[12]

Roger Kahn added to the racial suggestions when he wrote, "Remarks by some Dodgers in the clubhouse and at their hotel indicate that the problem of Negros in baseball is still to be finally resolved."[13]

Both Robinson and Joe Black, two of the club's three African American players, tried to neutralize the damage by publicly lauding the defensive virtues of Billy Cox and downplaying any racial inferences. In attempting to defuse the situation, Jackie said, "The only issue was the benching of Billy Cox, the best third man in baseball and the most underrated player in baseball, without telling him what it was all about. That I was taking his place had nothing to do with it."[14] Black was quoted as saying, "I'll miss Billy's glove at third. That was a big help."[15]

Robinson also said, "Someone has moved him out of his position and he has a right to be upset. I don't think it makes any difference to him whether that someone is white or Negro."[16] Carl Erskine, liked and respected by both players and writers, was the team's player representative and, as such, was often consulted on issues that players found to be disturbing for one reason or another. He is emphatic when he says, "I never heard any racial slurs behind Jackie's back or directed towards the other fellows." The only negative remarks came from reserves who always felt some resentment when a player was brought up and might be used over them. "It was odd," Erskine said, "Cox was a fantastic fielder, but every year there were rumors that he would be replaced. His job was never secure yet he always wound up out there again."[17] Buzzie Bavasi stepped in and spoke to five individuals and the issue dissolved in a matter of days. Gross wrote, "It was a shameful and wholly unnecessary interlude which could have been avoided."[18]

Perhaps, but the specter of racial disharmony was yet to be subdued and would become more evident with several ugly incidents through the course of the season. Jackie Robinson remained outspoken and aggressive, especially where racial matters were concerns, and had stirred the pot that offseason. In an appearance on a popular television program, *Youth Wants to Know,* he responded to a question about whether the Yankees, who had yet to sign a black player, were anti–Negro. With no hesitation, Jack answered, "Yes." His reference, he pointed out, was not at the players, whom he said "were fine sportsmen and wonderful gentlemen," but to the club management.[19] The negative reaction to Robinson's remarks was swift, both from the Yankees and the press.

In a call from Ford Frick, the commissioner of baseball, Jackie was asked to avoid the issue if possible in the future. Robinson said he would but explained also that he merely had expressed an honest answer to the question.

While Don Newcombe was lost to the Dodgers again in '53 because of his military service brought on by the Korean War, others were returning from their hitches. The major leagues had a ruling that ex–GIs could not be sent to the minors without their consent; however, any players kept on the major league roster would not be counted against the player limit allowed. This meant, in effect, that rosters could be increased. Whitey Ford returned to the

Yankees but would have no effect on the Dodgers season until the World Series. National Leaguers, however, were another matter. Pitcher Harvey Haddix was discharged in time to join the Cardinals in August of 1952. In '53 Haddix had his best year in the majors, going 20–9 for St. Louis.

Haddix is best remembered for his phenomenal performance while with the Pirates on May 26, 1959, against the Milwaukee Braves. He threw 12 perfect innings before losing the game on one hit in the 13th. An error by third baseman Don Hoak in the 13th ended the perfect game. The runner, Felix Mantilla, advanced to second on a sacrifice bunt by Eddie Mathews. An intentional walk to Hank Aaron preceded Joe Adcock's apparent home run. But Adcock passed Aaron on the bases and the hit was ruled a double. Milwaukee won the one-hitter, 2–0. Incidentally, Lew Burdette threw a complete-game shutout for the Braves.

The military rule allowed the Dodgers to keep two young pitchers on the roster, Glenn Mickens and Bob Milliken. Milliken pitched six shutout innings on March 25 against the Braves. Mickens appeared in only four games for 6⅓ innings before being sent to the minors, never returning to the big leagues. Milliken was around only for two seasons, but in '53 he went 8–4 in 117⅓ innings.

The episode involving Gilliam and Cox was, in a sense, a minor replay of 1947 with some unrest among the players and a settling down that would produce a pennant. Billy Cox played 100 games and hit .291, his best single-season average. Robinson split his time between third base and left field, hit .329, and drove home 95 runs. The rookie, Junior Gilliam, played in 151 games and hit for a .278 average. He scored 125 runs and led the league in triples with 17. Gilliam taught himself to switch-hit. A natural right-hander, he learned how to hit from the left side. He said, "Those curveballs bothered me, now they don't because they're comin' right at me."[20]

The Dodgers opened the exhibition season on March 7 and 8 with two games against the Braves, which they won. They then took two from the Phils. When Gil Hodges hit a two-run home run on March 10 against the Phillies, it was his first hit of the spring after 37 futile at-bats. In the game of March 11, Holman Stadium at Dodgertown in Vero Beach was dedicated. With 5,532 fans in the seats, the Dodgers beat the A's, 4–2, with Carl Erskine, the projected Opening Day starter, pitching four good innings and allowing only one hit. On March 18 against the Senators at Vero Beach, Gilliam started at second base and Jackie played third. Through the first nine exhibition games, Gilliam was hitting .300.

Rookie left-hander Johnny Podres had been suffering from an ailing back but on March 1 in an intra-squad game he threw three innings and felt no pain or twinges—a positive sign for Dressen and his pitching staff. Carl Erskine went to the hill in late March with the intent of going as far as he could. He went all the way, a complete-game shutout over the Philadelphia Athletics, allowing just two hits. The little right-hander seemed ready for the Opening Day assignment that was sure to be his come April 14 at Ebbets Field. Harold Burr was prompted to write in the *Brooklyn Eagle*, "It's still March but Brooklyn appears stronger than last year in young pitching and reserves."[21]

There was some skepticism expressed about the Dodgers' chances in '53. In some cases it may merely have been wishful thinking. The manager of the Philadelphia Phillies, Steve O'Neill, thought the Dodgers would not be able to retain their dominance over the second-division clubs as they had the year before. He noted also that his ace, Robin Roberts, had beaten Brooklyn six times in '52. As it turned out, the Dodgers went 6–1 against Roberts, and their record against the second-division teams was a collective 63–25, with a superlative 20 wins in 22 games against the lowly Pittsburgh Pirates.

Dressen told the press in March that Joe Black would remain in the same role in '53 as he held the previous year. But the season would herald the sad demise of the superlative pitcher that Black was in 1952. In his rookie year, Black had been named Rookie of the Year on the strength of a 15–4 record in 57 games. He saved another 15 games and had an ERA of 2.14. In spite of having started only one game during the regular season, Joe was named the starting pitcher in game one of the World Series against the Yankees. He bested Allie Reynolds with a complete-game 4–2 victory, becoming the first black pitcher to win a World Series game. Black also started games four and seven, and though defeated both times, he pitched well. Facing Reynolds, he lost, 2–0, in the fourth game and, 4–2, in the final game seven. Joe's World Series ERA was 2.53.

What happened in '53? His record was 6–3 and his earned run average ballooned to 5.33. "It has bothered me through the years," Black said, "not knowing if the circumstances and events curtailed my effectiveness or if, like a meteor, I was just a temporary flash."[22] Dressen felt that Joe had gotten by on just two pitches and needed to add to that repertoire. Don Newcombe warned him not to mess with his style, the style that had been so successful. Joe himself was uncertain but he followed orders. He worked on a forkball, knuckle ball, sinkers and changes off the fastball but seemed unable to master any of them. The real problem seemed to be physical.

Black was born with a deformed index finger that made it difficult for him to grip the ball properly when throwing any pitch other than the fastball and the quick, short curve. After weeks of futile attempts, Dressen told him to go back to his old style of pitching. However, it was apparently too late. "The trials and tribulations of different strides and pitches had deprived me of my rhythm and form," Black said. "I became flustered because of this turn of events."[23] Black won no games in 1954 while making just five appearances. The following year he was traded to Cincinnati, where he finished the season at 6–2 with a 4.05 ERA. He was gone in '57 after landing with Washington.

While there was cause for optimism, concern still existed regarding the recurrence of Furillo, Campanella and Hodges to the height of their former abilities.

The Yankees were departing St. Petersburg for the trip north and Casey Stengel was besieged with questions about the chance for a record-setting fifth consecutive World Series title. No one before—not Connie Mack, John McGraw nor Joe McCarthy—had been able to turn the trick. Casey was confident without being arrogant when he said, "I believe we can make it, mainly because of the depth of our pitching. However, I don't want to be quoted as saying that it is a sure thing."[24] He saw complacency as the Yankees' biggest hurdle, however. "Complacency," Casey said, "is a terrible disease in baseball. It withers ambition and dulls the intellect."[25]

There were memorable moments in 1953 and not all of them took place in or around Ebbets Field. On January 20 General Dwight David Eisenhower was sworn in as the 34th president of the United States. A truce in July brought the war in Korea to a halt. On March 26, Dr. Jonas Salk produced a vaccine to cure Poliomyelitis—polio—and no longer would the dreaded disease bring fear to families. Arguably the greatest all-around athlete America ever produced was the Sac and Fox Indian from Prague, Oklahoma. He won both the decathlon and pentathlon in the 1912 Olympics in Stockholm, Sweden, and played professional football and major league baseball. Jim Thorpe died on March 28.

Scientific research was breaking new ground by introducing a previously unfamiliar term to the vocabulary—Deoxyribose Nucleic Acid—DNA. The discovery of its nature would be one of the more significant stories of 1953. In Hutchinson, Kansas, on May 6, Dr. John H. Gibbons Jr. would perform the first successful use of artificial circulation in humans as he closed a hole between the upper chambers of the heart of an 18-year-old girl. The doctor would perform the first open heart surgery. On May 29 Sir Edmund Hillary of New Zealand and Tenzing Norgay of Nepal reached the summit of Mount Everest, in the Himalaya range, an elevation of more than 29,000 feet, the highest point on Earth.

Reports of unidentified flying objects (UFOs) were rampant in 1953, as they had been since the first reports in 1947. In March alone there were reported sightings in Hackettstown, New Jersey, Elmira, New York, and San Antonio, Texas. Hollywood stayed abreast of the phenomenon with 1953 alien-oriented films like *War of the Worlds* and *Invaders from Mars.* It also saw the light side when Universal Studios released *Abbott and Costello Go to Mars.*

The population of the United States was 160,184,192, the unemployment rate stood at 3 percent and life expectancy was 68.2 years. A magazine ad proclaimed that "Dollar for dollar you can't beat a Pontiac," and there were 26 million TV sets in 28 million U.S. homes. Konrad Adenauer of Germany was *Time* magazine's Man of the Year. Milk cost 32 cents a gallon, eggs were 24 cents a dozen, and a loaf of bread was 16 cents.

A new home could be purchased for $9,525, the average income stood at $4,011 per year, and the average rent for an apartment was $83 per month. A new car cost $1,651, gasoline was 20 cents a gallon, and you could mail a letter with a three-cent stamp. Earl Wilson's column of "Gossip, Gags, and Rumor" appearing in the *New York Post* always closed with the line, "That's earl, brother!" In March you could go to the Mayfair theater at Avenue U and Coney Island Avenue and see Ida Lupino in *The Roadhouse* and Richard Widmark starring in *The Kiss of Death* in a double bill. At the Kingsway on Kings Highway one could enjoy Red Skelton as *The Clown* along with Paramount's "thrill-packed" *Thunder in the East* with a cast that included Alan Ladd, Deborah Kerr and Charles Boyer in the second feature.

On television at 8:30 p.m. on CBS there was Arthur Godfrey's *Talent Scouts* immediately followed by *I Love Lucy* at nine on the same network. If yours was one of the diminishing number of homes without a TV, there was still radio. On March 23 at 2:25 p.m. the Dodgers-Athletics game was aired on WMGM. At 10:00 p.m. on WNBC the *Dinah Shore Program* featured guest Bing Crosby.

The April 22 edition of the baseball bible, *The Sporting News,* paid tribute to the song "Take Me Out to the Ballgame," which the article called "the national anthem of baseball." It was said that the composers, Al Von Tilzer and Jack Norworth, had not seen a baseball game before writing the song in 1908 and that Norworth attended his first in 1940.

On March 5, Russia's premier, Joseph Stalin, died of heart failure. An official Soviet announcement said, "The heart of Comrade Stalin has stopped beating." In early June Great Britain celebrated the coronation of Queen Elizabeth II in London. And on April 2 the Dodgers headed home to Brooklyn.

Four

April

"They were All-Stars at every position. A couple of more starting pitchers and they would have been unbeatable."
—Jerry Coleman, New York Yankees

With the onset of the month of April, the Dodgers left Vero Beach and began playing their way home. They faced the great southpaw, Warren Spahn, and the Braves at Sulphur Dell, in Nashville, Tennessee, the legendary and historic home of the Nashville Vols. A crowd of 12,059 watched Brooklyn defeat the venerable lefty, 3–1. The original name for the ballpark was Sulpher Spring Bottom when it was first used in the 1860s. It was christened Sulpher Dell by sportswriter Grantland Rice in 1907 because he reasoned that "Dell" was easier to rhyme with than the word "Bottom."

Sulpher Dell was a small park with a right field fence only 262 feet from home plate. In 1954, when Bob Lennon hit 54 home runs while playing for Nashville, pitchers began to call it "Suffer Hell." The park lasted until 1963 when it was razed and turned into a parking lot.

The Dodgers lost two games to the Senators at Griffith Stadium in Washington and finalized the training season with two at Ebbets Field against the Yankees, the world champs who treated their hosts badly. A bad omen was Erskine's final tune-up. He gave up four runs in the second inning and Brooklyn lost, 5–4. In the spring finale, the Dodgers scored six runs in the first inning off Jim McDonald before the rains came and after a 45-minute delay, umpire Bill Sommers called the game. Brooklyn finished the exhibition season with a record of 19–11.

It had been raining on and off in Brooklyn and was again threatening on Opening Day, April 14. The weather was bad throughout baseball and half the games during the opening week had been postponed due to rain, snow and frigid cold. The temperature in Brooklyn hovered at about 40 degrees and kept the Opening Day crowd down to 12,433. Brooklyn borough president John Cashmore threw out the first ball and a military color guard marched to the flagpole in center field and hoisted the stars and stripes. The Fourteenth Veteran's Band played and Everett McCooney sang the national anthem.

This was the 41st beginning to a new season at Ebbets Field. On another cold and raw Brooklyn afternoon on April 13, 1913, the first official league game was played. Baseball and its environs have often been referred to in religious terms, as a 2005 book about baseball stadiums was titled *Green Cathedrals*. One fan was quoted as saying, "Baseball was my family's religion, the Dodgers were our denomination, Ebbets Field was the church."[1] Bob McGee wrote, "The Brooklyn Dodgers were a religion. For those who bought into the faith, Ebbets Field was a holy place."[2] Indeed, if it can be said that Yankee Stadium was "a Cathedral on a Hill," then Ebbets Field was a "Chapel in the Valley" and was revered as such by those erstwhile parishioners that came to be known as the "Flatbush Faithful." There were 14,000 of them to watch the opening as Brooklyn's ace left-hander, George "Nap" Rucker, was defeated by Tom Seaton of the Philadelphia Phillies, 1–0. The lone run came on a muffed fly ball by right fielder Benny Meyer in the first inning and Ebbets Field's rich and colorful history was consecrated.

The new park contained 24,000 seats. The signature scoreboard was not even dreamed up yet—it was built in 1931—but there was the traditional sign of the bull, advertising Bull Durham tobacco. Although a grandstand ran part of the way around the field, the game could be viewed from a bluff overlooking the diamond. One enterprising gentleman erected a grandstand on the bluff and collected 50 cents apiece from 300 spectators.

The opening ceremonies had one of the owners, Steve McKeever, and his wife along with Charlie Ebbets, the Shannon 23rd Regiment Band and the entire Brooklyn team gather around the flagpole in center field, only to discover that someone had forgotten to bring the flag. It was uncovered in an office closet and rushed to center field where it was hoisted and the proceeding continued. Sunday baseball was barred in those days and Charlie tried every trick he could think of to circumvent the rule. In 1904 at Washington Park he had charged no admission to a Sunday game but required everyone entering the park to purchase a scorecard. To make his scheme even more obvious, Ebbets color-coded the cards to identify seats. The ploy failed, but Charlie was not one to give up easily.

He seized upon another idea in 1917. Instead of scorecards, he hired a band and sold "band concert" tickets. The fans would pay to hear the band and watch the game that followed for free. About 15,000 showed up and saw the Dodgers beat the Phils, 3–2, but once again Ebbets was stymied. Both he and manager Wilbert Robinson were arrested after the game. Although a Brooklyn court saw through the maneuver, the fine for violating the Sunday law was suspended. There were even judges who were Dodger fans.

Finally, in 1919 Sunday baseball was permitted in New York State. One of Brooklyn's early heroes, Charles Dillon Stengel, had been traded to Pittsburgh the year before. After serving time in the U.S. Navy during World War I, Casey returned to Ebbets Field as a Pirate for a game in late May. There were 20,000 in the ballpark on this Sunday afternoon. Casey struck out twice and grounded to short against the Dodgers' Sherry Smith, with the crowd getting on him more and more with each failed at-bat. Stengel, the right fielder, stopped at the Dodger bullpen each inning so as not to walk all the way to the dugout, and took the chance to visit with some old friends. One of them, pitcher Leon Cadore, liked to dabble in magic tricks. Cadore was holding a sparrow. Casey took the bird back to the dugout and slipped it under his cap until his turn to hit. As the crowd gave him the razz, Stengel turned towards them, bowed and lifted his hat. The sparrow flew away and the crowd roared its approval. Casey's solid reputation as a clown was cemented by the stunt. Dodger manager Wilbert Robinson commented, "Hell, he always did have birds in his garrett."[3]

Then there was the Ebbets Field moment when the park was raided by the feds. Game one of the 1920 World Series was played at Ebbets Field on Tuesday, October 5. Even though it was during Prohibition, owner Charlie Ebbets treated each of the writers in attendance to a half-pint of rye whiskey. Federal agents got wind of it and the next day they pulled a raid. The press box was thoroughly searched and Ebbets' private office was ransacked, but the feds found nothing. "Charlie had been tipped off and the hooch had been removed."[4]

The 1953 Dodgers club was a far cry from some of the past teams in Brooklyn, particularly in the twenties and thirties when the label "Daffiness Boys" was leveled at them by columnist Westbrook Pegler. These Dodgers were of baseball's golden age and were among the best who ever played the game. On this Opening Day 1953, Captain Pee Wee Reese, from the top step of the dugout, led the team out onto the field. Carl Erskine stood on the hill and all was ready for the new season. Expectations were high in Brooklyn as Erskine shut down the Pittsburgh Pirates for the first three innings. In the fourth, however, the Bucs scored four times and Erskine was replaced by Joe Black.

Pittsburgh's Murray Dickson had allowed only one hit in the same three innings, but with one out in the home fourth the Dodgers tied the score. After Reese singled and scored on Snider's double off the wall, Jackie Robinson beat out a grounder to short and Campanella tied it with a three-run home run. Brooklyn scored four more in the fifth, highlighted when Duke Snider hit a two-one pitch from the right-handed Dickson over the right field screen and onto Bedford Avenue. Pittsburgh scored a run in the ninth off Black, but the Dodgers' 13-hit barrage resulted in an 8–5 win.

As had been said in the spring, Gilliam opened at second base and Robinson at third, but Jackie pulled a muscle and Billy Cox went in to play third. He singled in his only at-bat. Gil Hodges beat out a hit in the fifth, which marked his first hit in his last 33 official times up. Since Ebbets Field opened in 1913, the Dodgers had won 18 openers and lost 20 times.

The next day, Wednesday, April 15, Russ Meyer made his Brooklyn debut. He went all the way while defeating the Pirates, 4–2, and striking out seven. Pee Wee Reese drove in two runs with a timely base hit.

At the time baseball was the only game in town, and the president tossing out the first ball had evolved into an American tradition. So when Washington Senators owner Clark Griffith paid the traditional visit to the White House to present President Eisenhower with a gold-plated season pass and an invitation to attend the opening game, the papers had a strong reaction when Ike turned down the invite to the opener, even to the point of calling it a political blunder.

The president was certainly not uninterested in sports. As a young man he played semi-professional baseball and football at West Point and was an avid golfer. In fact, he planned to be at Augusta on the links the day of the Washington opener. But the baseball gods intervened. It rained and the first game was delayed from Monday until Thursday. On that day Ike flew to Washington to deliver a luncheon speech, popped into Griffith Stadium to complete his presidential chore, stayed an inning and a half, and with the Yankees ahead, 4–0, flew back to Augusta and was on the course practically before the baseball game ended.

There was more notable activity at the Washington stadium that April. It was on the 17th that the Yankees' young star, Mickey Mantle, a switch-hitter, was batting right-handed against the Washington southpaw, Chuck Stobbs, and hit a monstrous drive that cleared the wall at the 391-foot sign in left-center field. It continued out onto a Washington street and ended up several houses down the block. It has been assumed that balls were hit as far or further off the bats of Babe Ruth and Jimmy Foxx, but they didn't have a Red Patterson around in their time.

Patterson was the Yankees publicity director and was in the ballpark. He decided to measure the distance the wallop traveled. He took the distance from the wall to the street and encountered a 10-year-old boy named Donald Dunaway, who supposedly showed Patterson where the ball had landed. The publicity man paced it off and came up with a travel distance of 565 feet. Although he didn't actually use a tape measure, the term "tape measure" home run was born. A tribute to the power of the Yanks' center fielder was the fact that while this particular homer remained the most famous of his clouts, it ranked only seventh among his longest drives. In 1953 alone he hit five that were measured at more than 530 feet. In 1963 Mantle hit one 734 feet at Yankee Stadium.

The same day as the Mantle home run, the Dodgers played a day-night doubleheader against the hated Giants at the Polo Grounds. In the first game Sal Maglie was the Giants' starter and rookie Johnny Podres was set to go for Brooklyn. A left-hander from Witherbee, a small town in upstate New York, Podres had been impressive from the very start of his career. A Dodger fan as a kid, he always remembered wanting to play with them. "When I was a kid in school, I wanted to be a Dodger," he said. "I always listened to the Dodgers on the radio, and when I had a chance to sign with them, that's what I wanted to do."[5]

In his first professional season, in 1951, Podres played in the Class D Mountain State League and won 21 games and lost only three. His earned run average was 1.67 and he struck out 228 in 200 innings. The next year he was sent to Montreal, the Dodgers' AAA affiliate in the International League. A bad back limited his activity to just 24 appearances and a 5–5 record. But the Dodgers retained their faith in the talented young southpaw and in 1953 brought him to Brooklyn.

On Opening Day Giants manager Leo Durocher stated that he would hold out his ace, Sal Maglie, until the Dodger series. Sal had gone 6–2 against Brooklyn in '52. Preacher Roe was the scheduled Dodgers starter, but when the 38-year-old veteran came up with a bad cold and dysentery, Dressen went with his 20-year-old rookie, Johnny Podres. It was not a surprise since the Dodger manager had been high on Podres for a while. The brash and cocky youngster pitched well, going seven innings and giving up two earned runs, both coming in the second inning when Daryl Spencer tripled into the left field bullpen and was followed by a home run by catcher Wes Westrum. It came off of a Podres' hanging inside curveball.

Although the Giants scored three off Jim Hughes in the eighth and won the game by a 6–3 score, Dressen was sufficiently impressed to include the rookie in a five-man rotation that included Erskine, Meyer, Loes, Roe and Podres. In the night game Brooklyn clobbered Jim Hearn with a six-run fifth inning and went on to a 12–4 victory. Billy Loes went the distance. Carl Furillo, apparently seeing the ball well after his eye operation, had a home run and a double. It rained in New York the next day and the Dodgers left for Pittsburgh.

The 12–4 win over the Pirates was Erskine's first of the year. Jim Gilliam was beginning to show himself as an effective leadoff man. Drawing three walks, he scored four times. In 20 at-bats so far he was hitting an even .300. Erskine walked six and gave up a first-inning home run to Pirate slugger Ralph Kiner and allowed eight hits but pitched the complete game. Showing no pain in his fingers or elbow, catcher Roy Campanella had a three-run homer for Brooklyn. In five games the catcher had driven in 12 runs to lead both leagues. Duke Snider also drove in four with two doubles and a single to increase his total to nine. The Dodger power was kicking in.

It snowed in Pittsburgh the next day, the 20th, and the Dodgers left by the 2 p.m. train for Philadelphia, where they were swept by the Phillies. The first eight games the Dodgers played in 1953 were evenly split, with four wins and four losses. Curt Simmons held them to five hits in a 7–1 win in the first of the two games, while Russ Meyer was knocked out in the fifth inning. Loes took the loss on coach Jake Pitler's 59th birthday, losing to Robin Roberts, who was pitching on two days' rest. The score was 6–1, the lone tally coming on a home run by Pee Wee Reese. And then the Giants came to town.

On Friday night Carl Erskine won his second game of the season, both complete games, 12–4. The Dodger bats came alive. Snider and Campanella both homered, Campy's coming with two on. On Saturday it was Maglie again. They called him "The Barber" because he shaved the hitters, but the name was actually given by his manager, Leo Durocher, who said that the scowling Italian face with the five-o'-clock shadow reminded him of the barber at the third chair where Leo got his haircuts. Either way the name fit. Maglie's theory of pitching was that he did not knock a hitter down when the batter expected it. "You don't scare a guy knocking him down when he knows he's gonna be knocked down," he explained. "You have to make the hitter afraid of the ball."[6]

Giuseppe Maglie grew figs and olives in his native Foggia, a village on the southern east coast of Italy. When he and his wife, Immaculata Maria, came to America, they settled in Niagara Falls, New York, where Salvatore was born on April 26, 1917. Sal preferred baseball over school and work and began playing semi-pro ball around home, earning five and 10 dollars a game. He began playing professionally in 1938 with a disastrous first outing at Offermann Stadium in Buffalo. Maglie came into the game in relief with the bases loaded against the Newark Bears and walked three in a row before being yanked. Sal's minor league career was undistinguished. Between '38 and '40 he won nine games and lost 30, but had a breakout year at Elmira in 1941. He won 20 games and lost 15 with 22 complete games and 280 innings. Sal later explained his success at Elmira. "They let me pitch regularly," he said. "That was all."[7]

Drafted by the Giants in '42, Maglie made his big league debut on August 9, 1945, and went 5–4 the rest of the year. In the winter of 1945–46 Sal went to Cuba to play winter ball and met Bernardo Pasquel. The Pasquel brothers were making generous offers to major league players to join their professional Mexican League. Maglie signed with the Pasquels and played two years in Mexico. Out of the experience came contact with Adolph Luque, a 20-year major league veteran and probably the most significant figure in Maglie's career. It was Luque who taught Sal a sharp curve and the mindset to set up hitters with the fastball up and in. Baseball commissioner A.B. "Happy" Chandler suspended all Mexican League jumpers for five years. Ultimately, the commissioner granted amnesty. Maglie was free to rejoin the Giants, which he did in 1950. Sal said later of the Mexico experience, "I not only made good money for two years, but I learned how to pitch."[8]

Baseball in the era was gritty and hard-fought and nowhere was it more epitomized than when the New York Giants and the Brooklyn Dodgers faced each other. On April 25 the Giants were at Ebbets Field and Roger Kahn wrote in the *New York Herald Tribune* the next day, "Bean ball, a game the Dodgers and the Giants sometimes play instead of baseball, made its annual debut at Ebbets Field yesterday." There was no minimizing the contentiousness that existed between the two ball clubs and no overstating the explosiveness that each game carried with it.

On this April day in 1953 Maglie was not his usual dominating self against Brooklyn. The Dodgers scored a run in the second when, after knocking down Roy Campanella, Maglie gave up a double to George Shuba and a single to Carl Furillo. In the next inning Brooklyn scored four times and Maglie was not in a good mood when next Furillo came to the plate in the third inning. Snider had tripled and Robinson drew a walk before Campy singled home a run. Maglie's first pitch sailed high over Furillo's head. The right fielder took a couple of steps towards the mound and exchanged looks with the scowling Barber.

On the next pitch, a breaking ball low and away, Carl swung and missed, but the bat came flying out of his hands towards the mound and settled on the grass just beyond the bump. Furillo began walking towards the pitcher with Giants catcher Sal Yvars beside him. Maglie took a few steps towards him and the two glared at each other. At this point the Dodgers outfielder caught sight of Leo Durocher, whom he detested. Furillo blamed Durocher for ordering his pitchers to throw at Dodger hitters. Carl was furious now and turned towards Leo. It took umpire Larry Goetz and Dodgers first baseman Gil Hodges to keep Furillo away from the Giants' manager.

Play was restored without further trouble. Afterward the Dodger right fielder explained that the bat slipped out of his hands. Why was he going out to the mound, he was asked. "I was just going to get the bat, that's all," Carl said.[9] Later Dodger president Walter O'Malley handed Furillo an envelope containing $50. That was the way they played the game, and Furillo and Maglie were invariably in the midst of the interminable confrontations that went on between the two clubs. The irony for the two battlers was that in May 1956 the Dodgers picked up Maglie's contract in a trade with Cleveland. Sal, the Barber of Coogan's Bluff, had become the Barber of Brooklyn. Remembering the day he walked into the Dodgers' clubhouse, Pee Wee Reese said, "Sal coming over to us was hard to believe. He spent a lifetime brushing us back."[10] The first meeting between Furillo and Maglie has been recorded by several individuals, including writer Jack Lang and Dodgers batboy Charlie DiGiovanna. All have the exchange as cordial, although Bavasi reported that Carl did not like the idea of Sal coming to Brooklyn at all. "Carl thought that Sal threw at him because he didn't like him." Bavasi pointed out to him that Maglie threw at Reese and Robinson also. "Yeah," replied Furillo, "but he throws at me every time I face him. With Jackie and Pee Wee, it's only once a game."[11]

The two were not only teammates but they became friends. The relationship began to head in the right direction when Sal told Carl he threw at him on orders from Durocher, confirming what Furillo already knew, but marking Maglie as a new and honest friend. The story of the dinner engagement was a favorite of Furillo's. Bavasi asked Carl to take Maglie out to dinner at Toots Shor's restaurant in Manhattan, hoping to ease any animosity that might still be festering between the two players. He told Furillo to pick up the check and he would be reimbursed. Shor wouldn't take any money from the players, and when Bavasi asked Furillo how much he'd spent, Carl said "$200." Bavasi gave him the money. "My dad loved that story," Furillo's son said.[12]

The 39-year-old pitcher went 13–5 in 1956 and on September 25 threw a no-hitter versus the Philadelphia Phillies. Furillo hit .289 that year with 21 home runs and 83 RBIs as the two men helped the Dodgers win their last pennant in Brooklyn. They shared a lot. Both were the sons of Italian immigrants,

Junior Gilliam backs up as first baseman Gil Hodges settles under a pop fly at Ebbets Field (author's collection).

both highly competitive. Enemies to the core, but in the end, teammates and friends, *paisans.*

Carl Anthony Furillo was born in Stoney Creek Mills, Pennsylvania, on March 8, 1922, the youngest of six children. Both his parents, Michael and Philomenia, had emigrated from a town near Naples, Italy, and in Pennsylvania where they lived Michael sold vegetables from a truck that was known as a "huckster wagon." Young Carl grew up fluent in the Italian language, which was spoken in the home. A man sensitive to any dishonors, which included getting decked by opposing pitchers, Furillo's emotions ran close to the surface. However, beneath the outer shell was a man of warmth and sincerity. He remained throughout his life a devoted family man.

Furillo dropped out of Pennside Junior High School in the eighth grade to go to work. He never held any expectations of being a major league ballplayer. In the seventh grade, "The principal asked me what I wanted to be," he said, "and at that time I wanted to be an undertaker."[13] He worked as an apple picker and as a bobbin boy in a mill, but always found time to play the game he loved. Furthermore, he had his brothers as mentors. Nick was the younger boy's inspiration, and the two played for local teams around the Reading area through the thirties. In 1940 when Furillo was 18 he signed to play for Pocomoke City in the Eastern Shore League of Maryland for $80 a month. Two weeks before he was scheduled to report, his mother died. It happened on March 8, Carl's birthday, and he was reluctant to celebrate his own birthdays for the rest of his life. Sad over his mother's passing and homesick, Furillo needed a push and his manager, Poke Whalen, provided it. "I'm going to make something out of you, you little Dago," he told the youngster. Furillo said, "He was the first one that really pushed me."[14] Before the season concluded, he was sold to the Reading club and he finished the year hitting .319.

In 1941 at Reading again he hit .313 with 10 homers in 125 games. That fall the Dodgers' Larry MacPhail bought the entire Reading team for $5,000. "This included the franchise, a set of uniforms, a broken-down bus, and 15 players, including Carl Furillo," recalled Emil "Buzzie" Bavasi, who would become a front office fixture in baseball for a half-century.[15] Carl's manager at Reading was another future Dodger front office executive, Fresco Thompson, and then when he played for Montreal, Furillo was managed by Clyde Suke-forth, remembered for his role in the scouting and signing of Jackie Robinson.

At Montreal in '42 Furillo hit .281 before the war intervened. In November he was inducted into the army and ordered to report to Fort George G. Meade in Maryland. Furillo served with the 77th Division for three years and saw combat action in the South Pacific at Guam, Leyte, and Okinawa. Cited for bravery in combat, Carl was hit by shrapnel and awarded the Purple Heart, but he refused all medals. "I didn't do anything to merit them," he said, with the humility befitting the man.[16] By 1946 he was home and back in baseball with Brooklyn. The outfielder with the rifle arm played in the Dodgers outfield with Pete Reiser and Dixie Walker and hit .284 while playing 117 games. The next season it was .295 and 88 RBIs. In the '47 World Series Furillo batted .353.

A good hitter with 20–home run power and very dependable in the clutch, Furillo became a regular in the Dodgers' lineup, but where he really shone was with an incredible throwing arm and the ability to play the tricky wall in right field at Ebbets. It has been said that Furillo had thrown men out at first base on singles. Actually it happened only once, although he threw out runners rounding the bag on seven occasions. On August 27, 1951, Pittsburgh Pirates pitcher Mel Queen singled to right field, where Furillo fielded the ball on one hop and threw the startled runner out at first. The right field wall was just 297 feet from home plate but it was a concave structure with advertising signs and a scoreboard. On top of the wall was a 20-foot screen. Depending upon the spot the ball hit, the rebound was wildly unpredictable. Furillo's uncanny ability to play the wall was not the result of a unique sense.

"I worked at it," he said. "Preacher (Roe) and Billy Cox hit fungoes to me. I worked every angle on the wall."[17] He became so adept at it that as the ball was heading for the wall, Furillo would position himself at a spot, at times some distance from where the ball was going to hit, and be perfectly positioned to play the carom.

The great Dodgers teams of the fifties, including the '53 squad, came together in 1948. They won a pennant in '49 and over an eight-year period would win five pennants and one World Series. They lost twice on the last hit of the last inning of the last game of the season, and both hits were home runs. Furillo has often been cast as out-of-the-loop among his teammates, but he developed close ties with many of them. He forged friendships with Gil Hodges, Roy Campanella, Carl Erskine and later the young pitcher, Sandy Koufax. Carl Jr. recalls how Joe Black called his father frequently "until the day he died."[18]

Joan Hodges said, "I didn't know Carl was supposed to be difficult," she said. "He and Gil got along very well; they never had a problem. They'd go fishing together, and I was friends with Carl's wife, Fern."[19]

Erskine recalls how after joining the club in 1948, Furillo went out of his way to befriend the rookie. "He invited me to go out with him and some of his Italian friends," the pitcher said. "He had a friend who owned a pizza parlor. In Indiana in those days, we had no idea what pizza was. I would watch those guys in the back sailing those things in the air and make pizza out of them."[20]

Tex's Restaurant and Pizzeria was a favorite eating spot for the Furillo family and friends. Located on Atlantic Avenue in the Brownsville section,

Carl Jr. remembers how his parents loved having pasta fagioli at Tex's. In fact, Carl's nickname, "Skoonj," referred to his preference for scungilli, Italian for conch. There is an Italian restaurant specializing in Neapolitan cuisine that Furillo frequented called Bamonte's at 32 Withers Street in Williamsburg. The owner, Anthony Bamonte, recalled some good times. "We had steak parties. Carl Furillo would come in with a few other players. We had bocce courts in the yard and he'd play with the fellows."[21] On July 6, 1946, Carl and Fern Reichart, a Pennsylvania girl, were married. A son, Carl Jr., was born in April 1949.

Furillo came by the sobriquet, "The Reading Rifle," in the 1947 World Series. It was hung on him by Yankees coach John Corriden, who warned his players not to run on Carl's arm. "He has a rifle hanging from his shoulder," he cautioned them.[22] Leo Durocher had platooned Furillo, using him against left-handed pitching, but it was Burt Shotton in 1948 who made him an everyday player. Ebbets Field became a special place with wonderful memories for the Furillos' "Right Field Family." They became so close to the fans in the seats there that Jimmy and Jean Riggerio, "Uncle" Jimmy and "Aunt" Jean, became godparents to Carl Jr., and the Marinos, Vinnie and Grace, stood up for brother Jon at his baptism. "In Brooklyn we lived among people," Carl Jr. said, "and I eventually wanted to live there permanently." Furillo told his son that he could do whatever he wanted to do, but reminded him, "Our family has never been broken up."[23] Young Carl went back to Pennsylvania where he still resides.

Beginning in 1955, when he came to the Dodgers, a strong tie developed between the bonus southpaw from Brooklyn and the Furillo family. The bonus rule in effect at the time forced the Dodgers to keep Sandy Koufax on the major league roster for a minimum of two seasons. The reasoning was meant to dissuade teams from signing players to bonus contracts for more than $4,000. The club roomed him with Furillo. Frustrated at his limited opportunities to pitch and his wildness when he did, the young Koufax confessed to the veteran that he considered quitting. Carl Jr. said that his father explained to the young pitcher that it was not yet his time, and encouraged him. "Your time will come," he told Sandy, "and when it does you will be ready."[24] Of course, it did, ... oh, how it did. Sandy became like a member of the Furillo family.

"My dad was like a father to him," Furillo's son recalled. "He ate dinner with us often."[25]

Fern Furillo, although not Italian, learned to cook Italian food, probably from her father-in-law. A Koufax favorite was Fern's macaroni and meatballs.

She also made a Pennsylvania Dutch buttermilk cake from her own recipe and over the years cakes would arrive for Sandy at the clubhouse at Dodger Stadium in Los Angeles. The two ballplayers became close friends. They hunted and fished together. At Furillo's funeral, Koufax did not want to view the body. He told Fern, "I don't want to remember him like this."[26]

When Charles Dickens wrote the immortal words, "It was the best of times, it was the worst of times," he certainly did not have Carl Furillo in mind during the 1949 season; yet the phrase fit the Dodger right fielder all too well.[27] He wasn't hitting well but it was not generally known of the burden he carried. His dad was gravely ill and Carl kept making trips home to Pennsylvania to be with him. Although below par at the plate, he nonetheless held his own until August. The Dodgers were in a pennant race with the Cardinals and in the last 46 games Furillo went on a tear. In one stretch he hit .431 and drove in 22 runs in 15 games. Brooklyn won the pennant by a game over St. Louis. Michael Furillo lived that year and the next and passed away on March 9, 1951, at age 74. A second son, Jon, was born to Carl and Fern on March 28 of the same year.

The animosity between Carl Furillo and Leo Durocher was more than a product of the intense and long-standing rivalry between the Dodgers and the Giants. It began as far back as 1946 when Durocher's attitude towards the rookie was not supportive and Furillo began to dislike the manager. It really turned sour when Leo went across town and Furillo resented his style of play. "He was a dirty manager," Furillo said. "'Don't let that son-of-a-bitch beat you.' That was the way he talked. 'Stick it in his goddamn ear.' I hated his guts."[28]

Furillo was beaned six times but it was the hit by Giants pitcher Sheldon Jones that stung the most because he knew Durocher had ordered it. On June 28, 1950, in the eighth inning after the Dodgers right fielder had hit a two-run home run and a single off him, Jones plunked Furillo just below the left ear. Carl spent the night in the hospital and returned to the lineup three days later. The previous 12 games before being hit, Furillo had batted .558. According to Carl Jr., Durocher once said that the three greatest outfielders he knew were Mays, Clemente and Furillo, but not in that order. When asked how he rated them, he refused to answer. Leo certainly respected Carl's ability. He told a young Willie Mays when he first came up, "Don't ever take a big turn at first on Furillo."[29]

Campanella said that a throw from right field would come on a fly and crack into his mitt like a pitcher throwing from 60 feet six inches. Furillo's hatred for Durocher extended to some of his players, like Dark, Rigney and coach Herman Franks, whom he felt tried to emulate their manager. "They were no-good bastards," he said. "They wanted to be like Durocher."[30] A man of strong emotions, Furillo would get his chance with Durocher late in the season ... and he would be ready.

Tough yet possessing a warmth not always visible, Furillo was protective of his family. His son Carl remembered an incident at Ebbets Field. The boy noticed that Ty Cobb had come into the ballpark and he asked his dad if he could meet the great Georgia Peach. Furillo knew that in addition to his other foibles Cobb was supposed to hate kids. Concerned for his son's feelings, he asked DiGiovanna to introduce young Carl to Cobb. "Tell him it's my son," he instructed the Dodgers batboy, "and if he's not nice to him, I'll come up there and make him sorry." Ty could not have been nicer. Carl Jr. had a pleasant and memorable visit with the great star. "He even signed a ball for me," he said.[31]

Carl went to California with the Dodgers and in 1958 hit .290 with 18 home runs and 88 RBIs. The next year he played in only 50 games, and in '60 he was released while recovering from an injury. He singled up the middle in the playoffs against the Braves to drive in the winning run as LA went on to win the 1959 World Series. Furillo was so angered by the Dodgers' action in releasing him while injured—which was against the players' contract—that he sued the ball club for his 1960 salary. He collected $21,000 but claimed the club had him blacklisted from ever getting another job in baseball. There was a reconciliation of sorts, but towards the end of his life, Carl said he was willing to forgive but not forget. "Regrets?" he said. "I don't regret nothin'."[32] Carl Furillo's creed allowed that a man's word was his bond and what was right was right. He never really forgave the Dodgers.

The 6-foot, 190-pound right fielder was a clutch player throughout his career, as highlighted by some of his World Series performances. In the '53 Series he hit .333 and drove in the tying run in the seventh inning of game one, though Brooklyn lost the contest. In the sixth game he hit a two-run homer in the ninth to tie the score at 3–3, but the Yankees won that game as well as the Series in the bottom of the ninth. In game five in '52 Furillo saved a 6–5 Dodgers victory with a spectacular leaping catch to take a home run away from Johnny Mize with one out in the eleventh inning. In '59 while with the Los Angeles Dodgers, his clutch hits won both a playoff and a World Series game. In his last major league at-bat, Carl drove in the tying run in the eighth inning against the Phillies and the Dodgers won it in the 11th.

Carl and Fern enjoyed retirement. They loved going to Italian feasts and attended many of them, especially the San Gennaro feast in New York's Little Italy. They traveled to Cape Cod, New Orleans and Las Vegas. Ted Reed wrote, "Furillo always had the capacity to find happiness within himself and his family."[33] He worked an assortment of jobs in New York, then went back to Stoney Creek Mills and was employed as a deputy sheriff, a night watchman and a security guard. He hunted and fished. When he developed leukemia, he didn't take to his bed. He worked and lived and beat the disease. While hunting with his sons on a later occasion, he began to sweat profusely and sat down to rest. The symptoms continued the next day and he went to see Dr. Leonard Scheffer, who found fluid around the heart. Carl's birthday was March 8 and the boys had been planning a fishing trip since the first of the year. It was on January 21, 1989, that Carl Furillo, the "Emperor of Right Field," died of a heart attack. He was 66 years of age.

He was eulogized by friend and teammate Carl Erskine, who said, "Carl was a sensitive person. His gruff exterior often obscured his more tender side. Carl was like steel and velvet."[34] One of Brooklyn's "Boys of Summer" immortalized by author Roger Kahn, Kahn wrote, "Carl Anthony Furillo was pure ball player.... I cannot imagine Carl Furillo in his prime as anything other than a ballplayer. Right field in Brooklyn was his destiny!"[35]

The second game of the Giants' series came on Saturday the 25th before 19,936 of the "Flatbush faithful." Russ Meyer was Brooklyn's starting pitcher and was relieved in the seventh by Joe Black after giving up a two-run home run to Monte Irvin that tied the score at 5–5. Black took the loss when Alvin Dark singled with the bases loaded in the eighth, and the Giants won, 7–5. The next day under alternate sun and clouds, Billy Loes took the rubber game, 8–4. Campanella homered and Furillo and Shuba each drove in three runs. But the Phillies won a doubleheader from the Pirates for their eighth straight victory to hold onto first place. The Dodgers were third, three games back.

In 1953 an L-shaped split-level three-bedroom home in Hicksville, Long Island, was selling for $12,990. A 10-ounce package of Seabrook Farms frozen peas and carrots sold for 19 cents. The population of the United States was 160,184,112. A loaf of bread cost 21 cents, a quart of milk 23 cents, and life expectancy was 68.8 years. Ringling Brothers and Barnum & Bailey brought their circus, "The Greatest Show on Earth," to Madison Square Garden where tickets could be had for prices ranging from $1.50 to $6.50.

The Redlegs of Cincinnati, fed up with having to change their name in order to distance themselves from the aura of communism, decided to go back

...And the fans loved every minute of it (Brooklyn Public Library—Brooklyn Collection).

to being called the Reds. They did it with the announcement, "Let the communists change their name, we had it first."

The war in Korea would soon wind down but the tragedy of war deaths continued. On April 16 the *Brooklyn Eagle* reported that Philip S. Romano of 1300 Halsey Street had been killed in action. A member of Company 4, 2nd Battalion, 3rd Marine Raiders, he died in defense of Vegas Hill on March 26. Pvt. Romano had arrived in Korea on March 19; he was 18 years old.

The Dodgers concluded the month of April with four consecutive victories, the last three a sweep of the Cincinnati Reds. They beat the Reds on a cold day at Ebbets Field. Preacher Roe, healthy again, gave up eight hits and won, 5–1. The shutout was spoiled by a ninth-inning home run off the bat of huge Ted Kluszewski. The next day Brooklyn won in the ninth on a passed ball with Joe Black getting the credit for the win. The victory on the final day of the month went to Brooklyn, 7–4, although Johnny Podres was hammered out of the game in the first inning and relieved by Ben Wade.

Television's *Hallmark Hall of Fame* presented a production of *Hamlet*, which starred British actor Maurice Evans. It was stated that more people watched that television performance than the total number who have seen the Shakespeare masterpiece in the 350 years since it was written. The number one pop record on the charts for the month of April was "I Believe" by the popular recording star Frankie Laine.

The Dodgers ended the month of April with a record of nine wins and five losses.

FIVE

May

"I wish they wuz all Reese and Robinson."—Charlie Dressen

There were 18,178 fans at Ebbets Field on the night of May 6, the night that the Dodgers' first baseman hit his 140th career home run to set the Brooklyn club mark. They were not cheering the record, but Gil Hodges' first home run of the season. They hoped it would be the beginning of the end of the terrible slump the popular Dodger still struggled with. In the previous 17 games he had but 11 singles and just one run batted in. They stood and applauded his drive into the upper deck in left field, which came off Joe Presko of the St. Louis Cardinals in the sixth. Hodges was elated by the support. "It was wonderful," he said. "Imagine them cheering me when they be should be razzing me. I'll never forget that."[1]

Fans, players, family and friends were all rooting and praying for the big slugger to regain his form at the plate, but it would take another month before that would happen. When it did, Hodges, of course, went on to have one of his finest seasons.

Hodges' homer helped the Dodgers beat the Cardinals by the score of 7–3, but as usual there was a lot more happening at Ebbets Field. An obstruction call by umpire Jocko Conlan in the sixth inning against Solly Hemus helped to contribute to Brooklyn's four-run inning. Snider was on third and Robinson on second when Roy Campanella hit a hard grounder to Hemus's right. The St. Louis shortstop dove for the ball, and it went through for a single. Robinson had held up until he saw the ball go into left field and then took off for third, tumbling over Hemus on the way.

Conlan made the interference call, sending Robinson home. Cardinals manager Eddie Stanky disputed the call and protested the game, claiming that Hemus did not block the runner intentionally. Conlan's interpretation of Rule 7.06-A was that it was still obstruction whether the fielder did so intentionally or not. The ump's verdict was upheld by the league office.

Though the season was only three weeks old, of the first 18 games they played, the Dodgers won 12. Dressen was not completely satisfied with his pitching, however. In the temper of the times, pitchers were expected to pitch nine innings, and the Dodgers' staff had completed *only* seven: three by Billy Loes, two by Erskine and one each by Meyer and Roe. It was the offense that was winning games, particularly the hitting of Roy Campanella, Duke Snider and Jim Gilliam. Campy had 24 hits, which included six home runs, a triple and two doubles. He drove in 28 and scored 12. Brooklyn's "Dook" of Flatbush had hit in 15 straight games. Junior Gilliam was a hot topic in the leadoff role. With 22 hits and 20 walks, he had been on base in every game. He also scored 17 runs.

Their tenth win came against the Chicago Cubs on May 1, 6–5, giving the Dodgers possession of first place. They went into the eighth inning three runs down and scored four. Captain Pee Wee Reese hit a 3–2 pitch into the lower deck in left field at Ebbets off knuckleballer Dutch Leonard, who relieved Turk Lown in the midst of the four-run barrage. Meyer went eight and got the win. Rube Walker hit for the pitcher and singled and Joe Black finished up. Though another cold day in Brooklyn, the 10,631 chilled fans had the chance to warm their hands at the Dodgers' outburst. It is interesting to note that of the 12 names in the Cubs' lineup, eight had at one time been the property of the Brooklyn organization.

In the 79th running of the Kentucky Derby at Churchill Downs, Dark Star, ridden by jockey Henry Moreno, held on to win the "Run for the Roses" over second-place finisher Native Dancer. The fifties was a golden age for baseball, but boxing also retained a significant place with the sports fan and the glamour division was with the heavyweights. Rocky Marciano held the title he won when he defeated Jersey Joe Walcott the previous year. On the 15th of the month the rematch was set in Chicago. Walcott went down in the first round from a left hook and a short right by the champion and he stayed down as Rocky retained his title.

The Pulitzer Prize for fiction went to Ernest Hemingway for his classic novel, *The Old Man and the Sea.* The United States had in January detonated an atomic warhead for battlefield artillery use, and in May the Joint Chiefs of Staff recommended air and naval operations include their use. They made it known that the bombing of Manchuria north of the Yalu River would be part of this plan. The president was pushing the Chinese and the North Koreans toward a truce in Korea.

Over in the American League, Bill Veeck, owner of the lowly "collection of old rags and tags known to baseball as the St. Louis Browns," was denied permission to move his club to Baltimore.[2] Veeck was perpetually on the wrong side of the owners because of the assortment of promotions, gimmicks and productions the consummate showman constantly engaged in, not the least being his stunt in 1951 of sending a midget up to pinch-hit in an official game. But not all of the unprecedented events that Veeck was a part of were staged.

In the spring of 1953 he paid $10,000 to the Syracuse ball club as a down payment on a minor league right-hander from Thomaston, Georgia, named Alva Lee "Bobo" Holloman. The agreement stipulated that Veeck would send another $25,000 should he decide to keep Holloman after the June 15 trading deadline. It turned out that the 26-year-old was a bit of a flake, referring to himself in the third person as "Big Bobo." "Big Bobo could out-talk me, out-pester, and out-con me," related Veeck. "Unfortunately, he could not outpitch me. He was hit harder in the spring trying to get the batters out than our batting practice pitchers who were trying to let them hit."[3]

Bombed each time he got the chance to pitch in a game, and on the verge of being sent back to Syracuse, Holloman begged manager Marty Marion for a chance to start. He was a starter not a reliever, he insisted, and so Marion and Veeck agreed to give him one crack as a courtesy before sending him on his way. He drew the Philadelphia Athletics, the only club in the American League that was worse than the Browns. He started on May 6 and was slammed around pretty good, but everything that was hit well was caught. There was intermittent rain that gave Big Bobo a chance to rest and he plowed on.

When it was over, Bobo had pitched a no-hit game. The 2,473 lonely fans at Sportsman's Park saw a bit of history unfold. Holloman was the first man to pitch a no-hitter in his first start and the only one to throw one in his only complete game in the majors. Veeck did not send him back to Syracuse. He didn't think it wise to send a man back to the minors after he had "become an immortal."[4] In his next start Holloman was knocked out in the second inning. He pitched 65⅓ innings and wound up 3–7 on the year, the only season anyone would see Big Bobo in a major league uniform. But he had his day in the sun and no one could deny him that.

Brooklyn won its sixth game in a row by defeating the Braves behind a three-hitter by Billy Loes, but was defeated the next day by Milwaukee with the help of a three-run home run by catcher Del Crandell, 9–4. It rained on Tuesday. The Phillies came in for a weekend series and the clubs split the first two games. The Dodgers won the rubber game on Sunday as Loes threw a complete-game shutout. The score was 5–0. The 23,843 in attendance were also treated to a hitting display by Roy Campanella at Ebbets Field. Over the last five games the catcher had hit five home runs and batted at a .571 clip. He drove in all five Dodger runs with a double and a three-run home run off Karl Drews. Campy seemed to have lost all traces of the previous year's injuries.

On May 10 the *New York Times* carried a book review of *Dodger Daze and Knights* by Tommy Holmes. Holmes, born in Brooklyn, was a columnist for the *Brooklyn Eagle*. The review, written by Gilbert Millstein, noted that the book showed the "same peculiar combination of crowing and yearning which seems to be endemic in all the passionate generations that have fixed, inexplicably, upon the Brooklyn Dodgers as their ideal of a baseball team."

The club traveled west, losing to the Cubs at Wrigley Field and then dropping two to the Cardinals in St. Louis. In the Friday night game, Erskine was knocked out in the first inning before he could get an out. Ralph Branca made his first appearance of the season by pitching the last two innings. The score was 8–3. It was a chilly night but the crowd of 17,653 was treated to a rhubarb, which always warms up the fans. It commenced in the third inning when after scoring two unearned runs, Jackie Robinson hit a drive high off the wall in left-center field.

Musial made a leap and the ball dropped back onto the field. Umpire Augie Donatelli called it a home run and the Cardinals were all over him. He conferred with plate umpire Jocko Conlan and reversed his decision to a ground-rule double. Now the Dodgers bolted from the dugout. Even the mild-mannered peacemaker, Gil Hodges, had to be pulled away. The decision, however, stuck and once more the Dodgers were involved in a donnybrook, a scene all too familiar to Brooklyn's fans.

By mid–May, Hodges had only 14 hits in 75 times at bat for a .187 average. He had one home run and no other extra-base hits. Manager Dressen sent Gil to the bench on the 17th; it would last for five games. In a doubleheader against Cincinnati and right-hander Bubba Church, the lefty-swinging Wayne Belardi played first base and Robinson played third. In the nightcap the Reds sent a left-hander, Ken Raffensberger, to the hill and Dressen countered with Jackie at first and Billy Cox at the hot corner. For the first time this season Dressen acknowledged that he would consider using Robinson in left field. He had given up on early tries with Don Thompson because the rookie did not hit. He used George Shuba, who flourished in two games that he started against the Giants. Shotgun Shuba had hit three doubles and driven in five runs. He used Dick Williams as well, alternating the left fielders according to the opposing pitching, but the manager was uneasy about the third outfield position and asked Robinson to work out in the outfield. Jack had neither objections to playing the outfield nor any concerns about his ability to do so. Manager Dressen said, "I've thought about it. Jackie says he can play it."[5]

The Dodgers split that doubleheader with Cincy. Loes was knocked out in the fourth after giving up four runs. Sadly, the Joe Black saga was winding down. He was proving to be ineffective in relief as Brooklyn went down, 13–5. The second game, however, was an entirely different story. It was all Carl Erskine.

The Cincinnati crowd of 18,536 expressed its displeasure when the hometown Gus Bell beat out a bunt in the sixth inning. They were very much aware that it was the Reds' first hit of the game, and, as it turned out, the only hit they would get against the little Dodger right-hander. In fact, only one ball was hit out of the infield. Rocky Bridges led off the inning with a walk and was forced at second when Bobby Adams grounded to first base. It was then that Bell beat out a bunt, putting runners at first and second. A double play ball served up to Jim Greengrass ended the inning. The gentleman from Indiana expressed no resentment towards the Cincinnati outfielder. "It was a good bunt," Erskine said. "It caught us by surprise. Me and Campy went for it, then we both looked at each other. Maybe the hesitation made the difference, but Bell could run."[6]

Asked if he was thinking of what would have been a third career no-hit game, Carl said, "You don't get serious about a no-hitter until the last inning, at least I didn't."[7]

The Dodgers mauled four Reds pitchers for 20 hits. Pee Wee Reese had four and Jackie Robinson and Billy Cox three each. Each of Robinson's three hits drove home a run. After lining a double to right-center field, Jackie took third on the throw. Still an explosive base runner, Robinson was on his way to another fine season. Following the three-hit day against the Reds, he was hitting .322. Jackie had more than proven his worth since the day that he and Branch Rickey had taken the first steps in initiating the so-called "Great Experiment." In spite of all he stood up to and endured in baseball, Robinson was no stranger to the fight against segregation and bigotry.

As an army officer during World War II, he had been ordered to the back of a bus traveling on army property and not subject to segregation. MPs were called and Jack stood a court marshal and was exonerated. This was the same Jackie Robinson who would not give in to death threats, intentional spikings or racial slurs in the big leagues. Milton Gross wrote, "A complete code of conduct was preordained for Robinson before he ever stepped on a field."[8]

Born in Cairo, Georgia, on January 31, 1919, Jackie moved with his mother Mallie and his four siblings to Pasadena, California, after her husband had run off with a neighbor's wife. She supported her family by getting work as a domestic. There is a familiar story of a 10-year-old Jackie getting into a name-calling and stone-throwing episode. He was in the fight even at so tender an age. Cared for by older sister Willa Mae when his mom went to work, he recalled those days years later. "I remember being aware of the constant protective attitude of my sister," he said. "She was dedicated on my behalf."[9]

Jackie spent his early years with the Pepper Street gang, kids of black, Mexican and Japanese heritage who got into constant trouble with the local police. He credits two men from steering him away from trouble. One, Carl Anderson, tried to talk him away from the gang. The other, was the Reverend Karl Downs. The Reverend Downs' influence on Jackie grew over the years and helped to direct his life in a responsible way. Sports were always big with Jackie, and at John Muir Technical High School he lettered in football, basketball, baseball and track. At Pasadena Junior College and at UCLA he continued to excel in all four sports. His bothers, Frank and Mack, were also great influences on the young man. Mack was an outstanding runner, finishing second by 0.4 seconds to Jesse Owens in the men's 200 meters in the 1936 Olympics.

Although Jackie came to be one of the greatest athletes to come out of Southern California, he quit school before getting a degree, believing that "no amount of education would help a black man get a job."[10] While at UCLA he met Rachael Isum, who would share the rest of his life and become an intricate part of it in both the sufferings and the successes. When Jackie left the army he joined the Kansas City Monarchs in the Negro Leagues in 1945 while seeking an opportunity to coach.

Branch Rickey was now running the Dodgers. It was the first opportunity he had to consider seriously his thoughts about bringing a Negro player to the major leagues. Certainly in St. Louis the plan could not be implemented considering the racial climate in the southernmost major league city. In Brooklyn both the climate and opportunity improved immeasurably. The pressure to integrate was increasing as well. There were half-hearted attempts made in Washington, Pittsburgh and Boston, but all came to naught. In July 1945 the Ives-Quinn Act was signed into law in New York State prohibiting employers from refusing to hire anyone because of race. When he read of the signing of the act by Governor Dewey, Rickey was elated. He exclaimed to his wife, " They can't stop me now!"[11]

The death of commissioner Kenesaw Mountain Landis on November 25, 1944, was a significant factor as well. Landis had been vehemently opposed to integrating the big leagues. The baseball owners would not be easily moved, and Rickey's first challenge came in finding the right man to fulfill the role he would be laying out for him. He came to know of Robinson with the aid of Wendell Smith, a writer for the *Pittsburgh Courier*, at the time the largest

Negro weekly newspaper in the country. Rickey's interest peeked when he learned that Jackie was one of the three players given the half-hearted trial with the Red Sox. He swore Smith to secrecy as Rickey considered it to be paramount while taking very few into his confidence.

As a subterfuge he announced on May 7, 1945, that the Dodgers would sponsor a Negro League team called the Brown Dodgers. This story was his cover for having Dodgers scouts seek out Negro ballplayers. In August Rickey sent Clyde Sukeforth to check out Jackie's throwing arm and, if acceptable, to bring him back to Brooklyn. Sukeforth arrived at Comiskey Park in Chicago on August 24 and introduced himself to Robinson as a scout for Rickey, the Brooklyn organization and the anticipated Brooklyn Brown Dodgers.

Clyde Sukeforth was a Rickey man, one of the last to be cut loose by O'Malley. Sukey's dismissal came after the 1951 playoff with the Giants; his crime was that he informed Charlie Dressen from the Dodgers' bullpen at the Polo Grounds that Carl Erskine had bounced a curveball. Sukeforth had played 10 seasons in the big leagues with Cincinnati and Brooklyn in the twenties and early thirties and came back to catch a few games in '45 when Leo Durocher found himself wanting in talent.

Sukey was born in Washington, Maine, and spent two years at Georgetown University before moving into the pro baseball ranks. A catcher, he was playing in the New England League when his contract was purchased from the Manchester Blue Sox by the Cincinnati Reds in 1926. In '29 he hit .354 in 84 games, but a couple of years later Sukeforth lost partial sight of his right eye after a hunting accident in the offseason.

He continued to play but his hitting suffered. Traded to the Dodgers in 1932, he ended his career with a .264 lifetime average and continued to work for the Dodgers in several capacities, including coach, minor league manager and scout. In the late summer of '45, when Rickey sent him to Chicago for his evaluation of Robinson, the old scout stepped into the history books. The story of the Rickey-Robinson "Great Experiment" is scarcely ever mentioned without the inclusion of the part played by Clyde Sukeforth.

Rickey had established a contact with Wendell Smith. Smith was a graduate of West Virginia State College with a major in journalism. He also captained the baseball and basketball teams in his senior year. In 1933 Smith was 17 years old, and after pitching his American Legion team to a 1–0 playoff victory, he met Detroit Tigers scout Wish Egan. On that day Egan offered contracts to Smith's battery mate, Mike Tresh, and the opposing pitcher.

"I wish I could sign you too, kid," Egan told Smith. "But I can't."[12] At that moment Smith vowed to dedicate himself to changing baseball's unfair color code. He wrote diligently over the years and pushed for change whenever he could. It was Smith who engineered the tryout for the three Negro ballplayers at Fenway Park on April 16, 1945, one of whom was Jackie Robinson. Though none of the three ever heard from the Red Sox, Wendell had no intention of giving up.

About a week after the writer informed Rickey of the events at Fenway, the Dodgers' boss called him. He told Smith of his interest in Jackie and about the Sukeforth trip to Chicago. In keeping with the almost-paranoid desire for secrecy, Rickey instituted the code words for Robinson: "The young man from the west." He hired Smith as a scout and asked him to accom-

Despite having broken the color barrier in the major leagues seven years earlier, Jackie Robinson and Roy Campanella were still confronted with bigotry in 1953. Painting is by artist Gabe Perillo (courtesy Gabe Perillo, Jr.).

pany Robinson on the road. As Smith later wrote, "I knew nothing about scouting. I was being paid to help Jackie jump the hurdles."[13]

When Sukeforth arrived in Chicago, he found that Robinson had suffered a shoulder injury and could not give Sukey the look he wanted, but the scout was impressed enough with the Negro ballplayer. "He was tough, he was intelligent, and he was proud," Sukeforth said of bringing Robinson back to Brooklyn anyway.[14] The historic meeting took place on the 28th at the Dodger offices at 215 Montague Street, and here the story played out. Clyde introduced the player by saying, "Mr. Rickey, this is Jack Roosevelt Robinson of the Kansas City Monarchs. I think he is the Brooklyn kind of ballplayer."[15] The scout then took a seat in the back of the office, the only eyewitness to the conference.

The first thing Rickey wanted to know was if Jackie had a girl. He advised him to marry her. Rickey revealed to Robinson that it was the Montreal Royals and possibly the Brooklyn Dodgers that he would be signing to play for and began to lay out very graphically the abuse that Jackie should expect to be subjected to. He emphasized that the ballplayer could not fight back or the entire project could fail. Then Rickey took a book from a desk drawer and showed Jackie a passage he had marked. The book was a favorite of Rickey's—*The Life of Christ* by Giovanni Papini. It was the passage about turning the other cheek.

"I come into second base," Rickey dramatized. "You tag me hard in the ribs. I jump up. 'You tar baby son of a bitch,' I scream. 'You can't do this to me, you coon.' I punch you in the face." Rickey swung his clenched fist under Robinson's chin. "What do you do now, Jackie? What do you do now?"

"I get it, Mr. Rickey. I've got another cheek. I turn the other cheek."

"Wonderful!" Rickey said. He was finally satisfied.[16]

Regarding Rickey's elation, Sukeforth said later, "I thought the old man was going to kiss him. What was I doing while this was going on? Listen, I was pretty uneasy. Remember, I still hadn't seen the guy's arm!"[17]

On October 23, 1945, Jackie Robinson signed to play for the Montreal Royals, Brooklyn's top affiliate in the International League. He had a spectacular year at Montreal, hitting .349 to lead the league in batting. But that was merely the tip of the iceberg. He ran the bases like a dervish and proved to be an excellent defensive second baseman. Rickey knew that Montreal would accept the black player but there were troubles in spring training in Sanford, Florida, which extended into the '47 season when Jackie joined the Dodgers. Following the suspension of Leo Durocher for the entire season, Rickey brought his old friend, Burt Shotton, in to manage the club. Before Shotton joined the club, however, Sukeforth managed the first two games of the season, adding to his historical resume as Jackie's first big league manager.

Another of the hopeful left fielders, Brooklyn-born Bill Antonello, homered into the right-center field bleachers for his first of the year. On Monday they lost, 2–1, on a 10th-inning homer by Reds behemoth Ted Kluszewski off Preacher Roe. Brooklyn left 18 men on base. They moved on to the newest National League city for a two-game set with the Braves in Milwaukee on the 19th and 20th and won them both. Russ Meyer scattered seven hits for a 4–1 victory, knocking the Braves out of a first-place tie with the Phils. Shuba and Snider homered. There were 36,439 fans in the seats at Milwaukee County Stadium, a fact no doubt noted by Walter O'Malley.

The next day Billy Loes won his fifth game, 7–2, during which Jackie Robinson homered for the second time this season. Still playing with some degree of inconsistency, they lost two to the Giants. The largest Polo Grounds crowd of the year, 46,778, saw Bobby Thomson homer off Black on Thursday night in a 7–2 Giants win. The next day Jim Hearn went all the way to defeat Carl Erskine, 5–1, adding insult to injury with a fourth-inning double. It was noted in the press coverage that this was the first complete game for Hearn in seven starts.

An item out of Washington, D.C., announced that the Supreme Court would once again take up the question of major league baseball's exemption from federal antitrust laws in the fall term. Was baseball a sport or a business? A decision could have an effect on the validity of the reserve clause. In a 1922 decision in the case of *Federal Baseball Club of Baltimore v. National League of Professional Baseball Clubs*, which grew out of a dispute between major league baseball and the upstart Federal League, the court upheld the status, preserving the reserve clause and continuing the game's exemption from the antitrust laws. Once again the court would keep the game free from antitrust laws. Owner Phil Wrigley of the Cubs said it as well as anyone could. "Baseball is too much of a business to be a sport, and too much of a sport to be a business."[18]

Baseball's conundrum, begun in the 1870s, was still being tossed about in 1953. Does a curveball really curve or as has been suggested, in some cases vehemently, is it an optical illusion? Major league old-timer Luke Sewell wondered, "Isn't it strange," he said, "that the optical illusion only happens when someone tries to throw a curve ball, and never when a fast ball or straight ball is attempted?"[19] To illustrate the discrepancies in the debate, two major magazines sponsored tests in an effort to settle the supposed controversy. One of them, *LIFE,* claimed that their tests concluded that the curve is indeed an optical illusion. The other, *LOOK,* insisted that its photographs proved "that a curve ball actually does curve."[20]

Over the years the dispute went so far as to involve philosophers and scientists. In an 1877 experiment, tests were made that used wooden posts driven into the ground. Super pitchers like Bob Feller were used, and the science of aerodynamics was ushered into the study. It was left to Igor Sikorsky, an expert in aerodynamics, to delve into the question utilizing the resources of his company, United Aircraft Corporation. The result, as summarized in a 1953 article by Joseph F. Drury, Jr., stated, "It can definitely be concluded that a pitched ball does actually curve, in addition to any optical illusion which may exist."[21]

Of course, ballplayers needed no such confirmation. Al Schacht, former big league pitcher and in the '50s known as "The Clown Prince of Baseball," liked to tell this story of the local baseball star who is trying out for a big league team. Writing home, he tells his folks, "Looks like I will be a regular outfielder. Now hitting .433." A week later came the lament, "Dear Mom," it said. "They started throwing curves. Will be home Friday."[22]

There were 31,532 at Philadelphia's Connie Mack Stadium on the 23rd when Preacher Roe hooked up with Robin Roberts in a pitching gem that saw Preach prevail with a beautiful six-hit 2–0 whitewashing of the Phils. Roberts allowed just four hits, but one of them was Roy Campanella's 13th home run in the fifth. Roy now had 45 runs batted in. Brooklyn scored its first run in the fourth inning on Gilliam's lead-off double to right field. Gilliam got to third on Reese's sacrifice bunt and came home when Duke Snider lofted a sacrifice fly to the right fielder.

Brooklyn had now beaten the Philadelphia ace right-hander three times this season. Roe went to 2–2 as the 38-year-old threw 131 pitches. The Dodgers had yet to take off, as their record to date was 17–14. Preacher's shutout ushered in a 10-game winning streak that seemed to signal the start of a turnaround. It would not be their longest streak of the year—that extended to 13 games and did not come until August—but this was a significant step.

Russ Meyer had managed to defy the "Mad Monk" image, at least until the 24th of May, when he stretched his tempestuous legs on Sunday in Philadelphia against his old teammates. In the fourth inning, Meyer began stomping around the mound, irate over the calls of plate umpire Augie Donetelli. Finally he had had enough. He stormed the plate at Donetelli but Campanella held him back. In his anger and frustration, Meyer grabbed the rosin bag and tossed it 30 feet into the air. According to Sir Isaac Newton, what goes up must come down, and as the object descended it landed square on the top of the pitcher's head. At this point Donetelli tossed the pitcher out of the game.

So far, not an unusual day for the Monk. But once in the dugout he made an obscene gesture towards the umpire that was caught by the television cameras, which created a bigger uproar than Meyer had. National League president Warren Giles levied a $100 fine and three-day suspension at him. Oddly, commissioner Ford Frick commented about the TV cameras turning towards the dugout, considering that to be an invasion of the players' privacy. Giles agreed and thought it better if the cameras stuck to the action on the field.

Unfortunately for Meyer, his temper tantrum cost him a win. The Dodgers went on an offensive onslaught. They scored 12 runs in the eighth and came away with a 16–2 victory. The Dodgers set a record for the most runs scored at the start of an inning before a single out was recorded. The inning proceeded in this way: Hodges walked, Cox singled and Snider doubled to right, scoring Hodges. Furillo was walked intentionally. Erskine, who threw four innings in relief, blooped a single to right, scoring Cox and leaving the bases loaded. This was against the Phillies' Curt Simmons, who was replaced now by Bob Miller, who walked Gilliam to force in a run. Podres and Hughes followed Meyer until Erskine took over in the sixth.

It was not unusual for the ace of the staff to come in and relieve during the era; Erskine made six relief appearances during the season. It was certainly a different time in baseball. "Between starts we would throw," Erskine said, "and sometimes the manager would tell the pitcher to wait until late in the game to do his throwing in the bullpen, he'd say, 'I might need you for an inning' and would use you between starts."[23] Erskine is quick to point out what he refers to as a major breakthrough in baseball. "In my time in the majors I had four pitching coaches who were catchers," he said. "They never signed former pitchers to the job. The catchers couldn't tell you about mechanics or the grip on the baseball. The Dodgers signed Ted Lyons but he only lasted a year because the manager paid no attention to him. But it was the start of a new idea and former pitchers became the new pitching coaches."[24] A notable exception at the time was the Yankees' Jim Turner, who coached the New York staff from 1949 to 1959 under Casey Stengel.

In the absence of more qualified coaches, pitchers of the day sought advice from the veterans. Erskine, for example, was treated to some excellent advice when he first joined the Dodgers from Hugh Casey. The veteran cautioned the rookie to expect the really good hitters in the league to get their share of safeties off of him, but he advised that he bear down against the guys ahead of them in the lineup. "Keep those weak sisters off the bases," Casey said. "Then when Musial and Mize get their hits, you don't get hurt."[25] Erskine listened to veterans like Casey and Preacher Roe. "I leaned on Preacher a lot," he said. "But the changeover happened in that time and led to former pitchers serving in the role."[26]

Reese tripled to clear the bases and Robinson singled off Andy Hansen, the next Philadelphia pitcher. Campanella walked and Hodges singled. The new Phillie pitcher was Paul Stuffel and he walked Cox and Snider, forcing in another run. Kent Peterson replaced Stuffel and Furillo tripled over Ashburn's head in center. Erskine struck out for the first out. Gilliam hit a ground ball and Furillo was thrown out at the plate. Reese struck out to end the inning that had lasted 44 minutes. There were seven Dodger hits, six walks and 12 runs scored.

The pounding of the Phillies continued the next day. Brooklyn won, 11–9, with Robinson and Campanella hitting home runs. The Dodgers were in third place but just percentage points behind Philadelphia. Loes started the game but gave up three runs in the Phillies' first and was relieved by Ben Wade. Wade threw two innings and was followed by Bob Milliken, whose 5⅓ innings earned him the victory. The Dodgers trailed, 6–4, going into the sixth inning when they tied it up on a single by Billy Cox and Carl Furillo's third home run of the year, which came off Karl Drews.

The club returned home to Ebbets Field to host the Giants for two games on Wednesday and Thursday, the 27th and 28th. In keeping with the tradition of Dodger-Giant games taking longer than Brooklyn's games against anybody else, this one lasted three hours and three minutes. Brooklyn trailed New York by a run going into the ninth inning when, after a Gilliam groundout, Pee Wee walked. He moved to second after Snider flied to center for the second out and before Jackie Robinson reached on an error by shortstop Al Dark. It set the stage for three unearned runs as Roy Campanella homered off Jim Hearn for Brooklyn's 5–3 victory.

Another late win came in the tenth as the Dodgers broke a 6–6 tie and scored the tie-breaker on a rash of Giants misplays. Reese struck out but reached first safely when catcher Ray Noble was charged with an error. On Snider's sacrifice bunt, Pee Wee scampered to second while the Duke made it safely to first. Both runners moved up when Hoyt Wilhelm delivered a wild pitch with Robinson at the plate. The Giants then walked Jackie intentionally to load the bases, and Reese scored the winning run on a passed ball. Dodgers win, 7–6. Joe Black got credit for both victories in relief.

After winning five in a row, Brooklyn completed the streak by sweeping the Pirates in a five-game set at Pittsburgh. Russ Meyer picked up his fourth win against only one loss on Friday as the Dodgers defeated Johnny Lindell, the old Yankee outfielder who was back in the majors as a knuckleball pitcher. The score was 7–4. The Brooks went ahead with two in the top of the first when Reese scored on Campy's sac fly and Snider came in on Gil Hodges' single. Lindell gave up another run in the fifth and two more in the sixth but stayed in to complete the game. Meyer went five before being replaced by Jim Hughes.

The next four games were back-to-back doubleheaders on the Memorial Day weekend. The Dodgers won the opening game, 7–4, with a 12-hit attack against three Pirate pitchers, the loss going to starter Murray Dickson. Preacher Roe started for Brooklyn but left during a Pittsburgh four-run fourth inning. He was relieved by Ben Wade, who hit a home run that chased Dickson in the top half of the sixth. Gil Hodges hit a three-run homer in the same inning as the Dodgers scored five. Wade got credit for the victory, his third of the season.

In the second game of this Memorial Day weekend pair of doubleheaders, Podres won his second game against an equal number of losses by a 4–1 score. The loser was Bob Friend. Carl Erskine threw three scoreless innings in relief of Johnny Podres. On Sunday, May 31, Brooklyn squeaked one out of the Pirates. The Dodgers went into the ninth with a two-run lead, but Billy Loes needed help from Jim Hughes to get the final out of the game. Danny O'Connell began the last inning with a double and scored on a pinch-hit single by Pete Castiglione. Hughes came in to get Eddie Pellagrini on a foul pop-up behind third base that Billy Cox squeezed for the final out. The score was 4–3.

Brooklyn's 10th win in a row came as the nightcap of the Sunday doubleheader with a score of 4–1. Rookie Bob Milliken won his second game against no defeats. Bob Milliken would be 27 years old in August and was getting a much-longed-for chance after serving the last two seasons in the army. He did some pitching at Camp Atterbury, Indiana, and was a teammate to the Phillies' Curt Simmons while there. But Milliken had already lost the 1950 season before entering the military because of an arm injury in April while with the Montreal Royals.

Milliken, from Majorsville, West Virginia, had been a highly regarded prospect for the Dodgers. He began his professional career at Nashua in 1947 where he was 11–6. He split the '48 season between Danville and Fort Worth and had a fine year at Fort Worth in 1949, winning 12 and losing five with a 2.65 ERA. While getting a chance with Brooklyn this year, he had not pitched as a pro since 1949. Used as a swingman between the rotation and bullpen, he proved effective, going 8–4 in 117⅔ innings and making 37 appearances, 10 as a starter. His last gasp in the majors came the next season when he won five and lost two games in just 62⅔ innings. His ERA was 4.02.

In the month of May 1953, a young writer from Brooklyn began to cover the Dodgers for the *Brooklyn Eagle,* taking over for Harold C. Burr, who had broken his hip in a fall. Dave Anderson had worked as a summer copy boy at the *New York Sun* while attending Xavier High School in Manhattan and was later sports editor of the Holy Cross student newspaper.

"I wanted to be a sportswriter since I was twelve," Anderson said, "since I spread the sports sections on the floor of our Bay Ridge home and read the best sportswriters of the era."[27]

Following graduation in 1951, Anderson was hired as a clerk in the *Eagle* sports department at $40 a week. After Burr's accident, the kid from Brooklyn found himself covering the Brooklyn Dodgers on a daily basis. "The best beat in the business," he proclaims.

When the paper folded in January 1955, Dave recalls with relish how six months later he was at Yankee Stadium when Brooklyn won the '55 World Series, now as a writer for the *New York Journal-American*. He can recall his favorite memory of Jackie Robinson, though not on a great day in Brooklyn. It was immediately after Bobby Thomson cleared the left field wall in the third playoff game in 1951. "While the other Dodgers have turned towards the clubhouse in center field at the Polo Grounds, he is still standing near second base, his hands on his hips, staring at home plate to make sure Thomson steps on it."[28]

Anderson was assigned to cover the last game to be played at Ebbets Field on September 24, 1957. Dave and Bill Roeder of the *World-Telegram and Sun* were the last writers to finish their stories in the press room. "When we got to the night watchman's door near the marble rotunda," he remembers, "I stepped aside to let Bill walk out, then I walked out—the last writer to leave Ebbets Field after the last Dodger game.

"Put that on my tombstone!"[29]

Anderson went to work for the *New York Times* in 1966, and in 1981 was given a Pulitzer Prize for commentary, only the second sportswriter to be so honored.

On May 12 the last of the DiMaggio brothers retired. He hit .294 the previous year but this spring suffered from an eye infection, and though it cleared up, the Red Sox preferred to go with the young players, and Dom DiMaggio was relegated to the bench. Not happy with his lot, the "Little Professor " decided to retire with the statement, "It is doubtful that I will ever return to baseball."[30] In his 11 seasons, all spent with Boston, DiMaggio hit a collective .298 and was considered among the finest defensive center fielders in the game. Dom started his professional career following in the steps of his older brothers, first Vince and then Joe. All broke in with their hometown San Francisco Seals. Of the three DiMaggio brothers, Vince retired in 1946 and Joe followed after the '51 season.

With his 16 home runs in 35 games, Campanella was ahead of Babe Ruth's 1927 pace. Both he and Hack Wilson, who holds the National League record at 56, did not get number 16 until their 43rd game. Brooklyn won their fifth consecutive game the next day, 7–6, on a passed ball by Giants catcher Ray Noble and a wild pitch from reliever Hoyt Wilhelm, both coming in the 10th inning.

The Dodgers concluded the month of May with 10 straight wins and a season record of 27 wins and 14 losses. They were now in first place by a half-game over the Milwaukee Braves.

Six

June

"The '53 Dodgers were the most awesome team Brooklyn would produce."—Richard Goldstein, *Superstars and Screwballs*

"What he (Snider) showed me in the Series, he can take from there ... and be as great as he wants."—Joe DiMaggio

Brooklyn opened the month of June on the second with a three-game set against Milwaukee at Ebbets Field. They dropped the first two, leaving them a game and a half out of first place. There should have been some regret in the Dodgers' front office in that first game because it was Andy Pafko who hit a two-run home run in the ninth to give the Braves the win by a 4–3 score. The next day Milwaukee jumped all over them, winning, 14–9, as the Braves scored six runs in the fifth inning and five in the eighth. The Dodgers recovered enough to pull out the third game, 10–5, dropping the Braves' lead back to a game and a half. Duke Snider walloped his ninth homer of the season; he was joined by Furillo, Hodges and Bobby Morgan, who also connected for circuit blasts.

There were more than 20 future Hall-of-Fame players on the 1953 major league rosters and the Milwaukee Braves had two. Hank Aaron debuted in the major leagues in 1954, but now there were Eddie Mathews and Warren Spahn building those great credentials. Although the Dodgers, with their tremendous right-handed power, were usually deadly versus left-handed pitchers, some, like Curt Simmons of the Phillies and Harvey Haddix of St. Louis, gave Brooklyn hitters trouble. Oddly, the winningest southpaw in baseball history, Warren Spahn, always had difficulties with the Dodgers, especially at Ebbets Field. In 1952 he lost to Brooklyn five times without gaining a victory. However, in the spring he almost became a Dodger. They made a bid for him, offering Andy Pafko, Billy Cox, a couple of pitchers and a ton of cash for Spahn and outfielder Sid Gordon, but were turned down. Having gotten wind of the rumors, Spahnie ran into Dodger skipper Charlie Dressen in January.

"Am I going to your club?" Spahn wanted to know.

"Don't look like it," snorted Dressen. "We offered them half the ball club for you, and they wanted the uniforms too."[1]

Spahn came up in 1942 and threw 15⅔ innings before going off to war. He went overseas with the 276th Combat Engineers Battalion and saw constant action, including the Battle of the Bulge and the fight at Remagen Bridge across the Rhine. Spahn won the Bronze Star and a Purple Heart. He came back to baseball in time for the '46 season and stayed for 21 years, retiring at 44 years of age. The stylish lefty won 363 games overall, 13 times winning 20 or more games in a single season. In 1953 he would post a 23–7 record, a winning percentage of .767.

Milwaukee's third baseman was only in his second year in the big leagues but would lead the National League in homers in '53 with 47. In a 17-year career, Eddie Mathews hit 512 home runs and drove in 1,453 runs. He led the league in round-trippers again in 1959 and was an all-star nine times. Mathews was inducted into Cooperstown in 1978.

The Dodgers' attack was beginning to look awesome and in the vanguard were the two established outfielders. The Duke of Flatbush was in center and the Emperor of Right Field was Carl Furillo. They would play alongside each other for ten successive seasons in Brooklyn. They were different men. Edwin Donald Snider was the blond, handsome Californian, an Apollo with steel springs in his legs and a left-handed swing that was as sweet as a bottle of Log Cabin syrup. Snider could be moody, particularly in the earlier years, and at times temperamental. Furillo was old-world, a laborer, ruggedly handsome, confident, and with a powerful throwing arm that stopped major league speed in its tracks. But how they jelled on the field.

"No two outfielders ever communicated better than we did," Snider said. "Skoonj would take anything in right-center that was deep and I would take anything that wasn't. Films of those years show Carl gliding in back of me and me running a few feet in front of him, still leaving plenty of room to prevent a collision. You see other plays where I'm going for a ball hit to right-center and he's hustling over in case he's needed, but we're nowhere near running into each other. It was a pleasure playing alongside of him."[2]

Snider was born in Whittier, California, on September 19, 1926, and named "Little Duke" by his father Ward, "Big Duke." The elder Duke worked as a jackhammer operator at the navy shipyard in Long Beach. Ward entered the Navy in 1943 at a time when his son was drawing the attention of baseball scouts as well as college recruiters for his prowess on the gridiron. Duke played baseball, football and basketball at Compton High School, once tossing a 68-yard pass that had the colleges on his doorstep. He earned sixteen high school letters and was All-Southern California in three sports. A natural right-handed hitter, Snider was turned around by his dad when he was six or seven years old. "My father put a bat in my hands and told me, 'Hit left-handed. Most ballparks are built for left-handed hitters. Besides, you're a couple of steps closer to first base.'"[3]

Although scouted by Cincinnati, no offer was made and it remained for Tom Downey of the Dodgers to offer Duke a $750 bonus. He signed and was sent to play for Class B Newport News under manager Jake Pitler, later a Brooklyn coach. "We weren't rich," he recalled, "and I thought I should bring in some cash money for the family."[4] His first spring training in 1944 was held in Bear Mountain, New York, because of wartime travel restrictions. When the kid from California stepped off the train, he saw something he had never seen before—snow. And he didn't own a topcoat.

It was at Newport News that Snider began to develop the bad boy reputation as a temperamental sulker. After getting a take sign on a three-one pitch, Duke struck out. He tossed the bat high into the air and came out on the short end of a $50 fine. He did hit .294 and led the league in doubles with 24 and home runs with nine, but he also struck out 96 times, which added a lack of knowledge of the strike zone to his negative portfolio.

Duke was drafted into the navy that fall and served 11 months aboard a submarine tender in the South Pacific. Upon getting his discharge in May 1946, he was sent to Fort Worth, where he was used mostly in a pinch-hit role. He struggled, both with the bat and with his temper, but the bursts of power kept the Dodgers hopeful. He came to Brooklyn on Opening Day in 1947 and stayed until July 4, when he was sent back to St. Paul where he clubbed 12 home runs and hit .316 the rest of the year.

There were two notable occasions for the Duke soon thereafter. Having gotten engaged to Beverly Null on Valentine's Day 1944, he and Bev were married at the First Methodist Church in Lynwood, California, on October 25, 1947. In spring training the next year, Snider came under the tutelage of Branch Rickey's college of baseball knowledge at the enormous complex at Vero Beach, Florida. In an effort to teach him the strike zone and to learn to lay off bad pitches, Rickey had Duke stand at the plate with orders not to swing but to watch the ball and call the pitches. Instructed by hitting coach and Hall-of-Famer George Sisler, the key to the project was for Snider to call the pitches and then compare his calls with the pitcher, the catcher and Sisler.

It seemed to work. At Montreal he hit well but his attitude didn't change much. Manager Clay Hopper called him, "the worst acting .330 hitter I ever handled."[5] But Duke kept hitting and displaying great power. By 1949 the Duke was ready for Flatbush.

He and Bev rented a second-floor apartment in a private home on East 18th Street between Beverly Road and Church Avenue. Duke remembers having "a lovely view of an eight-story apartment building. The only sky we saw was a narrow slit of blue almost straight up."[6] The Sniders eventually would become a part of the Dodger enclave in Bay Ridge when they rented a home at 178 Marine Avenue, creating a lasting memory for a Brooklyn Dodgers fan named Henry D'Amato. Hank grew up in his grandmother's brownstone on Carroll Street in Park Slope and with childhood friend Jimmy LaCerra attended school at St. Francis Xavier.

As a kid playing stickball on the Brooklyn streets, Hank was a Dodgers fan who idolized Duke Snider. D'Amato grew older, married a girl named Karen, and they had a daughter. In 1975 they purchased a home in Bay Ridge where a second daughter was born. A neighbor shocked D'Amato by telling him that the house he now owned at 178 Marine Avenue had once been lived in by his hero, Duke Snider, and his family. Hank was walking on air but the story wasn't yet completed. In the early eighties, his wife called him at work to say that a man was at the door who claimed to be Duke Snider and he had a camera crew with him. She was reluctant to let anyone in the house.

"By the time I got home," Hank said, "my wife and the Duke were sitting in the kitchen having coffee. I remember that the Duke wore a plaid blazer and baby blue pants and had a World Series ring on his hand. He was a real gentleman."[7] He was there to film scenes for the documentary *The Boys of Summer*, based on the book by Roger Kahn. There was another unexpected twist to the story that would keep Hank shaking his head for years to come.

His good buddy Jimmy LaCerra had moved away when they were still kids and the two had lost touch. The LaCerras had moved to a home at 177 Marine Avenue across the street from the Sniders. His parents still lived there when Hank and his family moved in.

"Jimmy said he was moving to Flatbush; we didn't know Flatbush from a hole in the wall. He moved to Marine Avenue. Wow," Hank said, "this is a big circle being completed."[8]

Duke hit .292 with 23 home runs in his rookie season but struck out eight times in the five games of the '49 World Series against the Yankees. The questions persisted: When would Duke Snider realize the tremendous potential many considered he possessed? It finally did happen. Perhaps the word is maturity; he learned how to handle himself. "With the help of my wife and a lot of people who didn't give up on me," he said, "I learned to stand on my own feet."[9]

Snider's defensive ability was never an issue. One of the most graceful and agile of center fielders, he ranked among the best in a field that was abundant with outstanding defensive center fielders. Composer Terry Cashman aided the concept when he penned a ditty entitled, "Willie, Mickey and the Duke," immortalizing in song the exemplary talents of Snider along with Willie Mays and Mickey Mantle. It was an extraordinary trio to play in the same city at the same time. Snider may not have gotten the full credit that he deserved because of the smaller confines of Ebbets Field, but the catch he made on a drive by Willie Jones of the Phillies achieved mythical proportions among the fans of Brooklyn. It happened in Philadelphia on Memorial Day when Duke literally climbed the wall to make the catch. The spike marks on the barrier reached as high as his head. It came in the 12th inning and Jones' drive would have scored the tying and winning runs, but the catch preserved a 5–4 victory for Clem Labine and the Dodgers.

Dave Anderson called Snider's catch the "greatest, absolutely the greatest, in baseball history."[10] The writer went on to call Duke "the best center fielder in baseball these days. And that means you too, Willie Mays, and especially you, Mickey Mantle."[11]

Coach Ted Lyons said he could hear "Snider's knee and torso bang the wall from the bullpen," and expressed just why it was such a great catch. "It meant the game," he said. "If he misses it, we lose."[12]

The World Series of 1952 was the break-out point for Duke Snider. His average was .345. He hit four home runs, drove in eight, and had 24 total bases. In 1953 Snider would have the first of five consecutive seasons hitting 40 or more home runs. He would complete his Hall-of-Fame career with 407. In 1954 the Duke hit .341 and the batting race between him and Mays and Don Mueller of the Giants went down to the final game of the season. Duke took the collar, Mueller went 2-for–5, but Willie had three hits and the batting title—Mays, .345, Mueller, .342, and Snider, who finished at .341.

In the '55 Series, Snider again hit four home runs as Brooklyn won the World Series. He was the first player to hit four Series homers on two occasions. He batted .320 and drove in seven. In the decade of the fifties no one hit more home runs or drove in more runs than Duke Snider. He leads in both categories among the all-time Brooklyn Dodgers as well. In the '56 pennant clincher, the last Brooklyn would ever see, Duke hit two homers, one of them a three-run blast off Pittsburgh's Vernon Law.

The move to Los Angeles, somewhat traumatic for all the players, was no less for Snider, although he was a native of the state. He would miss his Brooklyn neighbors in the Bay Ridge section where Duke and his family rented a home each summer. The Sniders had four children—sons Kevin and Kirk and daughters Pamala and Dwana. And he would miss the Brooklyn fans as well as the sheer joy of playing at Ebbets Field. Furthermore, there would be no more "Dook of Flatbush." In the final weekend of the '57 campaign, Duke hit the final major league home run ever at Ebbets Field. He told manager Walter Alston that he wanted to sit out the last two games. "I'd hit a home run," he explained, "and I wanted to remember that as my last Ebbets Field experience."[13]

Snider went to Los Angeles with the Dodgers in 1958 and stayed until '62 before coming back to New York as a member of the fledging New York Mets. He hit his 400th home run as a Met. There wasn't much in the press and that surprised teammate Jim Piersall, who had 99 lifetime round-trippers. He told the Duke, "I bet I get more ink when I hit my one hundredth than you got with four hundred."[14] He did. The flamboyant Mr. Piersall accomplished it by running the bases backwards.

As a great ballplayer who was at this time a seasoned veteran, Snider was revered by some of the young Mets. One in particular was a kid from Brooklyn named Ted Schreiber. Schreiber, incidentally, had hit the next-to-last home run at Ebbets Field when his two-run drive into the left field seats for St. John's University defeated Manhattan College on April 24, 1958. Signed by the Red Sox and then drafted out of the minor leagues by the Mets, Schreiber got to the big club where he spent the 1963 season as a teammate of Snider's.

"Duke was great," Ted recalled, "a real class guy. He always went out of his way to be friendly and helpful to kids like myself. I liked and respected him."[15]

After retiring, Snider managed a bit in the minors and enjoyed a second career as a broadcaster for the San Diego Padres. The eight-time All-Star hit over .300 seven times, six times driving in more than 100 runs. He arrived in Cooperstown and was reunited with Willie and Mickey in the place all three belonged. The Duke of Flatbush passed away on February 27, 2011, in Escondido, California, survived by his wife, Beverly, and the couple's four children. Occasionally booed in Flatbush yet eminently popular with the fans, the Duke is remembered in Brooklyn with great respect. As professor Lee Congdon reminds us, "In very important ways, baseball encourages us in the habit of remembering."[16]

When Duke and Bev made the trip east for the Hall-of-Fame induction ceremonies in 1980, they stopped in Brooklyn and had dinner one evening at

The 1953 campaign was the first of five consecutive seasons that Duke Snider would hit 40 or more home runs. In the decade of the fifties, no one in baseball hit more home runs than the Duke of Flatbush (Brooklyn Public Library—Brooklyn Collection).

the River Cafe, below the Brooklyn Bridge. Someone among the patrons recognized the Duke and began to applaud softly. Soon the entire restaurant joined in. Someone sent over a bottle of champagne. "The people of Brooklyn were still being nice to the Duke of Flatbush."[17] Carl Erskine, teammate and friend and Snider's roommate for 12 years put it in the best perspective when he said, "The Dook, as he was called in Brooklyn, was the royalty that gave the borough respectability."[18]

Since returning to the lineup Gil Hodges had recorded twenty hits in 45 at-bats to lift his average from an anemic .181 to .273. Morgan played third as Cox sat it out with a strain in his side. Robinson played left field. Brooklyn got on the board early with a first-inning run on Snider's double that scored Gilliam, who had led off with a walk. In the third two more crossed the plate on a single by Reese, a double by Furillo, and two walks and two fly balls.

In the third game against the Braves they faced Max Surkont and finished him off in the fourth inning by scoring three. A home run by Morgan, Gilliam's bunt single and Reese's double accounted for most of the damage. Hodges and Furillo hit successive home runs in the seventh as Brooklyn stole five bases in six attempts. Billy Loes won his seventh game against two losses and it was also his third straight win against the pennant-challenging Milwaukee Braves. Loes needed help in the eighth when the Braves scored three and he received it from Jim Hughes. The 6′ 1″, 200-pounder from Chicago, Illinois, had up to this point become Dressen's man in the bullpen. In ten appearances so far he had not given up a run.

The 29-year-old right-hander had spent seven years in the minors before joining the Dodgers in 1952. He threw just 19 innings for a 2–1 record but had a 1.42 ERA. Originally signed by the White Sox, he became part of the Dodgers' organization in 1948 and was 10–4 at Montreal in 1951. Jim served with the 1st Marines during World War II, doing time in the Palau Islands where he was decorated for "meritorious performance of duty" in the face of enemy fire. Moving to the bullpen at Montreal in '52, Hughes appeared in 45 games and pitched 95 innings. Dressen would utilize him on 48 occasions and Hughes responded with a 4–3 record in 85⅔ innings of work.

The Dodgers then swept St. Louis in a weekend series. On Friday night in front of 29,976 at Ebbets Field, the Brooks eked out a 5–4 victory, Black getting the credit in relief of Preacher Roe. On Saturday it was an inspired Gil Hodges who led Brooklyn's charge with two home runs, including a three-run shot in the ninth. Again the score was 5–4, but on Sunday the Dodgers unloaded. The 10–1 win went to Carl Erskine and Hodges homered again. In winning his fifth game Erskine gave up just four Braves hits, two of them to third baseman Ray Jablonski. Brooklyn scored three each in the fourth and fifth innings. Four singles by Robinson, Hodges, Furillo and Morgan did it in the fourth, and the next inning three scored on singles by Snider and Campanella. Gilliam was hit by a pitch and Robinson walked in the inning that also included a costly error by shortstop Solly Hemus.

On this weekend the Phillies' Robin Roberts won his 100th career game while topping the Braves. Milwaukee then took a doubleheader from the Pirates and went back on top of the Dodgers by a half-game.

The Reds came in for four and dropped the Dodgers back by one game when they beat Russ Meyer in the opener, 8–5. Gus Bell and Ted Kluszewski had circuit blasts. Big Klu was a monster. He wore his sleeves cut to the shoulder and those biceps bulged out like the trunks of two trees. Cal Abrams, an old Dodger, was playing right field with the Cincinnati Reds when he took a single by Jackie Robinson. Having known Jackie as a teammate, he knew his propensity to make a huge turn and try to draw a throw. Abrams fired behind him, but Kluszewski was caught by surprise. "Jackie had stopped on a dime," Abrams said, "and suddenly the ball was at first base before he got back to the bag. But the ball hit Kluszewski in the chest, didn't even faze him because he's so strong."[19] It was Leo Durocher who once observed that Gil Hodges was the strongest human being he had ever seen in baseball.

"How about Kluszewski?" a writer asked.

"He don't count," Durocher told him. "He's not human."[20]

But the man was more than muscle. He was a good hitter who knew what he was doing with the bat. He had hit over .300 three of his first five years in the big leagues. He worked on his hitting until he got it right. One offseason he spent his time chopping down trees. He reported in the spring so tight and muscle-bound that he could not swing properly. As he loosened up, he cut down on his swing. His manager at Cincinnati, Bill McKechnie, suggested he go to a heavier bat—from a 34-ounce model to 40 ounces. Another problem he encountered was "stepping into the bucket." He would stride with his left foot towards third base. He solved that one by moving closer to the plate.

"The guy has no real weakness," said Dodgers chief scout Andy High, "unless it's his tendency to go after pitches outside the strike zone."[21] Ted won batting titles in each of his two minor league seasons, and in 14 major league seasons he hit for a .298 average with 279 home runs. He hit 40 of them in '53, 49 the next year, and 47 in 1955. Back problems were the cause of his power production tailing off after that. But a striking stat, especially for a slugger of Klu's proportions, were his strikeouts, or rather, the lack of them. In those 14 seasons he averaged just 26 per year.

By winning the next three, Brooklyn snapped the Reds' five-game winning streak. In the Tuesday 10–6 win, home runs by Furillo, Snider, Reese, and Hodges provided the offense. The Dodgers won the next two games, 13–3 and 9–6. Preacher Roe got the win in the first of the games with the assistance of a Dodgers offense that pounded Cincinnati pitcher Frank Smith for seven runs in the eighth inning. In the final game they beat a former Dodger, Bud Podbielian. In the last five games the Brooks had posted 70 hits and still remained a game out of first as Milwaukee kept up its winning ways.

Brooklyn took over first place when the Dodgers beat the Cubs, 7–4, with Jim Hughes tossing five shutout innings in relief. Among the 17,764 fans at Ebbets were two Bushwick High School students and a 21-year-old man who decided to climb down from the seats and run across center field. They explained that they were winning a bet with some friends. All three were held on $500 bail for disorderly conduct and arraigned in night court.

As the result of a rain-out on Saturday the two teams played a Sunday doubleheader. Brooklyn won the first game and took a four-run lead into the ninth inning of the second game when Ralph Kiner hit a grand slam, the 12th of his career, tying him with the Reds manager Rogers Hornsby. The game was halted in a 6–6 tie.

A magazine article called Roy Campanella "baseball's greatest catcher." A full-page ad for Camel and Cavalier cigarettes promoted Father's Day, June 21; it would be later this year that an announcement linking cigarette smoking to cancer would be made. A photo sequence in *LIFE* magazine showed a Russian MIG fighter jet being shot down over Korea and the pilot bailing out. The pictures were taken by a camera mounted on the wing of an F-86 American Sabre jet. It was the first time such film had ever been taken. The F-86 was piloted by 2nd Lieutenant Edwin Aldrin of Montclair, New Jersey. The lieutenant would join the NASA space program in 1963 and in 1969 would be the second man to walk on the moon.

The Dodgers began a losing road trip on the 16th when they were swept by the Cardinals in three. Before O'Malley struck, St. Louis was the westernmost city in the majors. Travel was primarily by train, long and tedious trips and hot and uncomfortable in the days before air conditioning. But there was a positive side. Teammates spent many hours together and got to know each other very well. Writers also traveled with the teams, and there were plenty of relaxed moments. There was much talk of baseball among the Dodger players and the chance to relive games and correct mistakes. Another mainstay of train trips was card games, very popular with the Dodger players, bridge and gin rummy among the favorites.

Jackie Robinson was an avid card player, and in a bit of an odd-couple pairing teamed with Billy Loes. Pee Wee Reese, Carl Erskine, Billy Cox and Duke Snider were among those who indulged in card games regularly in the clubhouse and on the train. The Dodgers talked baseball. They understood you don't win by laughing off defeats and Captain Reese and the other veterans brought the rookies into it by going over games and opposing pitchers. Among others they spoke of Sal Maglie, high and tight and low and away. Furillo seethed over the Barber and Durocher all summer. There was the Braves' Lew Burdette, who would go to his cap, his belt and anywhere else he might be able to wet one up. At least he made the batters think he was. Pitchers suspected of throwing spitballs always said that what the hitters *thought* they were doing served them as well as when they actually did it.

In the second game against the Cardinals, the Redbirds scored five times off Joe Black in the seventh inning. The great star of the previous year was struggling and becoming less reliable. In the final game of the set, St. Louis chased Carl Erskine for his third loss and came away with a 12–4 win. Stan Musial had been battling a slump, hitting just .251 on the year, but seeing the Dodgers was always like a gust of wind to a dead sail and "The Man" busted loose in grand style. He drove in four of the Cardinals' runs with a bases-loaded double. He had four doubles and five RBIs in two days against Brooklyn. The Dodgers were three behind Milwaukee.

The next stop for the Dodgers was Chicago. They played five games and lost three. The breeze blowing off Lake Michigan was a hot one and the temperature reached 100 degrees as the Brooks split a doubleheader with the Cubs. Randy Jackson hit a grand slam and Ralph Kiner swatted a three-run homer in an 11–8 win, but Brooklyn came back to win the second game by a 7–1 score. They won the third game of the set when Jackie Robinson came off the bench where he had been nursing a sore knee and hit a pinch-double to ignite the winning rally in the seventh. The Dodgers lost the last two games when ex–Dodger Eddie Miksis hit a 10th-inning homer off Bob Milliken and Warren Hacker beat Erskine, 9–4. Kiner and Hank Sauer went deep in that one.

Cincinnati won the first two of three at Ebbets Field on the 23rd and 24th. Brooklyn won the rubber game, 12–3, behind Preacher Roe. Dodger power was explosive again with five homers coming from Furillo, Snider, Hodges, Reese and Belardi. Still two games behind the Braves, they went into Milwaukee for a three-game series, beginning on the 26th. Brooklyn had won four of seven so far this season against the Braves, but Milwaukee had formidable power with Mathews, Gordon, Pafko and Adcock through the middle of the order. Their pitching staff consisted of Warren Spahn, Lew Burdette and Bob Buhl as the big three. The Dodgers were second to none in baseball in the potency they displayed but the pitching had been inconsistent. In game one, 35,145 screaming Braves fans came to see their boys push the Dodgers further back and grab a tighter hold on first place, but they went away disappointed.

Both Duke Snider and Gil Hodges hit two-run home runs and the Brooks won, it 4–3. Game two also wound up 4–3 in Brooklyn's favor when Pee Wee Reese hit a 10th-inning home run to win it. In the final game of the set, the Dodgers cut loose with 16 hits in an 11–1 romp. Russ Meyer went all the way, giving up only four hits, though one was a home run to Joe Adcock. Eight of the Dodgers' hits were for extra bases, three of them doubles by Carl Furillo and one a home run off the bat of Gil Hodges. It was the first baseman's 13th of the year, his 12th since returning to the lineup. The Dodgers hammered five Milwaukee pitchers—Spahn, Buhl, Burdette, Johnson and Cole—for their 11 runs.

Brooklyn got on the board in the first inning on a single by Hodges and Furillo's first two-bagger. In the third Gilliam walked, Reese sacrificed and Robinson doubled to right-center field. Campy's line single to left preceded Hodges' two-run blast off Bob Buhl. After the fifth inning, Meyer sat down 15 Braves in a row.

Furillo led the Dodgers' hitters on the road trip with a .340 mark. Snider was next at .320. Brooklyn had hit home runs in the last 12 consecutive games; the National League record was 19 set by the 1947 Giants. The Braves drew 102,880 in the three games. They had drawn to this time 692,281 in Milwaukee compared to 281,000 for the entire '52 season in Boston. O'Malley was taking notes.

The cold war was heating up. Julius and Ethel Rosenberg had been convicted of conspiracy to commit espionage, a capital crime, and were sentenced to death by Judge Irving Kaufman. In February 1953 President Eisenhower refused to grant a reprieve and both were executed at Sing-Sing prison in New York State on the evening of June 19. Politics were an undercurrent of Brooklyn baseball. A strong anti-communism prevailed throughout the ball club. Carl Prince called the Dodgers "the most overtly political sports team of the postwar decade."[22]

On the 15th the *Ford Fiftieth Anniversary Show* was telecast jointly on CBS and NBC. In the cast were two of the most formidable Broadway performers ever to grace a stage, Ethel Merman and Mary Martin. The show-stopper was a 13-minute duet by Merman and Martin as they sang a medley of 31 songs, concluding with "There's No Business Like Show Business" from the musical *Annie Get Your Gun* that both had starred in—Martin on TV and Merman on Broadway. The program was viewed by millions and the soundtrack recording set sales records across the country. This was live television; no changes, no retakes, no room for error. A little bit like throwing a baseball or swinging a bat, there were no do-overs!

In the American League the New York Yankees held first place but were beaten by the lowly St. Louis Browns, 3–1, to end an 18-game winning streak. Johnny Mize stroked a pinch-hit single for his 2,000th career hit and received a standing ovation from the 30,632 Yankee fans at the Stadium. Whitey Ford took the loss and was removed for Mize after giving up a two-run home run to Vic Wertz. It was the lefty's first loss of the season against seven wins. The Astoria, New York, native had gone 9–1 in his first big league season in '51 and then spent the next two seasons in the military. The Yankees' streak had begun on May 27 with a 3–1 victory over the Senators and ended with a 3–0 shutout over Cleveland.

The Yankees' Whitey Ford, Yogi Berra, Mickey Mantle and Phil Rizzuto would all be eventually enshrined in the Baseball Hall of Fame, but the '53 club also had Johnny Mize. The "Big Cat" was in his final season of big league play, totaling 15 in all, and though he hit just .250 in 81 games, his lifetime mark of .312 would get him into Cooperstown. Mize broke in with the St. Louis Cardinals in 1936 and won the National League batting title in '39 with a .349 average. Traded to the Giants for the '42 season, Mize stayed there until the Yankees picked him up late in the '49 season. Slipping with age, Mize still produced some big hits for the Bombers, particularly in the World Series, which was the reason they wanted him in the first place. He had two at-bats in that year's Series against Brooklyn and got hits both times to drive in two runs. He was with them in the record-setting five consecutive Series victories. In 1952 again against the Dodgers Mize hit for a .400 average, driving in six on the strength of three home runs. The Hall-of-Fame call came in 1981.

At the same time Bill Veeck's cellar-dwellers ended a 14-game losing streak, one short of setting a club record. The Browns' starting pitcher, Duane Pillette, pitched well into the eighth inning when he gave up a one-out single to Billy Martin. Manager Marty Marion went to his bullpen, and for the 26th time this season, a venerable old black gentleman employing sort of a dignified shuffle made his way to the mound. When the baseball showman, Bill Veeck, first brought Leroy Satchel Paige to the big leagues in 1948, it was derided as a stunt, a gimmick to bolster the gate, making a travesty of the game, but Satch proved them wrong. He went 6–1 in 72⅔ innings with an ERA of 2.48. In 1952 he won 12 games for St. Louis.

He faced Joe Collins in the eighth with one man out and Collins popped up, and so did Irv Noren. In the ninth he gave up a single to Gene Woodling but then retired the side to preserve the win for the Browns.

Paige had been disappointed when Jackie Robinson signed. "I should have been there," he said. "I got those boys thinking about having Negroes in the majors, but when they get one, it wasn't me."[23] It had to be a letdown for the Negro League star since age was creeping up on him. He admitted to being 42 years old at this time and no one really knew how accurate that figure was. When Veeck signed Larry Doby in the summer of '47, he received a wire saying, "Is it time for me to come?"[24] Veeck wrote back, "Have patience, it will happen."[25] He made his major league debut on July 9, 1948, becoming the first black pitcher in the American League. In 1953 he was named to the American League All-Star team.

When Veeck wired Paige to report to the Cleveland Indians, Satch wired back, "What took you so long?"[26] Veeck was accused of promoting and making a travesty of the game by taking the Negro ace who was past his prime. But on the way to the pennant in '48, Satch appeared in 21 games, won six and lost one. Always good copy, his quotes became the stuff of legend. When asked about his age, he said, "Age is a question of mind over matter. If you don't mind, it doesn't matter."[27] In the spring of '48 Paige threw two scoreless innings against the Dodgers.

After selling the club, Veeck bought the Browns a couple of years later and brought Satch to St. Louis, where he won 12 games in 1952. In 1965 Charlie Finley of the Kansas City Athletics signed the 59-year-old Paige for one game. He pitched three scoreless innings. Another of the era's Hall-of-Fame players, Satchel Paige was inducted in Cooperstown in 1971.

The 26th of June was an anniversary date of sorts for the Dodgers. It happened nine years before in 1944 that the International News Service ran a peculiar headline: "Dodgers Defeat Yankees, Giants Same Night in Craziest of All Games." Held at the Polo Grounds, the "Tri-Cornered Baseball Game" was the inspiration of some sportswriters and was presented by the War Bond Sports Committee. The objective was to sell war bonds in support of the Allied forces in World War II. The crowd of 50,000 paid $5.5 million dollars, with another 50 million being raised by the city of New York through mayor Fiorello LaGuardia.

Admission to the game was by purchase of a war bond. Forty thousand general admission seats cost one $25 bond, 5,809 reserved seats went for a $100 bond, upper and lower box seats cost the fan a $1,000 war bond, and bleacher seats were free to servicemen. Entertainment was provided by Al Schacht, "the Clown Prince of Baseball." The game lasted three hours and four minutes and was won by the Dodgers by a score of 5–1–0. The set-up for the actual game was confusing to lay out, but relatively simple.

The Dodgers and Yankees played the first inning while the Giants sat out; the Dodgers and Giants played the second inning while the Yankees sat out; the Yankees and Giants played the third inning as the Dodgers sat out. The same order was repeated two more times for nine innings. The managers were Leo Durocher for Brooklyn, Joe McCarthy for the Yankees and Mel Ott for the Giants. As odd as the game itself was, it was also unusual to see Durocher and McCarthy managing from opposite ends of the same dugout. The Dodgers scored one run off the Yankees in the first and two against the Giants in both the second and eighth frames. It was an odd but fun day for New York, but most important there was a total of $56.5 million raised for the Allied war effort.

The Dodgers came back home to Brooklyn on the last day of the month and lost to the Phillies, 10–9. Richie Ashburn executed a squeeze bunt that turned out to be the game-winner. Brooklyn scored two in the bottom of the tenth but fell short. The Dodgers ended the month of June with season record of 36–18 and held a half-game lead over the Milwaukee Braves. Although the lead was the slimmest of margins, Brooklyn would not look back again for the rest of the season.

SEVEN

July

"The collective talents of the 1953 Brooklyn Dodgers have seldom been equaled. In his decades of baseball, Branch Rickey put together many outstanding teams, but none to compare to his 1953 pennant winners in Brooklyn."—Donald Honig

July 7, 1953, was a red letter day in Brooklyn Dodgers history. On that day bells clanged and sirens wailed throughout the borough. Mozee Roe, the wife of Preacher Roe, was at home "with the boys that day and when I hit that homer, all the bells and sirens in Brooklyn started ringing. Mozee didn't know what had happened. Tommy came running into the house and said, 'Dad hit a home run! Dad hit a home run!' Well, then she knew ... Brooklyn was celebrating."[1] Preacher Roe, the skinny left-hander not known for his prowess with a Louisville Slugger, had indeed hit a four-bagger, the first and only one he would ever hit in his career 620 at-bats. When Preacher Roe, whose lifetime batting average was .110, hit a home run, it was an event of monumental historical proportion in Brooklyn.

With no red carpet available, his astounded teammates improvised. They paid homage by laying a carpet of white towels from home plate to the Dodgers' dugout for Preach following his third-inning blast against Pirate right-hander Bob Hall. Even Preacher was stunned. He hesitated out of the batter's box, and when he reached first base and coach Jake Pitler started needling him, the nonplussed slugger yelled over to him, "How should I know where to go. I never hit one of these things before."[2] Several days later at Ebbets Field, the Dodgers presented their newest power producer with a ten-foot Louisville Slugger autographed by all his teammates.

Elwin Charles Roe was a good old country boy from the Ozark Mountains in Arkansas; at least that's the role he liked to play. Blending home-spun humor and backwoods yarn-spinning, Ole Preach drawled his way through twelve big league seasons. He was born in Ash Flat, Arkansas, and said, "I am

Crafty southpaw Preacher Roe carried a big stick in 1953. His July home run was the only one he would hit in his career—620 at-bats.

proud to say I never lived more than 50 miles from Ash Flat.... We would go off to play ball but we always came back home."[3] He recalled the move to Viola, just a few miles away. The family loaded four wagons, each pulled by a team of horses. Preach's older brothers drove the extra horses and the cattle in front of the wagons. But Roe was no rube.

His dad was Dr. C. E. Roe, a country doctor who pitched a few years in the minors. He administered to the families in the community and kept good horses on the farm, horses he had purchased from the race track in Hot Springs. Preacher attended school in Viola and only played basketball, as the school had no baseball team. Dr. Roe schooled his son in the finer points of pitching and was convinced by the time Preacher was twelve that the boy would be a major league pitcher.

Roe attended Harding College and pitched in a semi-pro league on summer Saturdays and Sundays. After playing in a tournament in Kansas City during his sophomore year, Roe was approached by Frank Rickey, Branch's brother and a scout for the St. Louis Cardinals. This was in July 1938 and he stayed with the Cardinals for the rest of the season. Roe got into one game, threw 2 ⅔ innings, and gave up six runs. After that he spent four years in the minor leagues. That same year, 1938, on September 7, Preacher married Mozee Clay. They were married for 63 years before she passed away. "If you include the years we were friends before we got married," Roe said, "that makes 71 years we were best friends."[4]

In the offseason, Preach coached basketball and taught a class for two years and then accepted a coaching position at Hardy High School in Hardy, Arkansas. It was here that Roe suffered a serious injury. In 1946 Roe had an altercation with a referee and somehow was knocked unconscious. He spent 54 days in a hospital and lost his short-term memory; he actually had to relearn most of his pitching skills. He stayed at Hardy from 1942 through the '50 season while also serving time as a school principal.

While still in the minors, St. Louis sold him to Pittsburgh, and it was with the Pirates that he reached the major leagues in 1944. He was 13–11 and then 14–13 the next season, but in '47 he won only four games and lost 15 and was traded to Brooklyn. Preacher and Mozee had two sons, Elwin and Tommy, born in '40 and '46, respectively, and they lived in Hardy in the offseason. Preach was missing one thing, however, that kept him from being a more productive pitcher. He needed another pitch. Al Lopez was an outstanding catcher who was with Pittsburgh at the time and he worked with Roe on a new grip and the development of a slider, which the left-hander learned to master. He now had a fastball, curve, change and a slider and could throw at about six different speeds.

Preacher Roe blossomed in Brooklyn. In the second game of the 1949 World Series against the Yankees, after the Dodgers had lost game one, 1–0, Preach allowed the Yanks just six hits and shut them out, defeating Vic Raschi by the identical 1–0 score. He had great respect for his catcher, Roy Campanella, saying, "In my opinion, Roy Campanella was one of the greatest catchers of all time."[5] He garnered that viewpoint in part painfully. When he shook Campy off during that Series game and threw a fastball, the batter hit it so hard back through the box that it broke his finger. "That was the last time I ignored Campy," Roe said.[6]

Roe was a five-time All-Star, but at age 39 after the '54 season, the Dodgers traded him to Baltimore. Roe had a gentleman's agreement with Dodger owner Walter O'Malley that he would retire at the close of the '54 season, but O'Malley made the trade anyway. Roe never played for the Orioles. In a 1955 article in *Sports Illustrated*, Preacher admitted to having thrown a spitball during his career. He felt the article was exaggerated for effect and he didn't throw the outlawed pitch "near as often as they made out but it sure could psych the batter."[7]

Often called wily and crafty, Roe's assortment of speeds and great control allowed him to paint the corners. Said Campanella on a day Preach was scheduled to pitch, "They can cut the middle out and throw it away. Ole Preach ain't gonna use it."[8]

Preacher Roe was 92 when he passed away from colon cancer in West Plains, Missouri, on November 9, 2008.

Preacher's homer was not relegated to the dustbin of history, however, as the significance went beyond the Roe family scrapbook. It happened in the second game of a doubleheader against the Pirates at Forbes Field in Pittsburgh and represented the National League–record 21st consecutive game that the Dodgers had hit at least one home run. When the list of record breakers is displayed, there among the likes of Campanella, Hodges, Snider and Furillo is The Preach, forever enshrined in the annals of Dodgers power hitters.

The streak began on June 18 at St. Louis in a 12–4 Dodgers defeat. Jim Gilliam hit a homer off Harvey Haddix in the fifth inning with two on and one out. By June 30 it had extended to 13 games; the 14th came as a result of homers by Carl Furillo and Rube Walker against the Phillies on July 1. It ended with a National League–record 24 consecutive games on July 10 with a home run by Roy Campanella in the second inning off Sal Maglie of the Giants at Ebbets Field in a 6–1 Giants win. The major league mark of 25 was set by the New York Yankees in 1941. The Dodgers held onto the record until 1998 when the Atlanta Braves topped it with 25. The next day the Giants won again as Al Worthington shut out Brooklyn, 6–0, giving him a 2–2 record for the year. Russ Meyer took the loss; his record now stood at 7–4.

The most prolific slugger during the streak was Gil Hodges, who had distanced himself from that horrendous slump. The big first baseman hit eight.

Oddly just behind him was his understudy, Wayne Belardi, with six. Belardi was getting a look-see and played first base while Hodges went to left field. A left-handed first baseman, Wayne Belardi was one of the good-looking young Dodger prospects who never could get a full opportunity. As a first baseman, Belardi was caddying for the best in baseball in Gil Hodges, but his bursts of power allowed some maneuvering in Dressen's lineups. Born in St. Helena, California, the 22-year-old signed in 1949 for a $15,000 bonus. In '51 at Mobile and '52 at Fort Worth he connected for 22 and 20 homers, hitting .302 in 149 games in the latter year. Used sparingly in Brooklyn, Belardi hit 11 home runs and batted .239 in 69 games in 1953.

Furillo had five homers, Campy and Pee Wee Reese four each. Snider and Cox hit three, Jim Gilliam had a pair, and Jackie Robinson, George Shuba, Rube Walker and Preacher Roe each hit one. The total was 39 home runs in 24 games. The most explosive of the games came on June 25 at Crosley Field in Cincinnati in a 12–5 Dodgers win. There were five circuit blasts, coming from Reese, Snider, Hodges, Furillo, and Belardi.

As the month of July began the Dodgers were on top of the National League and singer Frankie Laine was number one on the pop music charts. His song of faith, "I Believe," stayed on the charts for 18 weeks. Laine said of the song written by Ervin Drake, Irvin Graham, Jimmy Shirl, and Al Stillman, "It said all the things that need to be said in prayer." The meaning of faith certainly was not lost on Dodgers fans. The rallying cry of "*Wait 'til next year!*" had become a standard lament and cry of hope in Brooklyn for decades.

On the first of July and with a slim half-game lead, the Dodgers defeated the Phillies and their ace, Robin Roberts, 5–4 in 10 innings. Brooklyn trailed by one going into the 10th when doubles by Carl Furillo and Roy Campanella scored the tying run. Campy was getting the day off and pinch-hitting as the starting catcher was Rube Walker, who went three-for-four, including a seventh-inning home run. Bill Antonello pinch-ran for Campanella and scored the winning run when lefty George Shuba came off the bench to pinch-hit for Podres and doubled to drive in Antonello. Roberts had thrown the complete 9⅓ innings but was charged with his sixth loss against 12 wins. Johnny Podres got the win for Brooklyn in relief.

Robin Roberts, one of baseball's greatest pitchers, was at the height of a Hall-of-Fame career. Though he lost for the third straight time to Brooklyn, he had thrown his 27th consecutive complete game. The antithesis of today's pitcher, the seven-time All-Star threw 305 complete games in a 19-year career and led the league in that category for five consecutive seasons, topping out with 33 complete performances in 1953 when he won 23 games and lost 16. He completed 30 in his banner year of 1952 with a 28–7 record.

Born in Springfield, Illinois, on September 30, 1926, Roberts served in the Army Air Corps and after World War II returned to Michigan State College to play basketball, with baseball being an afterthought. He became a pitcher because it was the position most needed on the school team. His major league debut came in June 1948, but in 1950 his 20–11 mark paced the Philadelphia Phillies to their first pennant in 35 years. The right-hander won 285 major league games and with it came induction into the baseball Hall of Fame in 1976.

On Thursday afternoon, July 2, Carl Erskine shut out the Phillies at Ebbets Field, 8–0. Reese and Hodges both hit home runs to bring the consecutive streak to 15. In keeping with the practice of the times, the Dodgers played a holiday doubleheader on July 4, Independence Day, at Ebbets Field against the Pittsburgh Pirates. They split the games, Brooklyn winning the first, 6–5, and losing the nightcap by a 5–2 score. Russ Meyer was the game one starter against Bob Hall, but neither was around at the finish. Pittsburgh scored four times off the Mad Monk in the third, as Joe Black came in to relieve and gave up a single to Toby Atwell that scored two more.

At the end of three, however, Brooklyn held a 6–4 lead, helped by a two-run homer off the bat off Roy Campanella, his 20th of the season. Reese's double and singles by Robinson, Belardi and Hodges knocked Hall out in the third. Hodges again played left field, allowing Belardi some more playing time at first base. The second game belonged to Pirate right-hander Bob Friend. Brooklyn used four pitchers. Bob Milliken was the starter and went into the sixth inning hanging on to a 1–0 lead. But Hal Rice belted a two-run homer over the scoreboard in right, then Shuba, batting for Milliken, drove in Furillo to tie the game. Billy Loes lost the lead in the eighth and took the loss, making his record 10–5 on the year. Friend went all the way for Pittsburgh; his record now stood at 13–8.

On the fifth the Dodgers were creamed at the Polo Grounds, 20–6. The same day the Braves split a doubleheader with the Cardinals, and the Dodgers' lead was 1½ games. They beat up on the Pirates at Forbes Field with a three-game sweep. The first was a 14–2 clobbering behind Russ Meyer and three Dodgers home runs by Cox, Furillo and Hodges. It was consecutive game number 19, tying the National League record. They took a doubleheader from the Pirates on the seventh, completing the sweep. The home run record was shattered with three in the first game and three in the second, two by Billy Cox and Preacher Roe's game-ender. They had now gone 20 straight games hitting at least one home run. The major league record of 25 set by the New York Yankees in 1941 was within reach.

The ball club traveled by train to Philadelphia where the Dodgers and Phillies split two. On Wednesday night they knocked out Karl Drews with a four-run fifth and Brooklyn's extra-base power accounted for seven doubles and two home runs, including number 17 for the big first baseman, Hodges, the slump almost faded from memory. Furillo had four hits and was the Dodgers' leading hitter at .331. Jackie Robinson was second at .329. The start of the game was delayed 24 minutes by rain and stopped again for another 13 minutes in the eighth. Campy and Hodges each drove in two; Campanella now had 70 RBIs and Gil 63.

There was a touch of the usual hubbub connected with the Dodgers in the third inning when Loes decked Richie Ashburn. The Phillies' center fielder started for the mound, bat in hand, then changed his mind. Cox's double in the eighth gave the third baseman a seven-game hit streak. Loes got the credit for his 11th win, and Billy's philosophy of just winning enough games seemed to kick in. He would gain just three victories over the second half, giving him 14 for the season. The Dodgers had a 7–3 July so far on their way to a 23–8 month.

As the Eisenhower administration prodded and pushed the North Koreans towards a truce in the war, a battle erupted that surpassed the most intense of World War II in terms of artillery expenditure. Designated as Hill 255, but to become known as Pork Chop Hill, it was located just north of the 38th parallel, only 70 miles from Panmunjom, where the peace talks were dragging on. Faust Sofo was a Brooklyn kid serving as a corporal with G Company in the army's 7th Division at the start of the advance. Over five days beginning on July 6, the ferocious battle ensued. Sofo remembers "getting shelled all the way up."[9] He recalled the enemy attack under cover of darkness and the glow cast by rounds of mortar fire revealing flickering glimpses of the Chinese attack. "They looked like ants coming up the hill," Sofo said. Casualties were devastating. Of the 180 men in G Company, only 11 returned. "I was lucky," Sofo said in a paradigm of understatement.[10] On July 27, by 10:12 a.m. the war was done. The Korean War had cost 142,091 American casualties; 33,629 dead, 103,284 wounded, and 5,178 captured or missing. Another horror chapter in American history had ended.

On the 11th of the month pitcher Ralph Branca was waived out of the National League and picked up by the Detroit Tigers. The next day he started a game for Detroit and lost, 3–2, to the St. Louis Browns. Used sparingly by Dressen with the Dodgers, he had made only seven appearances, all in relief. Born in Mount Vernon, New York, Ralph signed with Brooklyn and was sent to Olean in the PONY League in his first professional year and paid $90 a month. That winter he enrolled in New York University and played baseball and basketball. A hard thrower, he came to the Dodgers in 1944, was 0–2 that year and 5–6 the next. In 1946 he was 3–1, having thrown 67⅓ innings. It was during the '46 season that Ralph got a start against the Cardinals and threw a three-hit shutout.

"That game," he said later, "made me a pitcher, because after that, I believed in myself, that I could pitch and win a crucial game."[11] His greatest season came the next year, the pennant-winning season of 1947 when Ralph won 21 and lost 12.

Later in the month during a Saturday game at Ebbets Field against the Braves in which Russ Meyer shut out Milwaukee, 7–0, the biggest cheer of the afternoon came when public address announcer Tex Rickard announced that Ralph Branca had hit a triple with the bases loaded for the Tigers against the Yankees.

The Giants came to Brooklyn for a three-game series that preceded the All-Star break. Maglie beat them on Friday night, 6–1. The Barber had defeated Brooklyn for the third time this year and the 18th time in 21 decisions overall. The one run came on a Campanella home run, his 22nd, and the 24th consecutive game the Dodgers had hit one. Durocher's club had won seven in a row, and though in fifth place, was only six-and-a-half games out. The next day Al Worthington shut them out on four singles and ended the Dodgers' homer streak, one shy of the major league record.

Belardi was at first but his 0-for–16 slump seemed to signal Hodges' return to the initial sack. Brooklyn salvaged the final game of the series on Sunday when Billy Cox hit a ninth-inning home run to tie it and a bases-loaded walk by Hoyt Wilhelm in the 10th won it for Brooklyn. Going into the All-Star break, the Dodgers were 1½ games up on the Braves.

Billy Cox didn't hit a lot of home runs, 66 in 11 years, and his lifetime average was .262, but he was the best glove anyone ever saw in Brooklyn. Cox and Preacher Roe came to the Dodgers in the winter of 1947 from Pittsburgh in Rickey's most magnificent baseball acquisition. Billy and Preach roomed together for seven years and were the best of friends. Cox was the finest fielding third baseman of his or arguably any other time. The yardstick for measuring third basemen is Brooks Robinson, the Oriole Hall-of-Famer. Robinson was great, to be sure, but Cox was better.

"I never saw anyone better," said Pee Wee Reese, Billy's teammate in Brooklyn. "I did study Brooks Robinson. Cox had more range and a better arm than Robinson."[12]

Billy Herman, the Dodgers Hall-of-Fame second baseman, summed up Cox this way: "The best third baseman I ever saw was Billy Cox. He made the most outstanding plays I've ever seen. Brooks Robinson is great, and so was Clete Boyer; but Cox was amazing. He made your eyes pop; you couldn't believe how quick he was, going in any direction. And an arm like a rifle."[13] He had this little glove. The joke was, he bought it in a Whalens Drug Store, and he held it in his right hand until the pitch was actually on its way. He then would slip it on his left hand and crouch ever so slightly. If the ball was hit his way, he would snip it, as he used to call it, and then study the ball for a second or two before gunning it over to first, just nipping the runner. The fans in the lower deck behind third base could hear a frustrated Reese yell over from shortstop, "Throw the damn ball!"

Cox was born in Newport, Pennsylvania, on August 29, 1919, one of seven siblings. He played high school ball as a second baseman but realized he had some talent because he could throw harder and run faster than most of the other boys. Signed by a Pittsburgh scout, Billy was sent to Valdosta, Georgia, to play Class D ball. A reserved and introspective young man, Billy jumped the club and went home because he was homesick. Since the league soon folded, Cox was declared a free agent, and he signed with Harrisburg in the Inter-State League. He batted .288, and in '41, the 21-year-old hit a robust .363 to lead the league. Pittsburgh bought his contract and he joined the Pirates at the end of the '41 season. He appeared in 10 games and hit .270.

It was signing with Harrisburg that Cox called "the luckiest break I ever got. It was there I met my wife, Ann, and she is the best thing that ever happened to me."[14] Billy and Ann E. Radle were married on November 26, 1945, soon after Cox was discharged from the army.

Cox lost four baseball seasons to the military in World War II. Entering the service on February 9, 1942, Billy played some baseball at New Cumberland Reception Center while with the 1301 Service Unit. He soon went overseas with the 814th Signal Corps. Cox saw action in some of the toughest combat of the war, including battles in North Africa, Sicily, Italy, France and Germany. There were occasions when the shell-fire didn't stop for days at a time. Later his Pittsburgh teammates would relate how a display of fireworks or a sudden roar from the crowd would send Billy to safety beneath the bench in the dugout. This form of battle fatigue lingered with him until 1952. He was never wounded but once revealed that he had his helmet blown off during a bomb explosion.

Watching Cox play third base from the buck-and-a-quarter seats at Ebbets Field was like watching Michelangelo sculpt. It may have been rough-hewn at times, but the result was art. Always a good clutch hitter, in the closing days of the '51 pennant race his two-out double won a game against the Giants in the 10th inning. In game six of the '52 World Series, Cox scored the winning run in the 11th inning after singling to left. In the '53 Series after clutch hits in the first two games, he dropped a perfect squeeze bunt in game three to score Jackie Robinson with the tying run.

Traded to Baltimore after the '54 season where he played just 53 games and hit .211, Cox was sent on to Cleveland later that year but he refused to report and retired. He tended bar at the Elks and then the Owls club in Newport. Billy Cox died of esophageal cancer on March 30, 1978. He was just 58. His dear friend, Preacher Roe, took Billy's death hard. "It broke my heart when he died. We were roommates for seven years. I guess he knew me better than anyone," Preacher said. "Yes sir, that death hit me hard."[15]

Roger Kahn said of Cox: "This broad-shouldered, horse-faced, sad-eyed fellow was the most glorious glove on the most glorious team that ever played baseball in the sunlight of Brooklyn."[16]

The 20th All-Star Game was played at Crosley Field in Cincinnati on July 14. Manager Casey Stengel had taken his New York Yankees to four consecutive World Series titles from 1949–1952, but as All-Star manager his American League squads had lost the last three previous games. He would lose his fourth in a row as the Nationals came away with a 5–1 win. Dodgers in the starting lineup included Pee Wee Reese at shortstop and Roy Campanella behind the plate. Gil Hodges, Duke Snider and Jackie Robinson also were selected to the team. Both Pee Wee and Campy contributed to the victory, Reese with a single and a double to drive in two runs and Campanella scored an eighth-inning run on a single by the Cards' Enos Slaughter. He had doubled off Satchel Paige, who set an All-Star record as the oldest pitcher in the game's history. Satch admitted to 46 years of age, though no one really knew for sure. No one doubted, however, that the Browns' pitcher had more years than anyone else.

Both the starting pitchers, Robin Roberts for the National League and the American League's Billy Pierce, the fine lefty from the Chicago White Sox, threw three scoreless innings. The win went to Warren Spahn; the Yanks' Allie Reynolds suffered the loss.

Days after the Korean truce was signed, French paratroopers jumped into Lang-Son in Vietnam and recaptured an area held by the communists. French General Henri Navarre informed his superiors in Paris, after the Viet Minh slipped away into the jungle, that this war *could not* be won. Intervention by the United States was discussed, with General Mathew Ridgeway vehemently opposed. President Eisenhower would echo those sentiments, saying that in his opinion a ground war in Vietnam could not be won.

At least two motion pictures released that spring and summer have been listed among the great American films. On April 23 the western classic *Shane* opened at Radio City Music Hall in Manhattan and on July 1 one of the great films of World War II was released. Locally both *Shane* and *Stalag 17* were seen at such Brooklyn venues as the Paramount, Loew's Kings and the Benson theaters. Both films brought in a bevy of Academy Award nominations, including a winner for Best Actor for William Holden in *Stalag 17*.

Nineteen-fifty-three would also be the year that would see the onset of a sea change in popular music. A Cleveland disc jockey named Alan Freed would dub the new genre "rock 'n' roll," and would host a big bash in Cleveland. The first recognized rock 'n' roll song was recorded in April of the year by Bill Haley and the Comets. The song, "Crazy Man, Crazy," was also written by Haley and Marshall Lytle. By late May the Essex label recording had reached number 12 on the American *Billboard* chart. On July 18, a recent high school graduate entered Sun Records studio in Nashville, Tennessee, and paid to make a recording. The young man, Elvis Presley, recorded "My Happiness," a song for his mother Gladys.

The Dodgers opened the second half with a four-game sweep of the St. Louis Cardinals at Ebbets Field. On Thursday night, the 16th, Preacher Roe went all the way in a 9–2 win. Gil Hodges hit two homers, one a grand slam, and Brooklyn's lead went to 2½ games. They won the Friday doubleheader as Johnny Podres shut out the Cards in the first game, 14–0, with the help of another grand slam, this one from Billy Cox. In the *New York Times*, Joseph Sheehan called them the "Torrid Dodgers." They were certainly starting to act like a juggernaut, rumbling over the National League. The 29,793 in attendance saw a Jackie Robinson three-run home run in a 7–4 victory in the second game.

It was when the Cardinals played that Jackie Robinson spoke with writer Roger Kahn. "The shit has started again," Jackie said, "the shit from the other dugout. The bench. The Cardinals. Starting that shit again."[17] When Kahn confronted St. Louis manager Eddie Stanky about the racially motivated name-calling, the Cardinals' skipper told Kahn that he hadn't heard anything out of line. "So I wrote the story," Kahn said, "Jackie Robinson charges, Eddie Stanky denied."[18]

Once more confronting Stanky, "The Brat" told Kahn that he heard "black bastard" and "nigger," but didn't consider that to be out of line. "You gotta understand this game," he said. "That is not out of line."[19] Stanky was just warming up for a disgraceful exhibition later in the season.

In the final game of the set, Brooklyn staggered the Cards with a nine-run fourth inning and a 14–6 win. For the third time in four games, the Dodgers hit a grand slam; this was in a pinch-hitting role by Wayne Belardi. Unfortunately for the young first baseman, his .239 average did not bode well for keeping him in the starting lineup.

Brooklyn split a Sunday doubleheader with the Reds, losing the first when Ted Kluszewski hit two home runs and winning the nightcap with a five-run eighth inning that included a round-tripper from Billy Cox. The Cubs came in next for five games in four days, but on Thursday torrential rains washed out that game, setting up a replay on August 25 as a twi-night doubleheader. The Dodgers won the remaining four games. Russ Meyer shut out the Cubs for 8⅓ innings and allowed three hits, but after a hit and a walk in the ninth, Dressen brought in Jim Hughes to close out the 3–0 win. It was Meyer's eighth victory.

Seldom did a Dodger game go by without one or two anxious moments, and this one came in the second inning. Following Campanella's 24th home run into the left field seats, Chicago pitcher Bob Rush went to a count of two balls and one strike on Carl Furillo. The next pitch, high and inside, caught Furillo on the left side of the head, and he was carried from the field on a stretcher. According to Dr. Eugene Zorn, the Dodgers' club physician, an examination revealed no serious injury. Tough as nails, Furillo was never gun-shy at the plate, but he nurtured a seething resentment against anything he thought was intentional, generally storing such resentment for Leo Durocher and the Giants. He never blamed Rush, but the 21,877 Ladies Day crowd booed him mightily.

In the spring Furillo had spoken with writer Roger Kahn and Kahn described the conversation he had with the right fielder over a beer. "It's gotta stop," Furillo told him.

"What's gotta stop?"

"Maglie throwing at my head. I know why he's doing it. Durocher orders him to do it. Next time Maglie throws at me, I go for him."

"Who?"

"Durocher. I'm gonna get him."[20]

His time with Durocher would come soon, and when it did, Carl would be ready.

Brooklyn now held a 5½-game lead over Milwaukee as the Braves came in for four games. They defeated Billy Loes on Friday night before 27,948, 11–6. The Braves' manager, "Jolly" Charlie Grimm, noted for his left-handed banjo playing, had said recently that he was not impressed by the Dodgers, but Meyer's four-hit 7–0 victory on Saturday may have had him wavering just a bit. Dodger pitchers had now thrown seven shutouts. Erskine and Roe had two each, and Meyer, Podres and Loes had fired one apiece. The final piece for Brooklyn, the pitching, seemed to be well in place. The Dodgers had a five-run fifth off Jim Wilson and Dave Jolly. Gilliam tripled to open the inning, Pee Wee Reese walked and Snider bounced a single up the middle, scoring Gilliam. Jackie Robinson knocked Wilson out with a run-scoring base hit and Hodges singled off Jolly ahead of a Furillo single off Mathew's glove at third base. Campanella then drove in the fifth run with a fly ball to left. Campy had hit a two-run home run in the second.

On Sunday the 26th, Brooklyn won both ends of the doubleheader, each by one run, 3–2 and 2–1. The Dodgers', ace, Carl Erskine was beginning to hit his stride. Before the largest Ebbets Field crowd since 1951, 33,421, the little right-hander struck out 10 in the second game, getting the last 15 Milwaukee hitters in a row, five of them on strikes. The lone run for the Braves was a home run by Sid Gordon. In the eighth, Erskine's roomie, Duke Snider, made a leaping catch of a Billy Bruton drive to the wall in left-center field. For Erskine it was another complete game. He would have 16 of them for the season. Brooklyn's "Oisk" had now beaten every National League team at least once, the only Dodger pitcher to accomplish the feat.

In the first inning, after Gilliam walked and Reese singled off Lew Burdette, Robinson dropped a bunt down the third base line and beat it out for a hit. There were words exchanged between Robbie and the Braves' pitcher, and as they moved towards each other, umpire Babe Pinelli stepped in quickly and prevented any further altercation. Robinson said that he heard Burdette call him "a black bastard."[21] It would not be the last time this season that race would come up. A week later it involved Campanella and the same Lew Burdette.

Although trailing the Braves, 2–0, in the eighth inning of the opener, Brooklyn scored three, capped by a Carl Furillo single that drove Robinson home with the winning run. Brooklyn's attendance reached 834,660 in 54 home games on its way to another million gate. They were 114,539 attendees ahead of last season, though it was not enough to satisfy the Dodgers' owner. Los Angeles was not as far into the future as some might have thought.

They took two of three from the Cubs. The 13–2 score in the first game came with the aid of homers by Snider, Hodges and Furillo. Podres was the winner. In game two, Meyer got the win in a 6–5 game but needed help from Clem Labine. Bob Rush halted the Dodgers' win streak at five with a seven-hit 3–2 victory. The Dodgers held a seven-game lead in the National League.

Clem Labine emerged as a bulwark of the Dodgers' staff, both as a starter and coming out of the bullpen. The right-handed sinkerball pitcher made his major league debut on April 18, 1950, but he was sent back to the minors and didn't return until August of 1951. He won his first start on August 28 with a complete game over Cincinnati, but a decision that put him in manager Charlie Dressen's dog house may have cost Brooklyn the pennant. Facing the Phils in a September game with the bases loaded and Willie "Puddinhead" Jones the hitter, Labine wanted to pitch out of the stretch, but Dressen insisted that he use a full windup.

"I was stubborn in those days," Clem admits, "and I took a stretch and Jones hit a grand slam."[22] Dressen refused to use Labine again for the final three weeks of the season.

There were two superb performances by Labine that are relegated to a minor role because of the eventual outcomes, but they should not be overlooked. In the second game of the '51 playoff, Dressen was forced to finally use Clem and the right-hander shut out the Giants, 10–0. In the sixth game of the '56 World Series, the game that followed Don Larsen's perfecto, Labine got the ball with the Dodgers needing the win to stay alive. He hooked up with Bob Turley and Brooklyn broke a scoreless tie in the 10th to win it, 1–0.

Labine's 1953 performance was a major contributing factor to the Dodgers' success, especially out of the bullpen. He made 37 appearances, 30 in relief, and won 11 while losing six.

These were Roger's Boys, this 1953 club. Kahn wrote some excellent books and hundreds of great columns, but as so often is the case, posterity allows for one's body of work to be summarized in a single entity. For da Vinci it is the *Mona Lisa*, for Bogart it is Rick Blaine in *Casablanca*, and for Roger Kahn, who grew up on Lincoln Place in Brooklyn, close enough to Ebbets Field to "hear the crowd roar," it will forever be *The Boys of Summer*, his classic narrative of Brooklyn's Dodgers of the '52 and '53 seasons.[23]

Kahn's parents were intellectuals; his mother, Olga, taught English literature and composition at Thomas Jefferson High School. A lover of great literature and music, she majored in ancient history at Cornell. His father, Gordon, also a high school teacher, was the co-founder of the popular radio quiz show, *Information Please*. Roger's sister, Emily, was stricken with polio when she was 14. This was the Kahn family unit during his early years in Brooklyn.

It was Gordon's love for baseball and the early teaching of the fundamentals of the game to his son that made Roger yearn to someday play first base for the Dodgers. His mother, however, was so distraught over her son's growing obsession with the game that she prayed, "Please, God, let him become interested in a book. One book. Please. Any book."[24] He did. It was called *Pitching in a Pinch* by the great right-hander, Christy Mathewson, published in 1912. In time Roger, not unlike hundreds of thousands of Brooklyn kids, realized that he didn't quite have enough for the Ebbets Field first-base job and looked elsewhere for gainful employment.

While attending the Bronx campus of New York University and failing organic chemistry, Kahn was asked by a professor what he would like to do. "Well, sir," said the young man, "I believe I'd like to be a writer."[25] His dad's ties with the *New York Herald Tribune* helped him land a job as a copy boy. This was in 1948. From there it was writing high school sports to covering college football and special assignments for the Associated Press. By the spring of 1951, Kahn was allowed to cover baseball; first it was college ball, then a call from Bob Cooke, the sports editor of the *Tribune*. "On Tuesday," he said, "you'll be covering the Dodgers."[26] And so it was that the 24-year-old kid from Brooklyn went south with the team of his youth in the spring of 1952, and so too the genesis for the *Boys of Summer* had begun.

On the last day of the month, it was Erskine against the Cardinals in St. Louis. In winning his previous five decisions, Erskine ran his record to 10 wins and three losses. His money pitch was an overhand curveball that began near the waist and broke sharply downward, often winding up in the dirt, frustrating hitters who were swinging over it. Erskine never feared passed balls or wild pitches when Campanella was behind the plate. Campy would tell him, "You bury it and I'll catch it."[27] His six-hit, 2–1 victory was his sixth straight win. The right-hander had struck out 31 in his last three games. The loss dropped the Cardinals to fifth place, one percentage point below the Giants. Furillo's two hits extended his consecutive game streak to 11. Gilliam had three hits. The Dodgers began to take off in July. They were 23–8 in the month. They had played 100 games, winning 65, losing 34, and playing one tie in Chicago. They closed out July with an eight-game lead in the National League.

EIGHT

August

"It could have developed into the most violent racial incident since Negroes entered organized baseball."—Dave Anderson, *Brooklyn Eagle*

Anyone growing up in Brooklyn during the '50s can remember how they hung around the candy store waiting for the news truck to pull up and, sometimes barely stopping, toss out a bundle of the latest edition. We could scarcely wait to read about the latest Dodger game and get all the details. Don Honig explained, "We already knew every pitch that was thrown. We had listened to the game on the radio. We had discussed it for three hours. Now we were going to read about it. Now it would become scripture."[1]

There were no shortage of tabloids: the *New York Daily News*, the *Daily Mirror*, the *Post*, the *Times*, and they were just the morning papers. In the afternoon, there were the *Journal American*, the *Herald Tribune*, the *World Telegram* and, the borough had its own sheet, the *Brooklyn Eagle*. And there were some fine writers. Roger Kahn was with the *Tribune*, Mike Gavin with the *Journal*, Tommy Holmes and Dave Anderson wrote for the *Eagle*, Jimmy Power's "Powerhouse" column ran in the *News*, Dan Parker was sports editor at the *Mirror*, and Roscoe McGowen wrote for the *Times*. One of the best writers in New York was Dick Young, whose often acerbic prose ran in the *Daily News*.

Young was not particularly popular with the Brooklyn players. Carl Furillo said, "Dick was a bastard, and some guys were ready to beat the living hell out of him."[2] Jackie Robinson called him a bigot, Duke Snider wanted to "punch him in the nose," and Gene Hermanski "pushed him around the clubhouse."[3] Young's writing was frank and went beyond the game, which infuriated some players. He didn't endear himself with them when he wrote, "The tree that grows in Brooklyn is an apple tree, and the apples are in the throats of the Dodgers," insinuating that the team choked.[4]

Dick Young grew up in Washington Heights, New York. His parents divorced and after he graduated from high school went to live with his father in California so he could attend Los Angeles Junior College and then UCLA for free as a resident of the state. When the school learned that Young's mother in New York had custody, the free ride ended, and he had to quit. He worked for the Civilian Conservation Corps until he learned that the *New York Daily News* was initiating a program of developing their own writers, a farm system, to put it in baseball parlance, and Young got a job with the paper. Since he was not a college graduate, a prerequisite for the reporter positions, he began as a messenger in the publication department. After working up to copy boy in the editorial department, the war broke out and Young was deferred because by this time he had a wife and son.

Jimmy Powers, the sports editor, gave the ambitious young man some minor assignments. That worked into Opening Day 1946 when Young took over the Dodgers beat. It lasted until they left Brooklyn in 1957. He initiated what came to be called "the new journalism," which Roger Kahn described as "a frankness in reporting that had never been seen before. If a player had a weakness, Young would write about it, explain it, analyze it."[5] The resulting effects caused some resentment among the ballplayers and thus the antagonism some of the Dodger players felt towards him.

The Dodgers opened the month with two final games of the three-game series in St. Louis, which they split. Preacher Roe won his seventh of the year, his sixth in a row, 11–4, in front of 32,471 Cardinal fans. Brooklyn bombarded St. Louis pitching with 17 hits. Campanella continued his hot hitting with two home runs and Billy Cox hit a three-run homer. On Sunday Harvey Haddix stopped the Brooks with a strong six-hitter, the score was 10–1 as the temperature in St. Louis reached 110 degrees on the field. But the boiling point wasn't touched until the Dodgers opened a four-game set in Milwaukee on Monday.

Racial trouble in major league baseball, though Robinson was in his seventh season, had not disappeared from the scene. Six weeks after Jackie broke in, Bill Veeck brought Larry Doby to Cleveland, and by 1949 the Dodgers had Campy and Don Newcombe among the regulars. Yet in 1953, only six big league clubs had a black player in their regular lineup. In the National League, other than Brooklyn and the Giants, only Milwaukee, with Billy Bruton and Sam Jethroe, carried an African American as a regular. Other than the Indians and the Browns, thanks to Bill Veeck, in the American League, only the White Sox had signed black players. Worse yet, the vulgar name-calling and bigoted displays were still in evidence on major league diamonds.

Both Robinson and Campanella were cast in pioneering roles but saw their respective positions in different ways, which caused a riff to develop between them. The dissimilarity was illustrated in 1953 in an incident at the Chase Hotel in St. Louis. The Chase maintained a segregated policy among its guests but was finally willing to let down some barriers. They would allow ballplayers to stay as guests with the team, provided they avoided using the dining room, the pool area and the ballroom. With the exception of Robinson, the black players refused to accept the new conditions. To Jackie it was a positive step, but Campy wanted to wait until all conditions had been lifted. It was not until '55 that the remaining restrictions were removed.

On the third of August, Meyer opposed Lew Burdette of the Braves and Brooklyn won, 1–0. Don Thompson, running for Shuba, scored on Meyer's single off the glove of Jack Dittmar in the seventh for the game's only run. Duke Snider hit an eighth-inning home run that was nullified when the rain that had persisted throughout the contest caused the game to be called, reverting to seven complete innings and a 1–0 score. There were 32,739 fans who sat through the inclement weather but were given some eighth-inning excitement. Burdette had a history of confrontation with black players. He had beaned Jim Pendleton in the minors, and ever since Robinson stole home on him in Boston in 1951, he seemed to have it in for the Dodger.

Following the Snider homer, Burdette knocked down Campanella. That was not unusual as baseball tradition dictates that after a home run, the next hitter goes down. But Hodges was the next batter and he saw nothing close as he popped out. The first pitch to Campanella was at his head. Then with a count of two balls and two strikes, Burdette sat Campy down a second time. After striking out, the Dodger catcher started for the mound, bat in hand. Both dugouts emptied as Carl Furillo pulled the bat out of Campanella's hand and Braves catcher Del Crandall along with plate umpire Tom Gorman restrained the enraged player. Campanella claimed that he heard Burdette scowl, "Black nigger bastard." Burdette afterward said that pitching inside was his bread and butter, but Campy's retort was, "My head ain't his bread and butter."[6] The incident was magnified because of the normally jovial Brooklyn catcher's reaction to the Burdette pitches. It lent credence to Campy's claim of having heard a racial remark from the Milwaukee pitcher. Nevertheless, the game was Russ Meyer's 11th win of the season.

Roy Campanella was happy just to be in the big leagues. The talent was there but the unwritten Jim Crow laws made such dreams unapproachable for a ballplayer whose skin was black. When Jackie Robinson signed to play with the Montreal Royals, a AAA affiliate of the Brooklyn Dodgers, the situation

1953 Most Valuable Player Roy Campanella goes over the hitters with pitcher Billy Loes (Brooklyn Public Library—Brooklyn Collection).

changed for players like Campy. Campanella had started out in the Negro leagues when he was only 15 years old, and he recalled in later years what a tough life it had been. "We traveled in a big bus, and many's the time we never bothered to take off our uniforms going from one place to another," he said. "The bus was our home, dressing room, dining room and hotel."[7]

Campy loved to tell stories of his time in the Negro leagues when he played for the Baltimore Elite Giants, especially once he was comfortably installed as a major league star. One of his favorites centered on catching four games in a single day. The first two were a daytime doubleheader in Cincinnati, Ohio, and the next two were also played as a doubleheader in Youngstown, 275 miles away.

Hence, the young catcher was understandably dubious when a meeting was arranged at the Dodgers offices at 215 Montague Street in Brooklyn with Branch Rickey. Believing the stories he had been told that Rickey was organizing a club to play in the Negro leagues called the Brooklyn Brown Dodgers, Campy turned down the offer. He was satisfied playing with the Elite Giants and told Rickey as much. Campanella was staying at the Woodside Hotel in Harlem as a member of the Negro League All-Stars, and it was there he encountered Jackie Robinson.

Over a friendly card game, Jackie told him he had just signed to play for Montreal and that it would be announced in a few days. Roy realized he had made a mistake turning Rickey down and the young catcher spent several anxious days hoping that the Dodger executive would call again. He did, just two days after the Robinson announcement, and on October 25, 1945, Campanella agreed to a $1,500 bonus and a monthly salary of $400 to play with the Brooklyn organization. He was assigned to Nashua, New Hampshire, a Class B ball club, because it was the only one that would take both Campanella and Don Newcombe, another player Rickey had signed out of the Negro League. The general manager at Nashua was Emil "Buzzie" Bavasi, the future Dodgers GM, and the manager was Walt Alston, who would come to Brooklyn in the same capacity in 1954. It was the right setting for the two rookies and both exceeded expectations. Campy hit .290 with 13 home runs and 96 RBIs and was named the league's Most Valuable Player. Newcombe was 14–4. Both would be in Brooklyn soon.

Roy Campanella's story had its origin in Nicetown, a section of Philadelphia, where Roy grew up. His mother, Ida Mercer, was an African American woman from Chesapeake City, Maryland, and his father, John, was a white Italian American. It took Roy a number of scrapes as a boy before he learned the meaning of the taunt "half-breed."

John Campanella sold vegetables out of a Model T truck and on Fridays sold fish. Young Roy learned how to hustle for a buck at an early age. He sold newspapers, shined shoes, delivered milk and loaded his daddy's truck every morning at 5 a.m. Big for his age, it was not long before Roy was playing baseball with the older boys at Hunting Park, sometimes cutting school to do it.

He played in the American Legion and with a team sponsored by a local Negro newspaper. At 13 he fought three bouts in the Golden Gloves tournament, but baseball was young Campanella's game and he was already playing it well. Offered a chance to play for money by Tom Dixon of the Negro semi-pro Bacharach Giants, Roy was able to convince his mother to let him, though he was just 15. For two games each weekend he was paid $35. The first time the youth stepped onto the field, it was at Beach Haven, New Jersey. He looked around and saw the men he was now associated with, and with some apprehension realized, "This wasn't Nicetown anymore."[8] Within the year Campy received an offer from Biz Mackey of the Baltimore Elite Giants, which was the big time of Negro baseball. Both Dixon and Mackey were catchers and both worked extensively with the young Campanella. They taught him how to handle a pitch in the dirt. He had a strong arm, but Mackey tutored him on setting himself properly and making his throws accurate.

Roy married young and had two daughters. The couple separated and Roy remarried Ruthe Willis, whom he had met in New York. When World War II broke out, Campanella was classified 3-A because of his dependents and for the most part he continued to play ball during the war years.

Campy was in the Dodgers' camp in the spring of 1948 but was sent back to St. Paul because Rickey wanted him to integrate the American Association. By June he could not be kept down any longer; he had hit 13 homers in the six weeks he was at St. Paul. With the Dodgers struggling, Campy came to Brooklyn along with outfielder George Shuba, who was hitting .389 in AA Mobile. Roy played 83 games for Brooklyn and hit .258 with nine homers and 45 RBIs. The next season he banged out 22 home runs, drove in 87 and hit .287. He also played in the first of eight All-Star games.

Campanella's career lacked a certain consistency because of injuries that seemed to come in even-numbered years. He was the National League Most Valuable Player in 1951, an award he also received again in '53 and '55. Coming off the injuries to his hands in 1952, he was healthy and having a tremendous year. Campanella went on to play 10 years in the majors and hit .272 with 242 home runs. With Campy behind the plate, the Dodgers won five pennants in eight years and the only World Series Brooklyn would ever know. Preparing to go to Los Angeles with the relocating team after the '57 season, Campanella was severely injured in an automobile accident on January 28, 1958, paralyzing him from the neck down and confining him to a wheelchair for the rest of his life.

On May 7, 1959, at the Los Angeles Coliseum, 93,103 fans came to pay homage to Campy at an exhibition game between the Dodgers and the Yankees. Roy cried when the crowd gave him a thunderous ovation. When he got to the microphone he told them, "It was a wonderful tribute. I thank God I'm alive to see it. Thanks a million."[9] Roy worked as a coach for the Dodgers and gave tips to young catching prospects, including a kid named Mike Piazza. "You wouldn't believe how comprehensive he was," Piazza recalled. "He could observe and critique as well as anyone."[10]

Roy Campanella passed away on July 26, 1993. He had spent his last 35 years in a wheelchair. His once-powerful body had been decimated but his spirit never waned. Two years before his death he spoke to writer Pete Hamill at Vero Beach. "It's beautiful here," Campy said.

"Baseball?" asked Hamill.

"No," Campy said. "The whole damned world."[11]

On the same day of the Burdette–Campanella confrontation, the National League batting race was led by the Cards' Red Schoendienst with an average of .341. The Giants' Monte Irvin was second and Carl Furillo, at .327, was fourth. Brooklyn held an eight-and-a-half-game lead over Milwaukee and was ahead by nine in the loss column. The Braves won two of the next three games, which were the first games they won over the Dodgers at home this season. In the first game of the Thursday doubleheader, Pee Wee Reese drove in the winning run in the 11th with a two-out single off Warren Spahn. Meyer was the loser in the nightcap, 3–2, after giving up a bases-loaded triple to Harry Hanebrink in the ninth inning. The lead was seven-and-a-half as the Dodgers traveled to Cincinnati for three games and the start of a 13-game win streak.

The nation's moviegoers were agog at Hollywood's newest sex symbol, and Marilyn Monroe would make three films in 1953. Two were musical comedies, *Gentlemen Prefer Blondes* and *How to Marry a Millionaire*, and the third was a drama, *Niagara*, in which she co-starred with a Hollywood perennial, Joseph Cotten. On August 12 the Russians tested their first thermonuclear device, the devastating power surprising even the men who built it. The cold war was heating up. Air raid drills, bomb shelters, anxiety and a certain amount of paranoia became the watchwords of the decade. The New York City Civil Defense Organization issued recommendations for building air raid shelters in private homes. A Los Angeles mother of three, Ruth Colhoun, built the first of them in 1951.

Ian Fleming published his first James Bond novel, *Casino Royale*. Hollywood icon John Wayne appeared in three films in '53, *Trouble Along the Way*, *Island in the Sky*, and a Wayne classic western, *Hondo*. The Dow Jones averages hit 281 while the minimum wage was 75 cents.

National League president Warren Giles announced there would be no action taken regarding the beanball incident in Milwaukee on August 3; however, he did issue a warning to both clubs to curb their pitchers' actions in the future. Dodgers boss Walter O'Malley suggested he might introduce a rule at the next major league meeting. It would require that a pitcher intentionally throwing at a hitter be ejected immediately from the game. The umpires balked at the concept, claiming they could not be expected to read a pitcher's mind.

On August 7 the Dodgers were at Crosley Field in Cincinnati for three games against the Reds. They swept the series and opened up a 13-game win streak. They had gone 23–8 in July and would have an even better month of August. On Friday night they defeated the Reds, 9–4, behind Johnny Podres' eighth win. Snider and Furillo both homered; for the Duke it was his 22nd of the year. Carl's home run came in the four-run eighth and Campanella and Hodges scored ahead of him. Podres went 8⅔ innings, taking a 9–2 lead into the ninth but ran into some trouble when he gave up three hits and two runs. Rookie Bob Milliken came in to get the final out after he walked George Lerchen with the bases loaded to force in the Reds' fourth run. He struck out Bobby Adams to end the game.

The Dodgers' power continued in a barrage over the weekend. On Saturday Campy hit two homers in Brooklyn's 7–4 victory and on Sunday the Duke hit a grand slam off Joe Nuxhall to ice a 9–1 win. In completing the sweep in Cincy, Loes and Meyer both won their 12th games; Loes had six loses, Russ Meyer had five.

The Brooks came back to New York for three at the Polo Grounds and on Tuesday, August 11, Carl Erskine faced Sal Maglie. They led the National League by seven games while Durocher's Giants lingered in fifth place, 16½ games behind Brooklyn. Yet the standings hardly mattered when these two clubs met, and the fans turned out. On this evening there were 45,604 in the seats, the second-largest crowd of the National League season. The largest had been on May 21 when 46,778 showed up, against the Dodgers. Like his ball club, Maglie was struggling. He came into the game with an 8–7 record, but three of those wins had come against Brooklyn. Monte Irvin, currently leading the league in hitting, was out with a sprained right ankle, and the Dodgers were minus the services of Billy Cox, who had a bruised left arm. Jackie Robinson played third and George Shuba went to left field.

The game, however, belonged to Brooklyn's "Oisk." The right-hander with the curveball that wound up in the dirt continued his string of near invincibility by shutting down the Giants, 4–0, on two singles, both coming off the bat of Hank Thompson. The win gave Erskine his 13th of the season against five losses, his eighth win in the last nine decisions, and his sixth complete game. Over the last 80 innings, Carl had an ERA of 1.24. In this one he contributed with the bat as well, getting as many hits as he gave up. Maglie, however, was far from his usual self. He surrendered nine hits and two runs in four innings, before coming out as he was warming up for the fifth due to a twinge in his right shoulder.

Gil Hodges, his slump just a bad memory, hit his 25th home run in the second and Carl Furillo banged out his 16th of the year in the eighth off Marv Grissom. A Dodger run came in the seventh after Gilliam singled and moved to second on Reese's bunt. Snider struck out but Robinson beat out a swinging bunt. The Giants' first baseman, Tookie Gilbert, thinking Jackie was out at first for the third out, tossed the ball to the pitcher's mound and Gilliam scored from second. Leo's crew had now lost 12 of their last 15 games and 10 of the last 11, dropping them 17½ games behind the Boys from Flatbush. Dodger pitching had given up just 10 hits in the last three games.

The Wednesday and Thursday games would result in Dodger victories, as well. Ruben Gomez held the Brooks to three hits for the first six innings before the roof fell in. With a runner on first, the Giants' hurler walked Belardi, Gilliam and Bobby Morgan to force in a run. Snider then hit "the longest homer I've ever hit" for his second grand slam in four days.[12] The Dodgers' Johnny Podres lasted only an inning and a third, giving up five runs and seven hits, but Milliken, Hughes and Labine held the Giants as Brooklyn won, 6–5. Labine was credited with his fourth win.

The Dodgers won game three, 9–8, as Campanella tied it with a ninth-inning home run off Hoyt Wilhelm. They won it in the 10th when Carl Furillo homered, also off the Giants' reliever. Labine won in relief, his second victory in as many days.

After the Giants sweep, Charlie Dressen tossed a phrase into baseball's lexicon when he announced to the gathered press, "the Giants *is* dead!"[13] Criticized more for his grammar than his content, as the Giants were now 19½ games behind his Dodgers, the Brooklyn Board of Education rode to Charlie's rescue. A spokesman explained that the Dodger skipper had been grammatically correct in using the term *is* instead of *are*.

Ted Williams returned from Korea. After completing his second stint as a Marine pilot in his second war and flying 37 combat missions, Teddy Ballgame came back to baseball. He signed a contract for the remainder of the 1953 season and all of 1954. On July 28, the day after the signing of an armistice truce in Korea, Ted was discharged from the U.S. Marine Corps. He arrived at Fenway Park on the 29th, a day the Red Sox were playing the White Sox in an afternoon game. After Williams met with Tom Yawkey, the Boston owner suggested that Ted go down to the field and hit a few. George Sullivan was a former Red Sox batboy who was a student at Boston University and was doing some writing for a newspaper. He was interviewing Yawkey and was a witness to Williams' first time in the cage since before he had gone to Korea.

There were only ushers and some concessions people present, and Ted started off with a couple of line drives before he hit one out. He then hit a second and a third. "He must have hit about twelve out," Sullivan said. "Then I noticed that blood was coming through his clenched fingers. Finally, he went back to the dugout. It was the greatest display I ever saw."[14]

Ted's first at-bat on August 6 came as a pinch-hitter and resulted in a pop-up to first in the ninth inning of a 10-inning, 8–7 loss to the Browns. Three days later he made his second appearance since returning from Korea, this time against the Cleveland Indians at Fenway Park. Again in a pinch-hitting role with one on and two outs in the seventh against Mike Garcia, Ted hit a 3–1 fastball into the center field bleachers 420 feet away, awing the crowd of 26,966 as only the Splendid Splinter was able to do.

He appeared in 37 games for the rest of the '53 season and had 91 official at-bats. He collected 37 hits, 13 of them home runs, drove in 34 runs and drew 19 walks. His average was .407. He had an on-base percentage of .509 and slugged at an astounding .901 clip. The Kid was back.

In mid–August Broadway was aglitter with the lilting melodies of hit musicals. Martha Wright was "Washing That Man Right Out of My Hair" in *South Pacific* at the Broadway Theater, on Broadway and 53rd Street. Yul Brynner was starring in *The King and I* at the St. James, and Rosalind Russell was doing *Wonderful Town,* voted the best musical of 1953. For other entertainment you could swing and sway with Sammy Kaye on the air-conditioned roof of the Hotel Astor. For Brooklynites who shunned the subway ride to Manhattan, comic Joey Faye was heading a cast of 50 in the musical revue *Top Banana* at the air-conditioned Brighton Theater on Ocean Parkway in Brighton Beach.

Pittsburgh began a four-game series at Ebbets Field on the 15th. On Saturday afternoon Campy hit his 32nd home run and Furillo his 18th as the Dodgers' 15 hits included four homers and four doubles in the 14–6 rout. The Reading Rifle upped his average to .338. Russ Meyer started but was removed in the third after getting into some trouble. The Mad Monk showed his disgust by flinging his glove against the dugout wall. Ben Wade got the win with 6⅓ innings of relief. The win gave the Dodgers an eight-game lead over the Braves. On Sunday it was a pair of wins over the Pirates, 3–1 and 9–5. Brooklyn had now won 28 of its last 34 games. Preacher Roe scattered eight hits in the opener, struck out seven and walked but one for his seventh victory in a row.

In the second game it was Erskine again, recording his 14th win against five losses. Carl ran into trouble in the eighth, but Clem Labine put the skids on the Pirates and saved the win for Oisk. The Duke of Flatbush hit a home run in the first game and two more in the nightcap, giving him 27 on the year. In 1953 Snider was clearly coming into his own and realizing the greatness his potential dictated. This would be the first of five consecutive 40-homer seasons for the Duke on his way to the Hall of Fame. Snider rationalized the developments in '53 as "more experience, a little bit more relaxed mentally, not applying as much pressure on myself as I had in earlier years."[15] Whatever the reasons, Duke had finally arrived.

Former Yankee outfielder Johnny Lindell was back in the majors as a knuckleball pitcher and was facing the Dodgers as a member of the Pittsburgh ball club. On this Monday afternoon he took a three-the hit shutout and a 2–0 lead into the ninth inning. Keeping Dodgers bats quiet for nine innings was no easy task for National League hurlers, and Lindell didn't quite make it. Morgan opened the last stanza with a single and Snider hit a knuckler onto Bedford Avenue for his 28th home run to tie the game. The Dodgers won it in the 11th on walks to Snider and Robinson before on a three-and-one slider Gil Hodges belted one out. Gil's RBI total reached 101, the fifth consecutive year the power-packed first baseman had driven in more than 100 runs. Brooklyn's lead was eight games and the winning streak hit ten games.

The Giants came to Ebbets for three beginning on the 17th. The opener lasted three hours, 31 minutes and 13 innings before Gil Hodges drove in Pee Wee Reese with a sacrifice fly to win it, 4–3. Meyer was the starter in the next game but was blown away in the Giants' five-run third inning. After Meyer kicked a water bucket in the dugout, manager Dressen bragged about how he has handled the tempestuous pitcher. "Meyer only blows his top in the dugout now—he don't do it in the game anymore."[16]

Brooklyn completed the three-game sweep of New York with their 13th consecutive victory behind another brilliant performance by their ace, Carl Erskine. He spun a four-hitter and walked none in shutting out the Giants for the second time in a row. He now had hurled 19 consecutive scoreless innings at Durocher's crew. The Dodgers had home runs from Jackie Robinson with two on in the third inning, Junior Gilliam in the fourth and Bobby Morgan in the fifth, and the 10–0 victory moved Brooklyn into a nine-game lead while New York dropped back 23½ games. Roscoe McGowen made reference to Charlie Dressen's "Giants is dead" comment in the *New York Times* when he wrote, "Charlie may not be a grammatical prophet, but he seems to be an accurate one."[17] Erskine was now 8–1 since the All-star break.

While the Dodgers were tearing up the National League, the Yankees were not exactly dormant over in the American. Following a pair of wins over the Philadelphia Athletics, the Bronx Bombers opened up a nine-game lead on the White Sox. The players, through their league reps, Ralph Kiner and Allie Reynolds, announced the hiring of a New York attorney, J. Norman Lewis, to aid them in their negotiations with the owners. A comment in *The Sporting News* pointed out that a study by the architectural firm of Bennett & Bennett of Pasadena reported that it would cost $2 million to adapt the Los Angeles Coliseum for major league baseball. On August 28 California governor Earl Warren visited Ebbets Field and spent the entire game in O'Malley's box chatting with the Dodgers' owner. There is little doubt as to what the subject of that conversation was.

The Dodgers had their 13-game win streak halted by little Murray Dickson in Pittsburgh. On his 37th birthday, the right-hander defeated Johnny Podres, 7–1. Podres could not get past the third inning and was followed by Ben Wade and Joe Black. Dickson was a dependable starting pitcher who was in his fifth year with the lowly Pirates after breaking in with the St. Louis Cardinals in 1939. He played on pennant-winners in St. Louis in 1942, '43 and '46. His best year with St. Louis was 1946 when he was 15–6 and led the league in winning percentage. In 1951 with the seventh-place Pirates, Dickson won 20 games and lost 16. On this day he scattered seven Dodgers hits and was boosted by a three-run home run by Frank Thomas off Ben Wade in the sixth.

The Dodgers took the next three from Pittsburgh. On the 22nd Preacher Roe won his ninth in a row, 5–3, but needed help from Labine to nail down the win. Clem had achieved a rare accomplishment in his career. He had gotten Stan Musial out a remarkable 49 consecutive times. The Brooks came back to Ebbets Field to open an 11-game homestand that began on the 25th against the Cubs. They lost two of the first three to Chicago, but won game four to begin a six-game win streak that took them through a series with the Cardinals that ended on September 1.

The Dodgers split the doubleheader on the 25th, winning the second game behind Carl Erskine's 16th victory. Brooklyn's five-run seventh put them up, 6–4. Erskine gave up a run in the eighth that brought Jim Hughes in to finish it up. The final score was 6–5. After a loss on the 26th, Russ Meyer won one on Thursday for his 14th of the year. Meyer went 8⅔ before Labine came in to nail the final out. The score was 7–5. Chicago tied it at 4–4 in the seventh with three off Meyer. Brooklyn scored one in the bottom of the inning on

Duke Snider's 33rd home run that came off Johnny Klippstein. In the eighth the Dodgers added two when Gil Hodges hit one with Campanella on third, the result of a lead-off triple.

This "Golden Age" of baseball was replete with future Hall-of-Fame players, and the Cubs had Ralph Kiner, an extraordinary home run hitter. Kiner had spent his first eight years in the majors with the Pirates before the trade this spring brought him to Chicago. His career would total 10 seasons but his 369 home runs made Kiner the most prodigious slugger of all-time, averaging nearly 37 home runs per year. He led the league in homers for seven consecutive seasons through the '52 campaign, tying for the lead in 1952 with the Cubs' Hank Sauer at 37. Ralph was elected to the Baseball Hall of Fame in 1975.

The St. Louis Cardinals came to town on the 30th and with them came their own Hall-of-Fame entourage. Stan "The Man" Musial was the leader of the pack. Stan's lifetime batting average was .331. Enos "Country" Slaughter, the .300-hitting outfielder, would hustle his way into Cooperstown in 1985, and St. Louis' second baseman, Red Schoendienst, contesting for the 1953 batting title, wound up finishing second to Carl Furillo with a .342 average. In the opener of the set with the Cards, the Dodgers "tore up the pea patch" with a 19-hit attack against four St. Louis pitchers, but the day carried with it some ominous overtones.

Robinson was favoring a sore knee as he came to bat in the seventh. Stanky yelled at him from the Cardinals' bench and Jackie yelled back. After striking out, towels came sailing out of the St. Louis dugout; crying towels, to be sure. Stanky mocked a limp to the water cooler with a bandage wrapped around his knee, emulating Robinson. Robinson held up a sign referring to a mistake the Cardinals' manager had made a few days earlier when presenting his lineup card to the umpires. By this time most of the 16,781 Ebbets Field fans that could look into the visitors' dugout were doing just that. There was more attention being paid to the happenings in the dugout than there was to the play on the field. The fans started waving handkerchiefs at the Cardinals' bench.

The *Brooklyn Eagle* captured photographs of the entire incident. One was of famed Dodger fan Hilda Chester, who had made her way from the center field bleachers to a spot behind the St. Louis dugout. She is seen waving a hankie at Stanky while leaning over the dugout roof. Another, although sketchy at best, appears to show Stanky scratching near his armpits like an ape and hanging from the dugout roof. Carl E. Prince noted the Cardinals' manager in action: "Fists under armpits, lips out, jaw thrust forward, grunting, shuffling, and scratching as he moved from one end of the dugout to the other."[18] It seemed, however, that not everyone interpreted the pictures the same way. Roger Kahn in the *Herald-Tribune*, Tommy Holmes in the *Brooklyn Eagle*, and Roscoe McGowen in the *New York Times* all wrote accounts the next day and none indicated that it was anything more than bench-jockey charades with none of the racial overtones that Prince mentioned.

Kahn said the two had "turned comics," Holmes had Stanky "limping over to the water cooler several times," and McGowen wrote in the *Times* that "the Cardinals manager, ridiculing Robby from the bench, finally got up, wrapped a towel around his leg, and went back and forth to the water cooler with an exaggerated limp."[19] The photo caption read "Ebbets Field Frolics," and while not at all definitive, in one shot Stanky is seated on the dugout bench clearly with both hands at his ribs, fingers extended. The photo caption includes, "The Card manager makes like an ape." Another has Stanky holding his knee, obviously mimicking Robinson's sore knee.[20]

"Just like Durocher," Jackie said of the Cardinals' manager. "Everything's lovely as long as they're ahead. When they get behind they start their yapping."[21]

Dave Anderson of the *Eagle* was at the game and he saw no ape imitation. One thing that is clear is that the fans at Ebbets Field that day had a blast booing Stanky. The Dodgers were leading, 6–3, when the Stanky antics began, and according to Tommy Holmes in the *Eagle*, "Stanky brought it all on himself."[22]

The fans were treated to a double feature. That same inning Brooklyn scored 12 times; six runs following Robinson's strikeout, and six more after the second out was recorded. The Dodgers got seven hits, including a home run by Bobby Morgan, and there were five walks issued by St. Louis pitchers. Stanky trudged out to the mound to make three pitching changes, each time greeted by the hoots and howls of the faithful fans of Flatbush.

Roy Campanella had homered earlier in the game, his thirty-fourth, and his five runs batted in tied the National League mark for catchers, shared by Gabby Hartnett and Walker Cooper at 122. The 12-run seventh inning tied the National League record set by the 1925 Chicago Cubs.

In the first half of the year paced by the Levittown building boom in Long Island, new construction costs in the United States hit $16 billion. On August 17 a new film was released by Warner Brothers with the title *Big Leaguer*. It was Robert Aldrich's first feature direction and it starred Hollywood legend Edward G. Robinson. Robinson played a real-life former big leaguer, Hans Lobart, who in the film ran a tryout camp for the New York Giants. Young players in the movie had their dreams realized or smashed to smithereens. It was similar to such Dodger hopefuls as Wayne Belardi or Bobby Morgan, who could not get past the Reeses and the Hodges and had to settle for the handful of games and the few miscellaneous at-bats that were meted out to them.

On the last day of the month, Brooklyn defeated the Cardinals, 6–3, behind rookie Bob Milliken. Campy drove in two more, securing the RBI record all for himself. Milliken lasted 8⅓ innings when he walked both Ray Jablonski and Del Rice with a strikeout of Steve Bilko sandwiched in between. It remained for the ever-trusty Clem Labine to come in and throw a double play ball to pinch-hitter Sal Yvars, Gilliam to Reese to Hodges.

The Dodgers now led the league by 10½ games with a record of 90 wins and 40 losses for the season. Since the All-Star break, Brooklyn had played at a torrid pace, winning 40 games and losing only nine.

NINE

September

*"Bean ball, a game the Giants and Dodgers sometimes play instead of
baseball, made its annual debut at Ebbets Field yesterday."*
—Roger Kahn, *New York Herald Tribune*, April 26, 1953

The Dodgers clinched the 1953 National League pennant in Milwaukee
and Dave Anderson, writing for the *Brooklyn Eagle,* submitted the best lead.
The Braves had made three costly errors in the game and Anderson wrote,
"The Milwaukee Braves died with their boots."[1] Dick Young and Roger Kahn
both speculated as to whether it would make it into print that way.

"Two to one they change it on you," Young said.

"If not the deskman, then the printer," Kahn ventured.[2]

Sure enough, the next day's article led with, "The Milwaukee Braves died
with their boots *on.*"[3]

The clincher came on September 12, the score was 5–2, and it was win
number 19 for Carl Erskine against just six losses. It was the earliest clinching
in National League history, and no Dodger team had ever won two consecutive
pennants. In throwing a complete game, Erskine walked one and struck out
five while giving up seven hits. One Braves run was unearned. Behind 1–0, the
Dodgers scored two in the fourth on only one hit, aided by two Milwaukee
errors. In the sixth the three runs that crossed were the result of one hit, three
walks, and another Braves error.

The clubhouse celebration was low-key but jubilant. Dressen was the
only Brooklyn pilot to win two pennants in a row, which had him thinking
of a new multi-year contract. Russ Meyer stepped to the microphone and said,
"Thank you, Steve O'Neill!" in appreciation to the Phils' manager for trading
him away.[4]

Some of the players celebrated that night. Duke Snider recalled "coming
to the ballpark the next day with some admirable hangovers."[5] But the Duke

had a 26-game hitting streak going and wanted to keep it alive. Even the Cubs tried to cooperate. An arrangement was made that would have Chicago pitcher Johnny Klippstein groove one to Snider so the Duke could get his hit. Then with some help from Snider, Klippstein would pick him off first base. Everybody wins. However, in spite of seeing fat pitches all afternoon, the Duke could not get a hit. Finally, in his last at-bat, Klippstein hollered from the mound, "Bunt one!"

"I popped it up," Snider said. "I went 0-for-4 and my hitting streak was snapped with the fix on the whole game."[6]

The ball club opened the month with three wins in the first five games. Brooklyn's 17-hit barrage against the Cardinals on the first added to Stanky's humiliation, coming just two days after the 20–4 shellacking his Cardinals had taken at the hands of the Dodgers. This one was 12–5 and Preacher Roe got the win. They lost two in a row to the Braves at Ebbets Field. On Wednesday it was oppressively hot and muggy in Brooklyn for the 30,877 fans who witnessed a slugfest with a total of 29 hits and a 9–8 Milwaukee victory. Labine, the fourth Dodger pitcher, took the loss. The next day in a 6–1 Braves win, Eddie Mathews hit his 44th home run of the season. His total of 47 would lead the National League. Brooklyn still held a nine-game lead as the Dodgers went into the Polo Grounds for three games.

They swept the Giants on the fourth, fifth and sixth. In the 8–6 opening win, the Dodgers benefitted from four Giants errors to score five unearned runs. The sad demise of Joe Black from his tremendous '52 season also saw the rise of Clem Labine as a relief specialist. He relieved Black after the latter gave up a game-tying home run to Alvin Dark in the sixth inning. In Brooklyn's last 25 games, Labine had made 13 appearances, winning six, losing one, while saving five. Hodges hit his 30th homer and the Dodgers scored three off Hoyt Wilhelm, appearing in his 63rd game of the year.

As Red Barber often said from the broadcast booth, "Anytime these two clubs get together, there's gonna be a rhubarb!" And as sure as the Gowanus is in Brooklyn, there was. In the seventh inning Labine low-bridged Bobby Hofman. In the eighth Larry Jansen retaliated by putting Duke Snider on his butt. After both Snider and Robinson bunted, Snider for a hit and Jackie for a sacrifice, Jansen knocked Campanella down. Umpire Bill Stewart called Dressen and Bill Rigney together for a little talk. Rigney was managing the club because Stewart had run both Durocher and Wes Westrum in the fourth for arguing a ball four call on Reese with the bases loaded. After Stewart issued his warning, both clubs went back to playing baseball, at least for a while.

It was on July 12, 1938, that Robert Joyce sat in Pat Diamond's bar and

At war with the Giants. The rivalry was never more intense than in the Golden Age when Leo Durocher managed the New Yorkers. Willard Mullins' wonderful cartoon captures the fervent mood of the era (courtesy Shirley Mullin Rhodes).

grill on Ninth Street and Seventh Avenue in the Park Slope section of Brooklyn. Joyce was a Dodgers fan and he took their losses seriously. On this afternoon in spite of the fact that the Brooklyn Robins had defeated the New York Giants, 13–5, he still came in for some ribbing from the other patrons. William Diamond, the son of the proprietor, although a Dodger fan himself, was having some fun teasing Joyce. Another patron was Frank Krug, and Krug was a Giants fan. His barbs stung more deeply until Joyce had had enough.

He leaped off the bar stool, screamed at Krug and stormed out of the place to the derisive laughter of the crowd. In a few minutes he was back and had a gun in his hand. He shot Krug through the head, then turned on Diamond, putting a bullet in his stomach. Overcoming the shock of what had just transpired, the bartender said, "Jesus, Bob, looka what you done to Willie!"[7] Joyce tossed the gun and fled the bar pursued by patrons until police officers in a cruising patrol car caught him. He was sobbing hysterically, saying he didn't mean to harm anyone. William Diamond recovered from his wound, but Krug died in the attack. Robert Joyce's actions may have been extreme, but it does testify to the passion and intensity of emotions that some fans felt when the Dodgers and Giants were involved.

Baseball historian Lee Allen has referred to this longstanding clash as "Baseball's Fiercest Feud," and has stated unequivocally that the exact moment the rivalry began was Friday, October 18, 1899, at the old Polo Grounds at precisely 3:07 p.m.[8] That was the starting time for the first game of an unofficial World Series between New York and Brooklyn.

At a meeting on October 17, the two club owners, John B. Day of the New York team and Charles H. Byrne of Brooklyn, arranged the post-season series. It was agreed that the first team to win six games would be declared the winner. The series commenced on the 18th and lasted until the 29th. After Brooklyn took a lead of three games to one, the Giants swept the next five, winning six games to three. While this may have been the first exchange between the clubs, it might be called an unofficial opening salvo. The official start came the following spring. Brooklyn joined the National League and the two would square off all season.

It was the only time that two clubs from the same city played in the same league, and the opponents would face each other 22 times during the regular season for the next 67 years, providing plenty of opportunities for the pot to boil over. It was on May 3, 1890, that Brooklyn defeated New York, 7–3, before 3,774 fans. The starting gun had been officially fired.

Brooklyn won pennants in 1890, 1899 and 1900, while the Giants topped the league in 1904 and '05. It was in this latter year that the Giants' "Little Napoleon," John J. McGraw, and Brooklyn owner Charles Ebbets first locked horns and began a feud that would last until Ebbets' death in 1925. During a game in 1905 in which the Giants were ahead, an argument arose on the field with McGraw going at it with the umpire. Somehow Ebbets from his box and McGraw managed to exchange some livid language. Charley complained to the league but nothing came of it, and the two remained bitter enemies thereafter. It seemed that any time the Giants visited Washington Park, the home of the Dodgers, the potential for riotous behavior existed. On June 23, 1910, there was an eruption. Giants third baseman Arthur Devlin was being ridden by a group of fans in a nearby box. At the end of the inning, Devlin walked over and slugged one of the fans. Challenged further, Devlin, now joined by teammates Josh Devore and Larry Doyle, began swinging at the crowd. Ebbets and McGraw began screaming at each other, Ebbets threatening to have Devlin barred from baseball. The police broke it up and the game went on, the Giants winning. Nothing further came of the matter, although there was a court appearance by Devlin that was dismissed.

The rivalry's intensity increased when "Uncle" Wilbert Robinson was hired to manage the Dodgers. Robinson was not a calming influence. He and McGraw had been friends and teammates in Baltimore at the turn of the century, even to the point of running a successful business together in that city. But sometime during the 1913 season, a riff developed between the two. After Uncle Robbie took over the management of Brooklyn in 1914, any time that the two teams met, anything was liable to hit the fan.

By 1916 when Brooklyn won the pennant, Robinson was settled comfortably in the job. He was lovable old "Uncle Robbie," and the team was called the Robins in his honor. The last series that year saw the Giants visit Ebbets Field. The Giants were out of the race, and McGraw publicly derided his team, accusing them of not trying. There were even cries for an investigation, but nothing came of it. Brooklyn won the series and the pennant. The Robins won another pennant in 1920.

The Giants then won four consecutive pennants from 1921–1924, while the Robins challenged in the last of those years. Even so, it was never peaceful. In a 1922 game at Ebbets Field before a sellout crowd, the Robins took a 4–1 lead into the ninth. When umpire Bob Emslie called Heinie Groh safe on a close force play at second, someone threw a pop bottle from the stands. Soon there were dozens of them littering the field. After the grounds crew cleaned up, the Giants created their own mess by defeating Brooklyn, 5–4.

In September of that 1924 season, Brooklyn climbed to second place, New York was first, and on Sunday, September 7, came the day that Lee Allen called "the wildest day in the history of Ebbets Field."[9] It was anticipated that as many as 50,000 would try to see the game. Fans battered the gates, climbed the walls, and crossed the field. There were ambulances to administer to the many injured and it was estimated that at least seven thousand entered the park without any tickets. By some minor miracle the game was played, with the Giants winning, 8–7. Ed McKeever was in charge of the park that day, and he explained the next day, "The crowd tore back the sliding doors of the rotunda, and crashed through the turnstiles by the hundreds."[10] The Giants beat out the Robins by 1½ games and won their fourth straight pennant. Perhaps enthusiasm is not a strong enough word to explain the happenings at Ebbets Field, but Brooklyn fans were getting a reputation for being a rowdy lot. The next year the Giants came away with victories in the first five games they played against the Robins. Nothing seemed to happen just by chance and get passed over. In a game in which Burleigh Grimes hit the Giants' Frankie Frisch with a pitch and caused a bit of a ruckus, Ross Youngs and Jimmy Johnston went at it after a collision on a play at third.

In the Brooklyn ballparks, both Washington Park and Ebbets Field, the fans were as much a part of the game as the players. They were referred to as "tart and tempestuous" by James R. Harrison in the *Times*. "They were vicious and venomous."[11] The last game on the last day of the 1931 season saw the last of Robbie and McGraw. The Dodgers were now managed by Max Carey, followed by Casey Stengel in 1934. Bill Terry took over the Giants in 1932 and won a pennant the next year. Terry would be a Hall-of-Fame player, having hit .401 in 1930 and batting .341 lifetime. In the winter of 1934 he was asked how his club would do this season. "We should win again this year," he said, and proceeded to evaluate the chances of other contending clubs. The Cubs, Pirates and Cardinals were mentioned, but not the Dodgers. "What about Brooklyn, Bill?" asked Roscoe McGowen of the *Times*.

"Brooklyn?" Terry asked. "Is Brooklyn still in the league?"[12] The off-the-cuff remark, probably said with no real malicious intent, produced a violent reaction from the fans of Brooklyn. Terry received hundreds of letters, most of them from Dodgers fans, containing threats and words of hate. When the Giants came to Ebbets Field on Memorial Day and faced the largest crowd ever to squeeze into the tiny ballpark—41,209—Terry was booed and hissed all day long. But Brooklyn's revenge had to wait until the final two games of the season; when it came, it was oh so sweet for the fans of Flatbush.

The Cardinals and Giants were deadlocked in first place and the Dodgers were in their customary sixth place when Brooklyn came into the Polo Grounds. St. Louis had two with the Reds at home. The Dodgers pitcher was Van Lingle Mungo on Saturday and he stifled the Giants, 5–1, as the Cards defeated Cincinnati. On Sunday, Casey Stengel's Dodgers beat the Giants again, 8–5, and the Cardinals were National League champions. To add insult to injury, New York had jumped ahead with four runs in the first inning. But Brooklyn came back, and the teams went into the 10th tied, 5–5. The Dodgers won it against Carl Hubbell pitching in relief.

To say that there were fireworks when the two got together is not a total exaggeration. In 1935 the Giants obtained Dick Bartell, a scrappy, brawling type of player who was hated in Brooklyn. The first time the Giants came in, there were firecrackers from the stands tossed at Bartell and Terry all afternoon. The game had to be stopped and the field cleared. The Dodgers won handily,

12–5. The next day fans brought more firecrackers, but this time the man they called "Rowdy Richard" hit a triple and a home run and the Giants topped the Brooklyn men, 8–5.

On Opening Day in 1937 with the Giants at Ebbets Field, it did not take long for trouble to break out. The first pitch of the game from Van Lingle Mungo to Dick Bartell was a called strike. Bartell turned to holler at umpire Beans Reardon and was struck in the chest by an over-ripe tomato. Lee Allen noted the fact that it took "not more than two seconds for the first hassle of the season."[13] There was the day the next season when Giants first baseman Zeke Bonura, after being jostled by Leo Durocher on a play at first, threw the baseball at Leo's head in retaliation.

If winning was the most important thing to the fans of Brooklyn, clobbering the Giants was a close second. Any Dodger who made a contribution was a hero in Brooklyn. The Dodgers had a player named Packy Rogers who played only 23 games with them in 1938, the reason being that he hit a mere .189. But they loved Packy in Brooklyn because even though he batted an anemic .097 against the rest of the league, Rogers hit a rousing .667 against the Giants.

Larry MacPhail brought Leo Durocher to Brooklyn in 1938 and handed him the managerial reins the next season. Durocher was a stick of dynamite, explosive and notorious for his battles with the umpires. He and MacPhail clashed to the point of Larry firing Leo at least 30 or 40 times during their tenure together, once immediately following the Dodgers' pennant-winning victory in 1941. The next day, as always, it was business as usual and MacPhail never even mentioned his rash actions. With the exception of the three war years in 1943, '44 and '45, Leo kept the Dodgers in the thick of the pennant race each season. Off the field Durocher was a problem for the Dodgers' front office. A slick dresser, Leo hobnobbed with celebrities from Hollywood and politics and associated frequently with characters of dubious reputation, including known gamblers.

In 1946 Durocher uttered the phrase that would become one of those classic sayings used as much outside of baseball as within the game. As usual there were rollicking rhubarbs whenever the two clubs got together. The Giants had obtained an outfielder, Goody Rosen, and one day in August Rosen spiked Eddie Stanky while sliding into second base at the Polo Grounds, and a fistfight ensued. Durocher, in speaking with reporters, praised Stanky's competitive fire. Dodgers broadcaster Red Barber mentioned something about Giants manager Mel Ott being a nice guy. "Look over there," Leo said, referring to the Giants' bench. "Do you know a nicer guy than Mel Ott? ... And where are they? In last place."[14] The next day Frank Graham quoted Durocher's remark in the *New York Journal American* as, "Nice guys finish last."

It was primarily the gambler ties that led to Durocher's suspension in 1947. He also managed to get the Catholic Church through the CYO against him after his very public affair with movie actress Lorraine Day while she was still married and the subsequent wedding between Day and Durocher. Baseball commissioner A.B. Happy Chandler sat Durocher down for the entire '47 season because of his associations with undesirable characters.

The 1947 season, as significant as it was with the emergence of Jackie Robinson in the major leagues, was played without Durocher. Burt Shotton managed the club to a pennant and Durocher came back to his old job for the '48 season. Then the unthinkable happened. Branch Rickey realized that Durocher's days in Brooklyn were numbered. The club was not going well and their relationship had soured. Rickey had traveling secretary Harold Parrott pass the word to Durocher that Rickey wanted him to resign. Not surprisingly, it happened on July 4 during a game against the Giants when Jackie Robinson stole home and Durocher was thrown out of the game for arguing. Durocher refused to quit, and since the Dodgers won that game on a ninth-inning home run by Roy Campanella and five of the next six, the decision was put on hold. Rickey then approached Giants owner Horace Stoneham, who was ready to replace manager Mel Ott, and offered him the chance to speak with both Shotton and Durocher. Rickey knew that Stoneham would prefer Durocher and the deal was made. On July 17 it was announced, and Brooklyn fans were shocked. One day Leo was their fighting manager, and the next he was the fighting opposition.

Durocher returned to Brooklyn on July 26 as the Giants' manager. The lines began forming at 8 a.m., 12 hours before the game was to begin. Ebbets Field was packed, the overflow crowd was 33,932, and Durocher was greeted with a chorus of boos when he appeared on the field. He recalled how for nine years Dodger fans after a game would "yell to me from every corner to find out how we made out."[15] For Leo, it was a new day in Brooklyn.

The Dodgers under returning manager Burt Shotton finished third in 1948; the Giants placed fifth. The Giants in 1947 established the National League record for home runs with 221 and finished fourth. They were a slow, ponderous, yet power-hitting, team— not Durocher's kind of ball club at all. He began making changes. He got rid of players like Mize, Marshall and Cooper and added a new core that included Alvin Dark at shortstop and Eddie Stanky at second base. In May 1951 he brought up from Minneapolis a kid center fielder who was hitting .477. Willie Mays started off slowly but Durocher assured him that he was his center fielder come hell or high water.

Durocher's abrasive personality had not sat well with some of his Dodger players. In the spring of 1948 Jackie Robinson reported 20 pounds over-weight after hitting the off-season banquet trail. Leo embarrassed Robinson by ridiculing him and making him wear a rubber suit. He hit hundreds of ground balls to the second baseman and jawed at him all the while. "Stick a fork in him, he's done," he yelled in front of the other players. "C'mon, fatso, get moving."[16] Two men with large egos clashed. Robinson grew to hate Durocher. By the 1950 season the jockeying between the two became ferocious. Jackie was fond of alluding to Durocher wearing the perfume of his actress wife.

The other enemy Leo nurtured in a Dodgers uniform was Carl Furillo. On June 28, 1950, Furillo was beaned by Giants pitcher Sheldon Jones, and he blamed Durocher. Leo was a "stick-it-in-his-ear" manager and always had his pitchers throw tight to Furillo, an emotional man whom Durocher thought could be intimidated. But as far as the sensitive outfielder was concerned, the riff began even sooner. After coming out of the army in 1946, Carl had a minor league contract, but Leo was playing him regularly in the spring. When he was tendered a major league contract, the amount was minimal. When Furillo complained to Durocher, he was told to "take it or leave it." Said Furillo, "I hated Durocher's guts from that day on."[17]

As Durocher was building his kind of team in New York, the Giants were saddled with a right-handed pitcher named Sal Maglie, whom they were forced to take back after the Pasquel affair in Mexico. But it did not take long for Maglie to become Durocher's pride. He went 18–4 in 1950 and was particu-larly effective against the Dodgers. His lifetime record against them was 23–11. At Ebbets Field he went 11–3. As a result, the rivalry intensified during this era, with Durocher, Maglie and Furillo and Robinson facing off on a regular basis. Typical was the day in 1951 when Maglie tossed one at Robinson's head and Jackie pushed a bunt along the first base line. When Maglie came over to field it, Robinson bowled him over. Commissioner Ford C. Frick made a plea that this sort of behavior be toned down. Nobody listened.

In spite of all the tremendous successes enjoyed by the Dodgers and their fans during this particular era, the year 1951 has remained for most both a mournful and infuriating memory. Brookynites today can tell you where they were at the moment Bobby Thomson's drive entered the lower deck in left field at the Polo Grounds at 3:58 p.m. on Wednesday, October 3. The fact that the home run, poetically dubbed "the shot heard 'round the world," has been called the most dramatic home run in baseball history has not made it any easier for the faithful to accept.

As dramatic as it was, the fact remains that had the historic game not been between the New York Giants and the Brooklyn Dodgers, in all likelihood it would not have achieved such exalted status. For many Dodgers fans, however, as time heals most wounds, they have taken the philosophical approach and remember the season as one of the most exciting pennant races ever, even after coming out on the short end.

The animosity was present any time these two clubs faced each other. In the second game of their opening series beginning April 20, the popular General Douglas MacArthur was in attendance. MacArthur had just been recalled by President Truman and had been feted with a parade and a tumultuous reception. The teams put on a show that was typical. Durocher's distinctive voice could be heard from the dugout and his "stick-it-in-his-ear" style was unmistakably present on the field. When Larry Jansen hit Campanella with a pitch, Roy went after Giants' catcher Wes Westrum. Both benches emptied, eventually order was restored, and Brooklyn took a 7–3 victory. Early in that '51 season, with the Giants off to a slow start and the Dodgers beating them in a doubleheader, New York had a losing streak of 11 games. At Ebbets Field there was only a wooden door separating the two clubhouses. Following that double victory, the Brooklyn players were banging on the door with bats and yelling, "Eat your heart out, Leo, you sonofabitch."[18]

As the Dodgers built a lead that reached 13½ games by August 11, manager Charlie Dressen announced for the first time, "The Giants is dead."[19] But they went on a 16- game winning streak and won 37 of their last 44 games. Brooklyn didn't collapse; they played a bit better than .500 ball the rest of the way. But the fireworks never ceased. On September 27 in Boston, the Dodgers were tied at 3–3 in the eighth. With Braves runners on first and third, Earl Torgeson bounced one to Robinson at second. Robinson threw home, and after umpire Frank Dascoli signaled safe, Campanella threw a tantrum. He tossed his mitt on the ground and his mask in the air, and then Dascoli tossed him along with coach Cookie Lavagetto, who had joined Campy in violent protest. The 4–3 loss left the Dodgers just a half-game ahead of the Giants. After the game, somebody, presumably a Dodger, kicked in the door of the umpires' dressing room. In the aftermath, Robinson and Roe were fined $100 and $50, respectively, and Campanella $100. The Dodgers complained of the quick ejection of their catcher in light of the tight pennant race. Ford Frick acknowledged, lecturing Dascoli for being "too hasty" in ejecting Campanella in the heat of a pennant race and would not consider suspensions, saying, "I wouldn't think of depriving the Dodgers of player strength at a time like this."[20] The Giants were listening to the game on the radio, and Durocher's reaction was, "I think we've got 'em now."[21]

September 30, a Sunday, was the final day of the regular season and the two clubs were in a dead tie. The Giants defeated the Braves in Boston, 3–2, while the Dodgers were in the sixth inning in Philadelphia and losing, 8–5, to the Phillies. Brooklyn rallied to tie the game in the eighth. Don Newcombe and Robin Roberts were both pitching in relief, a mere 16 hours after both had thrown complete games. In the 12th, the Phillies had the bases loaded with two out when Eddie Waitkus rapped a low line drive towards the middle of the diamond. Robinson dove for the ball and caught it backhanded while sprawled on the ground. In the 14th inning Jackie hit a fastball into the upper deck in left field and the Dodgers remained alive.

The pennant-winning home run by Bobby Thomson off Ralph Branca made baseball history, but as might be expected, it was not the last word in Dodgers-Giants lore. Fifty years later writer Joshua Prager revealed that the Giants had an elaborate sign-stealing scheme set up and used it throughout the second half of the season. Hank Schenz, a journeyman infielder, had joined the Giants on the first of July and told Durocher that when he was with the Cubs, he had used a telescope to steal the opposing teams' signs. Soon Schenz had set up his Wollensak scope in the Giants' clubhouse and picked off the signs and signaled Sal Yvars in the Giants' bullpen, who passed the info to the hitter. They began it on July 20 and continued through the remainder of the season. Yvars confessed his role in the doings.

In early September at the Polo Grounds with the Dodgers holding a 10-game lead, Clem Labine decked Bobby Hoffman. The next inning Giants pitcher Larry Jansen knocked Duke Snider down. Never could a season pass without some kind of rumblings. In this last season series between the clubs, Joe Black, the Dodgers' pitcher, knocked down Giants outfielder George Wilson and Jansen dusted off Hodges and Black. Both teams were warned at this point, but Jansen decided to get in the last lick and hit Billy Cox in the ninth. Durocher was ejected from the game. A month or so before, National League president Warren Giles had issued a directive ruling that managers were responsible for beanball excesses. As a result, Durocher was kicked out of the game and suspended for two more. It was business as usual in the Polo Grounds or at Ebbets Field.

It had been six months since Carl Furillo told Roger Kahn that he would "get Durocher," and now his time had come. The pitching match-ups for the third game of the series, on September 6, had Preacher Roe opposing Giants rookie Ruben Gomez. Both threw complete games. The Dodgers won, 6–3. Roe's record now stood at 11–2, but as was so often the case, the fans, 25,331 of them, were treated to more than a mere ball game. Roe had given up just four hits but two were home runs—one to Alvin Dark in the first and a two-run homer to Bobby Thomson in the sixth. Trailing, 1–0, in the second inning, Jackie Robinson led off with a line single to left. Campanella then hit a line drive into the left field seats, giving Brooklyn a 2–1 lead. Hodges grounded out and Carl Furillo stepped in.

Gomez threw a fastball at Carl's head. When he raised his left arm to protect himself, he was hit on the wrist. Furillo started towards the mound, tossed some words at the pitcher, and as the umpires intervened, went to first base. On another day, in another town, with two other ball clubs, that might have been the end of it, but not in New York, and not between baseball's Hatfields and McCoys. With the count two and two on Billy Cox, Furillo yelled into the Giants' dugout from the bag.

"I know it was you, Leo," he screamed. "You told him to do that." Durocher yelled back, "That's right, you Dago prick, and the next time you come up I'm going to have him do the same thing."[22] Furillo saw red. He asked the umpire for time and bolted into the Giants' dugout. Monte Irvin stepped up to try to stop him, but the irate Dodger pushed past him and wrestled Durocher to the floor of the dugout. Those watching the game on television did not miss a thing. When the gesturing and the shouting started, the cameras stayed on Furillo and followed him right into the Giants' bench. Furillo was on top of Durocher with a stranglehold on the Giants' manager, and though it was only in black and white, the TV audience could see Durocher's bald head discoloring. In the confusion someone stepped on Furillo's hand and broke a bone. Later while it was being attended to in the clubhouse, he was asked how he thought he could get through the entire Giants team to reach Durocher.

"I wasn't worried about the other players ganging up on me," he said. "A lot of the Giants hate him too."[23] Fortunately, the biggest guys were peacemakers. Jim Hearn, Monte Irvin and Gil Hodges were seeing that things did not go any further. "That's when I found out how strong Gil Hodges was," Irvin said. "I looked up and saw Hodges picking up guys like they were babies and sifting them out.... I've never seen such strength."[24] Plate umpire Babe Pinelli rushed over to the scene and looked down at the combatants and saw Furillo on top of somebody. Remember, Durocher did not have many fans among the National League umpires. So when Pinelli asked, "Who's he got

Carl Furillo's left hand is in a cast following a September encounter with Leo Durocher at the Polo Grounds (Brooklyn Public Library—Brooklyn Collection).

down there?" and the answer came back, "Durocher!" the umpire fired back, "Kill him, Carl, kill him."[25]

Irvin remembered, "I was sitting on the bench. I had that bad ankle. Furillo left first base and started for the dugout. All I wanted to do was to keep Leo and Furillo from killing each other." Pee Wee Reese knew the emotion that was wrapped up in his teammate. "Knowing Furillo," he said, "I would not want to get him too upset, because Furillo would fight a buzz saw."[26] Irvin recalled the Dodgers players coming over to the Giants' bench and saying, "Let them fight. Let him kill him." According to Irvin, "We had one heck of a melee right there in front of the Giants dugout."[27]

Having helped to pull Furillo off Durocher, Irvin recalled that the next season Furillo, usually friendly towards Monte on the field, was acting funny.

Irvin asked Campanella what was wrong. "He hates your guts," Campy said. "Why? I never did anything to him," Irvin said. "You kept him from killing Durocher," Campy told him.[28] Furillo was hitting a lofty .344 and was sidelined the rest of the year. His average held up; the Cardinals' Red Schoendienst made a run but fell short at .342. Carl Furillo was the National League batting champion.

On the fourth of September Florence Chadwick swam the English Channel from England to France in 14 hours and 42 minutes. Swanson sold its first TV dinner and the American Security Council agreed to fund the French Navarre plan in Vietnam. The film *The Robe*, based on the best-selling novel by Lloyd C. Douglas, opened at the Roxy Theater in Manhattan. It was the first film in Cinemascope, the new wide-screen effect. The novel, with sales of 188,000, was the top-selling work of fiction for 1953.

The next day the Dodgers took both ends of a doubleheader from the Phillies by identical scores of 6–2. Both Billy Loes and Carl Erskine nailed down a victory and Campy hit home run number 39. Leo Durocher and Carl Furillo had been ejected from the Sunday game at the Polo Grounds, but league president Warren Giles announced there would be no action against either of them. As Brooklyn headed west, the magic number to clinch was three.

On a visit to the West Coast, Bill Veeck, owner of the St. Louis Browns, stirred the pot of California relocation when he announced that if the city of Los Angeles and county officials can purchase Wrigley Field in L.A., the American League will permit him to bring his major league ball club there next season.[29] Veeck, of course, was just blowing smoke. The American League would never grant him authority to relocate his club; in fact, the league forced him to sell the Browns before allowing the new owners to move to Baltimore.

Veeck, however, was right on the money as usual about what had to be done. O'Malley made the deal with Wrigley, which was announced on February 21, 1957, to swap the Dodgers' Fort Worth, Texas, franchise for the Cubs' Los Angeles Angels and Wrigley Field. O'Malley had dibs on LA. The fact remains that the California surge was not a last-minute inspiration that fell into O'Malley's lap in '56 or '57. It was also revealed by the Dodgers' boss that he had "received a letter from a prominent Angelino who is in politics and well-fixed financially asking that the Brooklyn club shift to the coast metropolis."[30]

Brooklyn defeated Cincinnati on Wednesday night, September 9, by a score of 6–0 behind Bob Milliken. Pee Wee Reese hit a grand slam and the Duke powered his 38th home run of the year. The magic number dropped to two. A 6–5 loss the next day snapped a six-game winning streak. Labine walked

Andy Seminick in the 11th with the bases loaded. On the 11th they lost to the Braves, 9–8, stalling the clincher one more day. The National League set the home run record with 1,102, topping the 1950 mark of 1,100, and the Dodgers' sluggers were contributing in a big way. The Dodgers had gone 8–4 from September 1 until the pennant-clincher on the 12th.

Brooklyn celebrated the pennant win, but a sad and tragic episode that combined drink and a passion for the game happened at the Furman Inn in downtown Brooklyn that evening. A heated argument over the Dodgers and the Yankees involving about a dozen patrons grew out of control. The proprietor forced them to leave and then bolted the door. The crowd outside picked up a bench and broke down the door. The owner took a pistol from behind the bar and after firing two warning shots into the floor, fired at the mob, killing one man and wounding another.

The next day super southpaw Warren Spahn won his 20th game by defeating Durocher and the Giants, 2–1. The same day Brooklyn lost to the Cubs, 3–2, in 10 innings when catcher Rube Walker failed to touch home plate on a force play. Duke Snider pinch-hit his 39th homer on the 15th against St. Louis as Clem Labine picked up the win. On the 17th Carl Erskine earned his 20th win of the season, beating the Cards, 4–3, and the Dodgers won their 100th game. Erskine trailed, 3–1, in the ninth against Harvey Haddix, but Brooklyn scored three in the ninth. Roger Kahn pointed out the fact that the Dodgers regulars chose to play. "As a sort of favor to Carl, all the able Dodger regulars passed up a chance to spend the afternoon napping and telling droll stories in the shade of the dugout."[31]

Jackie Robinson turned over to the St. Louis police a threatening letter he had received during the Cardinals series. Throughout the games of the 16th and 17th, two FBI agents as well as three local policemen were assigned to guard Robinson. The proper precautions were taken even though the letter was regarded as the work of a crank. Acting police chief Joseph E. Casey said that they decided to "play it safe," and the guards accompanied the player until he boarded the train the evening of September 17.[32]

Robinson opened the ninth against Haddix with a double into the left field corner. Campanella followed with a single, delivering Jackie, and then Cox singled. Haddix wild-pitched the runners to second and third. Dick Williams flied out, but Wayne Belardi delivered a clutch base hit, driving in two and putting the game on ice. Erskine's final decision of the regular season left him with a 20–6 mark, his best in the big leagues.

At the Stadium in the Bronx, the Yankees welcomed back Jerry Coleman. Like Ted Williams, the Yankees' second baseman had served in two wars. He had flown 57 combat missions in World War II over the Solomon Islands as a Marine bomber pilot. Recalled for the Korean War, Coleman flew another 120 missions and rose to the rank of lieutenant colonel. His brush with death came on one of his last missions when engine failure brought his Corsair fighter jet to the ground. Laden with three 1,000-pound bombs that miraculously failed to detonate, Coleman was pinned inside the plane with the straps of his helmet around his neck and choking him. The quick thinking of a navy corpsman, who reached inside the cockpit and cut the straps, saved his life.

On September 20, a rookie shortstop with the Chicago Cubs hit his first major league home run, the first of 512 that Ernie Banks, another of the era's future Hall-of-Fame stars, would hit in the big leagues. The Braves in Milwaukee set the National League attendance record of 1,826,297, topping the mark of 1,807,526 established by the Dodgers in 1947. The mark was duly noted no doubt by Walter O'Malley. At the Polo Grounds on the 24th in front of more than 44,000, heavyweight champ Rocky Marciano dispatched challenger Roland LaStarza in the 11th round. Marciano would go on to become the only undefeated heavyweight champion in history.

The Brooklyn Dodgers' final victory of the regular season came on the 27th, the last day of the year, by a score of 8–2. It was win number 105 for the Brooks, topping their franchise best of 104 in 1942. They beat Robin Roberts for the sixth time this season as the Phils' ace completed 346⅔ innings of work. Billy Loes won his 14th and also contributed with the bat. The Dodgers' pitcher had a double and a two-run triple. For the most part Brooklyn had its regular lineup in place. George Shuba played right field in place of the still-injured Furillo and Rube Walker went behind the plate to give Campanella a day off. Gil Hodges had two hits to culminate one of his best years, and it was especially satisfying to the big first baseman following the terrible slump and the hitless '52 World Series. In scoring his 100th run of the year, Gil joined Snider, Campanella, Gilliam, Reese and Robinson in the century class, tying the major league record set by the 1931 New York Yankees of five players scoring more than 100 runs. Brooklyn won the pennant over the Braves by a margin of 13 games. The club also set a mark for the fewest times being shut out. It happened only once, by Al Worthington of the Giants.

There were towering figures around in those days, both in and out of baseball. Ike was the president, of course, and Winston Churchill remained on the world scene. Churchill, nearly alone in his country, saw the oncoming threat of Nazism and rallied his countrymen to stave off the unending air attacks on London. In physics Albert Einstein and Enrico Fermi were both still alive in 1953; Einstein would die in April of '55, Fermi on February 29,

1954. Medical pioneers Dr. Jonas Salk and Dr. John H. Gibbons Jr. were redefining medicine.

On the 28th of September astronomer Edwin Hubble passed away. It was he who showed that the so-called "Island Universes" were in actuality vast galaxies other than our own and the universe was expanding by a constant and considerable rate. This led to the general acceptance of the big bang theory of the origin and formation of the universe. A science writer called the 1950s, " A boom era for American science, a time of optimism and technological advance."[33] In the same month that Hubble passed away, Clair Patterson and Harrison Brown, doing research at Caltech in Pasadena, California, determined a method of defining the age of the Earth through the radioactive decay of uranium. Their answer of 4.5 billion years was accurate and led to the correct dating of the age of the universe a few years hence.

In the American League the New York Yankees won their fifth straight pennant on September 14 in an 8–5 victory over the Cleveland Indians with six hitless innings in relief by Johnny Sain. Catcher Yogi Berra drove in the winning runs with a seventh-inning two-run home run. For Sain, his record went to 14–6. The Yankees ended the season 99–52, finishing 8½ games ahead of the Indians. But Cleveland would get a measure of pay back the next season. They won the 1954 pennant by eight games over the Yankees on the strength of their four starters who collectively won 78 games while losing just 29. Of the four—Bob Lemon, Bob Feller, Early Wynn and Mike Garcia—the first three are in Cooperstown. In 1953 the Yankees had four who made it there as well: Yogi Berra, Mickey Mantle, Phil Rizzuto and Whitey Ford. There were most certainly giants in those baseball days.

It had been a good year in the Bronx. On June 9 the Bombers won their 12th in a row by defeating Detroit, 3–2. On the 18th they held a four-game lead after Allie Reynolds won his ninth of the year against the Browns and the Yankees completed a triple play. At Yankee Stadium on September 17 Whitey Ford won his 17th game—he would finish at 18–6—in front of 34,691, defeating Billy Pierce and the Chicago White Sox. Berra led the club with 27 homers and 108 RBIs. Having won the previous four World Series, the Yankees stood on the threshold of a record-breaking fifth consecutive world championship.

Casey Stengel was delighted. When the Yankee manager signed for the '49 season, he was ridiculed in the media as a clown, someone not competent enough to skipper the elite New Yorkers. But since taking over the club, Casey had not had a losing season. Ironically, the October bane of the Dodgers actually began his career decades earlier in Brooklyn. Stengel broke in as an outfielder in 1912 and stayed in the majors for 14 years, ending up with a lifetime batting average of .284. He appeared in three World Series and hit .393. But Casey came by his clown reputation honestly, such as the time in the Southern League when he climbed out of a manhole that was in the outfield to snag a fly ball. Casey loved to clown around but was almost dissuaded while still in the minors. Not everyone enjoyed his fooling.

"Being a clown wasn't safe in the minors," he recalled. "Some of them bush-league managers could hit you with a bat at fifty feet."[34] On Saturday, April 5, 1913, Ebbets Field officially opened with an exhibition game against the Yankees. In the fifth inning, Stengel hit a drive to left-center field that bounced around as Casey completed the circuit of the bases for the first home run recorded at the new ballpark. However, "The house that Stengel built" never caught on in Brooklyn.

The problem with his reputation was that he had unsuccessful stints as the manager in Brooklyn and Boston. George Weiss, however, knew what he was doing when he tapped Stengel, who was managing Oakland at the time, to pilot his Yankees. The "Old Professor" went on to win 10 pennants in 12 years and seven World Series titles at the helm in New York. His special brand of double talk, known as "Stengelese," became immensely popular with the press and the fans, and in the end, the court jester wound up the king of the castle.

At season's end *The Sporting News* selected Roy Campanella and Al Rosen of the Cleveland Indians as the most outstanding players in their respective leagues. Pitching choices were Warren Spahn and Bob Porterfield of Washington. Campy cited his not getting hurt as the biggest reason for his supreme performance in 1953. He also received his second of three Most Valuable Player awards.

The World Series was scheduled to open on September 30 at Yankee Stadium. As the Dodgers went through their final workout, Reese had a sore shoulder but would play. Furillo, while using a sponge rubber grip on the bat, was hitting the ball hard. The pundits were giving Brooklyn the edge in power and the Yanks in starting pitching. The power part made sense. The Dodgers in '53 hit more home runs than any Yankee team ever did. How the two teams viewed each other can probably be summed up in one word—respect. Each knew what the other was capable of doing, each confident in its own abilities. In those days when the Series meant a good deal financially, both these formidable ball clubs were prepared to put it all on the line for a healthy paycheck and a chance to be called champions of the world!

Ten

October

Baseball was the sport, the World Series was its stage, and in Brooklyn, the Dodgers were the team. —Dave Anderson

October is World Series time in baseball. Beginning at the onset of the twentieth century, what is called "the modern era," the Brooklyn Dodgers won nine National League pennants, the first in 1916 and the final one in 1956, just one year before the exodus to Los Angeles. They won one world's championship, in 1955, but every Series had its drama, even beyond that which is normally inherent in the fall classic. Or at least it was until baseball debased it with second-place finishers and multitudes of playoff games. Every Series the Dodgers took part in seemed to involve something beyond the mundane. There was an unassisted triple play, a near no-hitter and a perfect game. In the 1920 Series against Cleveland, Bill Wambsganss, the Indians' second baseman, pulled off the unassisted triple play on the flabbergasted Brooklyn club. The Yankees' Bill Bevens nearly executed the World Series' first no-hitter in the '47 Series, and Don Larsen in 1956 not only did that but made it a perfect game.

After losing the Series in 1916 to the Red Sox and in '20 to Cleveland, the Dodgers did not win another pennant until 1941 when the tandem of Larry MacPhail and Leo Durocher turned the perennial sixth place club into champions. This was the first of the Yankee Series that would stretch to seven between '41 and '56. There were, however, a number of memorable World Series moments that took place at the home of the Dodgers. In game three in 1941, Fred Fitzsimmons of Brooklyn faced Marius Russo of the Yanks at Ebbets Field. The Series stood at one game apiece. Russo and "Fat" Freddie went into the seventh inning locked in a scoreless duel. With one out, Gordon walked and went to second on a ground out. Russo then cracked a line drive off Fitzsimmons' left knee. The ball was hit so hard that the carom allowed Reese at short to catch it on the fly for the third out. Fitz went out with a broken kneecap. Hugh Casey hurriedly warmed up but gave up two runs in the eighth and Brooklyn lost, 2–1.

The next day brought with it the game of the famous Mickey Owen passed ball. In game four the Dodgers took a 4–3 lead into the ninth inning with their ace reliever, Hugh Casey, once again on the mound. With just one more out to get to tie the Series at two games apiece, he faced Tommy Henrich with no one on base. With the count at 3–2, Casey broke off a tremendous curveball low and inside that Henrich missed, seemingly ending the game and knotting the Series at two all.

But catcher Owen could not handle the ball and it rolled all the way to the backstop, allowing Henrich to make it safely to first. After that DiMaggio singled, Charlie Keller doubled, and the Yankees went ahead, 5–4. Two more runs scored and the final was 7–4, Yankees. The suggestion was made that Casey had thrown a spitball. Owen and Henrich held that it was a curve. "It was a good pitch," the catcher said, "maybe the best curveball Casey threw all afternoon."[1]

"I was fooled," said Henrich. "Casey threw me a heck of a pitch. It was a great curve."[2]

One of baseball's most memorable World Series moments came in the sixth game of the 1947 fall classic. After Cookie Lavagetto's double had broken up Bevens' no-hitter and won the fourth game, the Yankees took a three games-to-two lead in the Series the next day when Spec Shea twirled a four hit 2–1 victory. In game six at Yankee Stadium, Vic Lombardi started for the Dodgers against Allie Reynolds. The Yanks led, 5–4, in the top of the sixth when Brooklyn scored four times to go ahead, 8–5.

Dodgers lefty Joe Hatten had come in to pitch in the bottom of the inning, the third Brooklyn pitcher of the day. The starting left fielder was Gene Hermanski, but manager Burt Shotton hit for him in the fifth with Eddie Miksis and Miksis went to left field. But in that same inning Hermanski experienced some difficulty with the sun, so Shotton decided to send in the better defensive outfielder, Al Gionfriddo, for the sixth inning. With two on and two out, Joe DiMaggio stepped to the plate against Hatten and sent a drive deep to left-center field for what looked like a possible three-run home run that would tie the game.

"I put my head down and ran," Gionfriddo remembered. "I looked over my shoulder once and knew I was going in the right direction." He looked back again as he got close to the bullpen rail and jumped. "I turned in the air and coming down hit the fence with my butt. I caught the ball in the webbing."[3]

Red Barber's technique of watching the outfielder instead of the ball resulted in his memorable call. Said "The Ole Redhead," "Here's the pitch. Swung on. Belted. It's a long one. Deep into left-center. Back goes Gionfriddo, back, back, back, back, back, back. He makes a one-handed catch against the bullpen. Oh-ho doctor!"[4]

As memorable as the catch itself was DiMaggio's reaction. Not normally given to visible emotion, the Yankee Clipper kicked the dirt in frustration as he neared second base. The Yankees scored a run in the ninth and Brooklyn won, 8–6.

In July the Baseball Hall of Fame in Cooperstown inducted two of baseball's greats, Dizzy Dean and Al Simmons. This month the newly formed Veterans Committee selected umpires Bill Klem and Tom Connolly, Ed Barrow from the front office, and players Chief Bender, Harry Wright and Bobby Wallace. Four of the 1953 Dodgers made it to Cooperstown, but 60 years later the committee was still ignoring Gil Hodges. Bill Veeck was forced to sell his St. Louis Browns and the new owners would be granted permission to relocate to Baltimore. The mayor of the city jokingly told Los Angeles newsmen not to worry, Baltimore may move to LA in 1955.

But this was 1953. It was said by some that if the Dodgers could not win with this club, they never would. The pundits were wrong on both counts. They lost the Series in six games but won it all two years later, just barely making the cut before O'Malley packed the club in his carpet bag and left town. Although they would lose the Series, Brooklyn fans would remember fondly the Series that belonged to Carl Erskine. It began on a sour note for the little right-hander, but the tide turned in the third game.

It was sunny and warm in New York as the Series got under way at Yankee Stadium in the Bronx. Lucy Monroe sang the National Anthem and Cy Young, the winningest pitcher ever in the major leagues with 511 victories, threw out the ceremonial first pitch. The 86- year-old was a veteran of the first modern World Series in 1903. The starting pitchers were Carl Erskine for the Dodgers and Allie Reynolds for the New Yorkers. A low-scoring pitchers' duel was anticipated. The Yankees won, 9–5.

Erskine was gone in the first inning, and though Reynolds took a two-hitter into the seventh, he was knocked out when the Dodgers tied it at five. In the Yankees' first, Hank Bauer tripled to right-center, driving in the first run. Berra struck out, but Erskine walked both Mickey Mantle and Gene Woodling to fill the bases. With a one-one count on Billy Martin, the pesky second baseman who hit .257 during the regular season slashed one into the gap in left-center, scoring three and getting Martin to third. Erskine retired

Rizzuto for the third out, but the Yanks had four and Erskine was finished for the day.

Jim Hughes pitched the next four innings, giving up a home run to Yogi Berra in the fifth, before being pinch-hit for in the sixth. Gilliam homered in the fifth and Brooklyn scored three in the sixth to rout Reynolds. To add to the Dodger woes, Roy Campanella was hit on the hand by a Reynolds fastball in the second. It was revealed after the game that Roy might have a small fracture in the little finger knuckle, but the catcher refused to have an X-ray taken and was determined to play in game two.

The three Dodger runs came on home runs by Gil Hodges and a two-run round-tripper by pinch-hitter George Shuba. Brooklyn tied it in the next frame off Johnny Sain when Furillo's line single drove in a run. Joe Collins' home run off Labine gave the Yankees the lead, and they scored three more off Ben Wade in the eighth. The time of the game was three hours and ten minutes. The gross receipts came to $465,267. Arthur Daley in the *Times* summed up the fatal first inning with a prize fight analogy: "As the bell sounded ... the Yankees bounded across the ring and fetched the Dodgers a clout. The savage assault floored them for a count of four."[5]

The next day, another beautiful early fall day in the city, the scheduled pitchers were usually referred to in the press as "crafty lefties." Both Preacher Roe and Eddie Lopat were veterans with the reputations of "painting the corners," making it tough on hitters to get solid wood on the ball. Both pitchers had the same approach—to throw off the hitter's timing—and in their careers they succeeded admirably. The Yankees got on the board with a run in the first, but the Dodgers came back with two in the fourth on three hits, highlighted by a Billy Cox double to drive in both runs. New York tied it in the seventh and scored two in the bottom of the eighth. The tying run was a homer by Billy Martin and the game-winner came on a two-run shot by Mickey Mantle. The Dodgers came home limping.

The World Series was a television event, though not the only one. Sixty-eight percent of all the TV sets in American had been tuned to the *I Love Lucy* show when in January Lucille Ball—as Lucy Ricardo—gave birth to Ricky Ricardo, Jr.—in life, Desi Arnez, Jr., the couple's first born. In the coming November RCA would air the first commercial program in color, *The Colgate Comedy Hour*, with Donald O'Connor, by special permission of the FCC. *Dragnet*, *Your Show of Shows*, and *Your Hit Parade* were attracting massive audiences in 1953. Television's great pioneer, Milton Berle, had drawn 94.7 percent of the television audience when he made his debut on the *Texaco Star Theater* in 1948. Ratings began to slip, however, by this year, and Texaco pulled the plug on its sponsorship. Berle signed with Buick and his *Buick-Berle Show* debuted in the fall. *The Red Skelton Show* premiered and would become the longest-running comedy show to appear on TV—it lasted 18 years.

As Brooklyn prepared for game three at Ebbets Field, the *Brooklyn Eagle* rallied the troops with the headline, "Egad, Men! Wake Up!"[6] It was a Friday afternoon and another beautiful day in Brooklyn. In the crowd of 35,270 was Governor Thomas E. Dewey, along with General Douglas MacArthur and Adlai Stevenson. The Dodgers set a record for Series receipts at Ebbets Field with a net total of $209,382.68. They brought out another veteran of the 1903 World Series to throw out the first ball. Fred Clarke managed and played left field for the Pirates in that Series.

Carl Erskine of Anderson, Indiana, pitched in Brooklyn from 1948 until 1957 and to this day he signs his correspondence "Oisk." In those 10 seasons he won 118 games and lost 71, a winning percentage of .625. He pitched two no-hit games and set a World Series strikeout record. There was no Cy Young award in 1953, but had there been Carl would certainly have been in the running. His 20–6 record gave him a league-leading percentage of .769. Close behind in winning percentage was the Braves' Warren Spahn with a record of 23–7. Erskine called the fact that he didn't win more than 20 a big disappointment since he had several more starts but was used in a limited role while gearing up for the World Series. After the '57 season, Erskine went west, packed in one of owner Walter O'Malley's carpet bags, but won only four games while losing seven in California. But that doesn't count. Carl Erskine never belonged in Los Angeles. He was Brooklyn, through and through.

Erskine recalled with great fondness the day he arrived in Brooklyn, from Fort Worth, Texas, where he had won 15 games by July, thus prompting the promotion to the Dodgers. Upon entering the confines of the old ballpark, he was recognized by a leather-lunged fan who announced in typical Brooklynese, "Hey, look, it's Oiskin from Fort Werth!"[7] From then on the gentleman from Indiana was Cal "Oiskin," and he was proud of it, almost as proud of the sobriquet as the fans who gave it were of him.

Although born in that Midwestern city on December 13, 1926, one glance at his name, Erskine, and you knew that he was born to play ball, as Brooklyn broadcaster Red Barber used to say, "On the banks of the Gowanus."

It was that spring while playing with the Fort Worth Cats that the young pitcher was given a psychological boost he deeply appreciated and never forgot. After throwing three solid innings against the parent club, he was sought out by none other than Dodgers second baseman Jackie Robinson, who told the

Carl Erskine is pictured following his record-breaking performance in game three of the 1953 World Series (Carl Erskine Collection).

kid, " Young man, I just want to tell you something. You won't be here very long. You're going to be with us before you know it."[8]

Erskine's money pitch was a devastating overhand curveball that wound up in the dirt and had batters swinging over it. In the third game of the '51 playoffs against the Giants it has been written countless times how coach Clyde Sukeforth informed manager Charlie Dressen that "Erskine bounced his curveball," prompting Dressen to bring Ralph Branca into the game to pitch to Bobby Thomson and give up the ill-fated home run. Erskine, however, suggested that another reason may have been even more paramount in the decision.[9]

Catcher Roy Campanella had been injured and was not playing that day. With the slow-footed Rube Walker behind the plate and the 75 or so feet between home plate and the stands at the Polo Grounds, Erskine thought that perhaps Dressen's decision was motivated by the fear that Carl's overhand curve may wind up in the dirt and get past Walker, a good catcher but not as adept as Campy was in hanging on to the tricky pitch. Campanella, whom Erskine calls the best catcher he ever knew, always told his pitcher not to worry about his dirt pitch getting by him. "You bury it," Campy would say, "and I'll catch it!"[10]

Erskine was taught the pitch by his dad when he was just a boy. The youngest of three sons, Carl, in trying to keep up with his brothers, threw straight overhand in an effort to get as much speed on the ball as possible. Matt Erskine showed him how to throw a curve by following instructions in a book. Carl laughs at the recollection of his dad standing in the living room, accidently releasing the ball from his grip and the sound of the glass in the china closet shattering. A costly lesson for Mrs. Erskine but one that gave Carl a career.

Erskine pitched for Anderson High School and played basketball at "The Wigwam," the name given to the school gymnasium. After graduation in 1945, Carl was drafted into the navy. Scouted by Stanley Feezle, the Indianapolis sporting goods dealer who operated as a part-time scout and also signed Gil Hodges, Erskine signed a contract with Branch Rickey at the Kenmore Hotel in Boston for a $3,500 bonus, not a bad sum in 1945. There was, however, a problem with the contract that was to prove beneficial to Erskine. Baseball commissioner A. B. "Happy" Chandler ruled that the Dodgers had broken a rule in signing Carl because he was still in the military and he was declared a free agent. Erskine received better offers but wanted to play with Brooklyn. He agreed to re-sign with the Dodgers and received another bonus, this one for $5,000.

Erskine played at Danville, Illinois, in 1947, a Class B Dodgers affiliate, where he went 19–9 in 233 innings. His ERA was 2.34 and he struck out 191. The next year he moved up to Fort Worth in the AA Texas League. It was July, the club was in Tulsa, and Carl had just won his 15th game. Burt Shotton, troubleshooting for the Dodgers, approached Erskine in the lobby of the Wells Hotel. He said the words that every minor leaguer waits to hear. "Well, son," he said, "I've just spent 45 minutes on the telephone convincing Branch Rickey that you're ready and he said OK. So you're going to leave here and join the Dodgers in Pittsburgh."[11]

The next morning upon leaving the Schenley Hotel for Forbes Field, he asked Billy Cox how to get there. "Get a cab," the third baseman told him. The rookie hailed a cab, and when he told the driver his destination, the cabbie said, "Your buddies are playing a trick on you. Forbes Field is around the corner, only a half a block away."[12] Welcome to the big leagues. When he reached Brooklyn, Erskine got a room at the YMCA on Hanson Place in the Boerum Hill section. His room had a small desk and a cot and the pay phone in the hall cost a nickel to make a local call. He took the short subway ride to Ebbets Field. After a while Carl bought a car, a 1948 two-door Pontiac, and he practiced by driving up and down Ocean Avenue.

On that first day in Pittsburgh he was brought in to relieve Hugh Casey. The Dodgers trailed when he entered the game but rallied to win it, giving Carl his first victory. He won six games that half-season but sustained an arm injury that could have ended his career and would plague him for the rest of his time in the major leagues.

After two wins in relief appearances, Erskine made his first major league start in a game against the Cubs on a rainy Thursday at Ebbets Field. In the seventh inning while pitching to Bill Nicholson, Erskine felt a sharp pain in his shoulder but finished the game for his third win. Reluctant to say anything about it, he started the next time against the Phils, but after five innings could barely lift his arm. He told manager Burt Shotton, who in complying with the prevailing attitude of the era said, "Why, son, you're pitching a shutout. Now you go right ahead out there."[13] Erskine beat the Phillies, 2–1, and won his next outing. Never in the next 10 years did he pitch without pain.

"Rookies were not expected to say much," Erskine recalls, "not if you wanted to stay. The Dodgers had 200 pitchers in their organization. You had a one-year contract and if you didn't produce, you were gone and someone else was brought up."[14] Erskine was 6–3 that season with three complete games. He estimates that he threw in the low 90s with a very live fastball, adding, "Oh, my arm hurt so bad."[15] He cannot say why it happened but the young hurler had thrown some 560 innings without a break. He went from spring training in 1947 to a full season at Danville, Illinois, to winter ball in the Caribbean, to spring training again in '48, followed by a half-season at Fort Worth and finally to the majors. "There was no break," he said. "I don't know, maybe that had something to do with it."[16]

He kept the injury from the front office. He took cortisone shots once a month. Only Duke Snider knew the extent of Erskine's pain. "Duke was my roommate for 10 years," Carl said. "We were as close as brothers. He was the only guy who knew my arm trouble. In those days it was the old macho way; no crying, no disabled list. The clubs had no investments to protect."[17]

Carl was 8–1 in the pennant-winning year of 1949. He won 16 games in '51 and in '52 went 14–6 with an ERA of 2.70. But it was on June 19 in an afternoon game at Ebbets Field against the Cubs that Oisk accomplished a pitcher's ultimate achievement—the no-hit game. It was an overcast day, and with an early lead Erskine was rushing to get the required five innings in so it would be an official game. In his haste he walked Cubs pitcher Willie Ramsdell on four pitches in the third inning. The game was held up because of rain and Carl played bridge in the clubhouse with Reese, Cox, and Snider for about 45 minutes before the game resumed. Erskine completed the 5–0 victory without giving up a hit and no other Cubbie reached base.

In the World Series that year he started the second game against the Yankees and lost it but came back in game five and got caught up in one of those sets of circumstances that sometimes develops in the oddest and most unexpected ways.

It was the *fifth* game of the Series on the *fifth* day of October and it was Carl and Betty Erskine's *fifth* wedding anniversary. Brooklyn jumped out to a 4–0 lead, but then in the *fifth* inning the Yankees scored *five* runs. Manager Dressen strolled to the mound. In an unusual bit of banter he asked Carl about his anniversary, asked if he and his wife planned to celebrate that night. Then he said, "See if you can get the side out before it gets dark."[18] He left Erskine in the game. The Dodgers tied the score in the seventh and won it in the 11th on a Duke Snider RBI. Carl had registered 19 consecutive outs from the time Dressen left him in the game in the fifth. Incidentally, as Erskine's last pitch struck out Yogi Berra, Vin Scully noted that the clock in the outfield at Yankee Stadium read 5:05 p.m.

The Erskines have four children—Danny, Gary, Susan and Jimmy—five grandchildren and seven great-grandchildren. During the Brooklyn years the family lived in the Bay Ridge section along with other Dodger families, and Carl always spoke highly of his neighbors. The Erskines lived on Lafayette Walk at 94th Street ,between Third and Fourth avenues, renting the home of a lady named Grace Coglin. Grace would go to visit her sister in Saratoga and Carl and Betty had the house for as long as the season lasted. The Reeses, the Sniders, the Rube Walkers and Preacher and Mozee Roe all lived near each other. They would carpool to Ebbets Field.

Dr. Morris Steiner, who lived on East Nineteenth Street, was the pediatrician who cared for the children. Joe Bossi was their butcher, and the guys all went to Cosmos for haircuts. Erskine recalled Abe Meyerson as the local grocer who would deliver two bags of groceries to the door every time Carl pitched, win or lose. Over Erskine's protests he would say definitively, "You guys shouldn't have to pay for anything. We love you guys here in Brooklyn."[19]

And the Erskines loved the people. They would spend hours over an Italian meal at the home of butcher Joe Rossi. After he retired, whenever Carl was in New York he would order 10 pounds of veal cutlets from Joe and the family would eat dinner in Indiana just as they had in Brooklyn.

A most poignant memory for the Brooklyn pitcher is of his friend and catcher Roy Campanella. In the winter prior to the 1959 season, Campanella had been injured in an automobile accident that left him paralyzed from the neck down. Carl went to LA with the Dodgers but in '58 knew that his career was reaching a climax. When he visited Campy in the hospital early in the season, he was deeply moved by what he witnessed. Always upbeat, the catcher never lost his unbounded enthusiasm and great spirit. Roy told him he would be watching the game the next night when Carl was due to pitch against the Phillies. He took the mound thinking of his friend and registered a 2–1 victory, the last complete game Erskine would ever throw in the majors. He announced his retirement from baseball on June 15, 1959. His last game was against Pittsburgh. Figuring that it was time to leave, Carl had second thoughts after striking out Bill Virdon, but then "a few bloop hits ensued and Dick Stuart took me deep."[20] As Alston came out to the mound to take the ball, Carl said, "'Walt, this is the last time you'll have to come to the mound for me.' I was done. Officially done."[21]

The following year Carl was offered employment by a shirt company to direct a group of athletes selling sportswear. At this time Betty Erskine gave birth to the couple's fourth child, Jimmy, who was born with Down Syndrome. When the parents found out about the baby's condition, Betty said, "I have had this child for nine months and I am taking him home with me."[22] The New York job was canceled and the Erskines went home to Anderson, Indiana. Carl started an insurance business and coached the Anderson University baseball program for 12 years, winning four championships. He also served as president and director of the Star Financial Bank until 1993. He would in time write several books as well, three of them relating *Tales from the Dodgers Dugout.* In a fourth, *What I Learned from Jackie Robinson,* the pitcher reflects upon his years as a teammate to Jack and the profound influence his friend had upon him.

Jimmy grew and flourished. He got a job setting tables at Applebee's in Anderson. He traveled with his dad to places like Vero Beach, Florida, for the Dodgers' spring training. The pixie-like expression of Carl lights up when he speaks of his youngest child. His eyes glimmer when he says of Jimmy, "He got himself in a golf tournament and you know what? The little bugger finished in third place."[23] Today Jimmy actively participates in the Special Olympics. Carl and Betty have worked in support of funding the Special Olympics over the years and Carl wrote a book, *The Parallel*, in which he relates Jimmy's struggles to those of his teammate, Jackie Robinson, as both faced bigotry and the insensitivity of others. The proceeds from the book go to the Special Olympics.

Erskine is 88 years old, and it was only yesterday that he pitched at that hallowed old ballpark in Brooklyn. Carl grew up in Anderson and returned to his hometown with his family to live out a busy yet tranquil retirement from the game. But *Cal Oiskin* lived the better part of 10 years in Brooklyn, years he will never forget. And the good folks of that borough will certainly never forget Oisk.

Carl Erskine warmed up for his second Series start. The greatest of all Dodgers teams had their backs against the wall and the ball belonged to their only 20-game winner. There were 35,270 fans jammed into Ebbets Field that afternoon. Ticket prices had struck an all-time high at $10 for a box seat and $7 for reserved seats in the grandstand. The bleacher seats cost two bucks. As he completed his warm-ups, Erskine may have thought of the humiliating one-inning stint in the opener or the fact that his ball club could not go down 3–0. One thing he was not thinking about was Howard Ehmke.

Ehmke pitched in the major leagues for 15 years and posted a distinctly mediocre won-lost record of 166–165. His best season was 1923 with the Red Sox when he won 20 games and lost 17. In 1929 his career was very near complete when he got to the World Series with Connie Mack's Philadelphia Athletics. He was 7–2 that year and pitched only 54⅔ innings. Prior to the Series Mack recalled telling Ehmke, "Howard, the time has come for us to part."

"Mr. Mack," said Ehmke, "I have always wanted to pitch in a World Series." He lifted his right arm. "There is one great game left in this old arm."

"All right, Howard," said Mack. "You are my opening pitcher for the World Series."[24]

Mack kept his plan a secret. He considered the element of surprise to be paramount if Ehmke was to be successful. Joe McCarthy, the Cubs' manager, later revealed his own concern when he said he was not afraid of the Athletics' Grove and Earnshaw. "We can hit speed," he said. "But they've got one guy over there that I am afraid of. His name is Howard Ehmke."[25] It was the slow "junk" that McCarthy feared would stymie his Cub hitters.

He was right. Ehmke dazzled the Cubs' hitters with his array of soft stuff. Among his strikeouts that afternoon were Rogers Hornsby, Hack Wilson,

In his favorite photograph, "Oisk" gets a victory kiss from wife Betty after striking out 14 Yankees in game three of the World Series (Carl Erskine Collection).

Gabby Hartnett and Kiki Cuyler until he reached 13 to establish the World Series strikeout record. It is unlikely that Howard gave much thought to Erskine either as he and Mrs. Ehmke were driving through the Pennsylvania countryside near Philadelphia with a casual interest in the game as it played on the car radio.

After his dismal performance and with Brooklyn being behind two games to nothing, Oisk was determined. "I told Duke," he said, "I gotta pitch like there's no tomorrow."[26]

Erskine struck out McDougald and Collins to open the game and then got Mantle and Rizzuto in the second. It was the first of four strikeouts in the game for the Yanks' center fielder. In the Yankees' third, Oisk got Raschi looking and then struck out Collins for the second time. Like the Mick, Collins would also register four whiffs on the afternoon. He got Mantle again in the fourth, but in the fifth the Yankees scored a run. There were three New York singles, though Erskine got Collins for the third time.

Brooklyn tied it in the bottom of the inning when Jackie Robinson doubled to right and went to third when Raschi balked. Billy Cox dropped down a perfect squeeze bunt and Jackie scored the Dodgers' first run. Erskine got Mantle and Woodling and his strikeout total after six innings stood at 10. It was about this time that Howard Ehmke began to take an interest. He said to his wife, "Let's park and listen to the rest of this."[27]

It was in the top of the ninth that Erskine tied Ehmke's record when he dispatched pinch-hitter Don Bollweg for his 13th strikeout. "Bolling was a low ball hitter," Erskine recalled. "I struck him out on three high fastballs."[28] But after the Dodgers scored a go-ahead run in the sixth when Jackie Robinson's single drove home Duke Snider, the Yanks came back in the eighth to make it a 2–2 game. Erskine gave up a base hit to Hank Bauer, hit Berra with a pitch, and then yielded an RBI single to Gene Woodling.

But in the bottom of the eighth, Raschi hung one inside to Roy Campanella, and he drove it into the left field seats for the game-winner. The record-breaking strikeout was Johnny Mize for the second out in the ninth while pinch-hitting for Raschi. Carl got two quick strikes on "The Big Cat," then he fouled one off before striking out on a wicked overhand curve. Brooklyn won the game, 3–2.

It had not been easy. Even after Mize struck out, Irv Noren walked, and with Collins up, Erskine knew that Collins was capable of clearing that short porch in right field. But Joe, in trying to avoid a fifth strikeout, tapped back to the box.

Ehmke said nothing as the game and his record ended. As related by Red Smith, "The record he had held for a quarter of a century was gone. He stepped on the starter. Nothing happened. The radio had drained his battery."[29]

Brooklyn's Oisk had set a World Series record. He was elated but tired. "I was more exhausted than after any other game I'd pitched," he said. "Strikeouts take so many more pitches out of you and I was beat after that game ended."[30]

That Friday evening, October 3, Edward R. Murrow premiered his new television show, *Person to Person*. Murrow would visit the homes of celebrities while sitting cross-legged in a chair in the TV studio, the ever-present cigarette between his fingers. On this inaugural show, his guest was Dodgers catcher Roy Campanella. The day before Murrow had suggested to Campy that he hit a World Series home run that day to win the game, giving them a good topic of conversation. Campanella, of course, obliged.

Eisenhower had promised the next Supreme Court appointment to Governor Earl Warren of California, not realizing the next call would be for a chief justice. Following the death of Justice Fred Vinson in September, Ike was true to his word. In early December the first oral arguments were heard in the landmark case of *Brown v. Board of Education of Topeka, Kansas*. The Nobel Committee announced the prize for literature would go to Winston Churchill for his monumental six-volume study, *History of the Second World War*. The greatest hoax of the twentieth century was exposed in November. Piltdown Man, believed to be an early modern human assigned to the genus *Eoanthropus* and whose skull fragments were discovered at Piltdown in Sussex, England, in 1912, was proved to be fraudulent. The so-called "missing link," proving that man evolved from the apes, was a fake. A 27-year-old named Hugh Hefner purchased a nude photo of a young actress who called herself Marilyn Monroe for the first issue of a new magazine he planned to call *Stag Party*. When the publishers of a hunting magazine with the name *Stag* threatened legal action, Hefner renamed his publication *Playboy*. The premier issue hit the stands in December.

Brooklyn tied the series at two games apiece with a 7–3 victory in game four. Once again the weatherman cooperated and the 36,775 fans enjoyed a beautiful day, the fourth great weather day in a row in New York. The Dodgers were slight game favorites at 6–5 odds, with the Yanks still favored to win the Series. In keeping with the theme of the 50th anniversary of the World Series, Tommy Leach, third baseman for the 1903 Pirates, threw out the first ball. The opposing pitchers were two kids from Queens—Billy Loes for Brooklyn and Whitey Ford for the Yanks.

The Dodgers jumped on the lefty with three runs in the first inning. Jim Gilliam hit a fly ball along the right field foul line that Hank Bauer seemed to have lost in the sun. As he crossed the foul line, the ball dropped two or three feet behind him in fair territory, then bounced sharply to the right and into the stands for a ground-rule double. Reese hit a grounder to the right side, moving Gilliam to third, who scored on a Jackie Robinson single to center. Hodges forced Robinson at second, but Ford uncorked a wild pitch with Campanella batting for ball three. Stengel then ordered his pitcher to throw the fourth ball, putting Campy on first. Duke Snider hit one off the screen in right to score two and the Dodgers had a three-run lead after one. Gil McDougald and Duke Snider hit home runs and Jim Gilliam had three two-base hits. Loes went eight innings and got the win. The score was 7–3. The Series was tied at two games apiece.

But Brooklyn would be unable to do anything more. On a sunny Sunday the Yankees took game five by an 11–7 margin. New York broke it open with five runs in the third inning, knocking out Johnny Podres. John left with the bases loaded, and Russ Meyer came in to face Mickey Mantle. He threw one pitch and the center fielder deposited it in the upper deck in left field for a grand slam. There were four Yankee homers in all. In the eighth, trailing, 10–2, Brooklyn scored four times. But it was too little too late for the Dodgers.

Back at Yankee Stadium, there were 62,370 in the seats as the Yankees completed the Series with a 4–3 win over Brooklyn. It wasn't a walk in the park, however, for Casey's men. It took a ninth-inning single by an unexpected hero, Billy Martin, to drive home the winning run. Reynolds got credit for the win with two innings of relief. Martin led everybody with his 12 hits in 24 at-bats for a .500 average. The New York Yankees under Casey Stengel had won five consecutive World Series, a feat not accomplished before or since in the major leagues.

Manager Charlie Dressen had accomplished three first-place finishes and two pennants in his three years in Brooklyn, but nine days after the Series ended, Dressen was gone as the Dodgers' manager. On October 14 at 11 a.m. the Dodgers called a press conference. The writers assumed it was to announce the signing of Dressen, but Walter O'Malley made the startling declaration that the Dodgers would have a new manager in 1954. He explained that the ball club would not deviate from its policy of tending one-year contracts only and apparently Dressen had asked for a multi-year deal.

Charlie's wife had penned a letter to O'Malley making the case for a three-year deal. Dressen had no doubt been riled earlier in the year when Eddie Stanky with the Cardinals and Leo Durocher of the Giants had been given multi-year contracts by their respective clubs despite finishing fourth and fifth in the standings. Of the mail received at the Dodgers' offices, one fan expressed his misgivings in typical Brooklyn fashion: "When that bum (Dressen) blew the pennant in '51 you hired him again. All of us knew better. Then, when he wins twice, you fire him. You and my wife keep me puzzled."[31]

The speculation as to the new manager began immediately, and a "virtual avalanche" of fan mail in favor of Pee Wee Reese inundated the Dodgers' front office. Apparently the Dodgers did not want him. Pee Wee said he wasn't sure if he wanted it but told writer Roger Kahn that he would not have taken it anyway after the way it was offered. "Bavasi came to me," Reese said. "I don't remember his exact words. But the sense was, 'Pee Wee, you don't want to manage this club, do you?' I knew I didn't want to manage after a proposal like that."[32]

In December the Dodgers announced the signing of Walter Alston as the new manager. Alston was a company man, a manager in the Dodgers' minor league system, unknown to the fans and scarcely recognizable to most of the writers. Alston would sign 23 one-year contracts with the Dodgers, in

Brooklyn and Los Angeles, and go on to the Baseball Hall of Fame. On October 28 O'Malley made another move. This one could not be blamed on team policy or long-term contracts. This was O'Malley, pure and simple.

"The Old Redhead," "The Verse of Brooklyn," Walter Lanier Barber, was unceremoniously dumped by the "Big Oom," the name that Harold Parrott used for the boss. Barber was more than a broadcaster to Brooklyn. His announcing brought fans into the ballpark; the Old Redhead put fannies in the seats. Writer Scott Simon referred to Barber's broadcasts as "the magnolia-scented voice of Red Barber coming in over the radio from Ebbets Field, softly diffusing the night, giving the feel of a front porch."[33] Barber was Brooklyn in those years.

Barber had balked following the 1952 World Series at having been paid only $200 per game without knowing what the figure would be beforehand and not having the opportunity to negotiate a reasonable fee. In '53 he wanted the right to negotiate in advance with Gillette, the Series sponsor. Gillette refused, determined to pay whatever they felt like. Take it or leave it. Barber chose to leave it. Red filled O'Malley in on the situation. Rather than putting his weight behind him, O'Malley told the broadcaster that it was his problem. O'Malley's inaction forced Barber out and he joined the Yankees the next season. O'Malley knew he had the young Vin Scully waiting in the wings, which made it a whole lot easier. "It's like marbles in a pipe," O'Malley said. "You push the cheaper marble in one end, and the expensive marble falls out the other end, and that's how you make money."[34] Barber was making $60,000; Scully was paid $18,000.

It is not too difficult to understand Barber's attitude. He said, "I was very happy in my work, very happy in Brooklyn. That's why I left. When I found I could not be happy broadcasting in Brooklyn under Walter O'Malley, the happiness that I had at Ebbets Field was too precious to me to dilute and vitiate, so I left."[35] In 1978 Red was the recipient of the Ford C. Frick Award and installed into the broadcasters' wing of the Baseball Hall of Fame.

Before joining a barnstorming team in the postseason, Carl Erskine went home in Anderson, Indiana, where he was feted to a "deafening tribute by 5,000 Anderson admirers" on October 9.[36] Before departing the scene, Chuck Dressen was quoted as saying that Jackie Robinson was the "best all-around player in the three years I managed the Dodgers.... He'd win games by doing little things that nobody ever realized."[37] That December young Jimmy Boyd recorded a new Christmas favorite, "I Saw Mommy Kissing Santa Claus," that would become a perennial and was still going strong more than 60 years later. On December 8, President Eisenhower gave his famous "Atoms for Peace" speech to the General Assembly of the United Nations.

The baseball rules committee made two significant changes. One, involving the balk, now allowed the offensive team to have the option of taking the play that ensued after the pitch was delivered. The second restored the sacrifice fly rule. Duke Snider, for example, had 11 sacrifice flies in 1953, which would have added six points to his batting average, making it .342. The Dodgers' team average would have benefitted by three points, to .288. On November 29, French paratroopers recaptured Dien Bien Phu, with Eisenhower still refusing to get involved in a land war in Asia.

The question of whether the '53 Dodgers were the best National League club ever is, of course, a subjective one to a point. The statistics don't lie but are not always definitive. Consider four other teams spanning 92 years for comparison.

The Chicago Cubs of 1906 played in the dead ball era and were no comparison to the Dodgers when it came to power production. The Cubs dominated the league in pitching, their top four starters winning 83 games, led by Mordecai Brown with a record of 26–6, as opposed to the Dodgers' 60. However, the pitching game was preeminent where the power was a dominating factor in the fifties. The Cubs' home run leader was Frank Schulte with seven, good for fourth in the league; the league leader hit 12. Both Campanella and Snider hit more than 40. Pitching in the dead ball era and power in the fifties made the games exceedingly different.

In an era where high averages rather than home runs were the primary ingredient, the Cubs had three .300 hitters in the regular lineup, the Dodgers five. Both clubs were exceptional defensively. The Dodgers should get an edge with perhaps the best infield in baseball in 1953, and with Snider and Furillo, they get the nod over the Cubs in the outfield. The Cubs had an incredible record of 116–36; the Dodgers won 105. The Cubs' team batting average of .266 was 19 points below the Brooklyn club.

The St. Louis Cardinals in 1942 won 106 games but trailed the Dodgers in all major offensive categories. With 680 RBIs as a team total, no one drove in more than 100. The leader was Enos Slaughter with 98. They hit only 60 home runs, again with Slaughter leading the way with 13, and had a team average of .268, with only Enos and Musial hitting higher than .300.

Consider the 1976 Cincinnati Reds, "The Big Red Machine." Cincy registered 802 runs as a team to the Dodgers' 887 and had 141 home runs. Brooklyn hit 208. The Reds' home run leaders hit 29, 27, and 19. Brooklyn's big three clocked 42, 41, and 31. George Foster led the Reds in home runs and RBIs, yet was fourth behind the Dodgers' big three in both power departments. The Reds matched the Dodgers with five .300 hitters and were only five points behind in team average at .280.

The Dodgers' weakest link was their starting pitching, the top four winning a total of 60 games. The Cardinals' top four won 69, but the Reds came in with 53 victories. Dodger pitching was not far off the mark, but they were so dominant in their offense and particularly the power the regular lineup generated that it would be their strongest point and bode well for calling the Brooklyn Dodgers of 1953 the best National League team ever. The greatest challenge might have come from the 1998 Atlanta Braves, who won 106 games. They hit more homers than Brooklyn with 215, but they drove in fewer (794) and had fewer .300 hitters (three). Their top four starters won 72 games.

Both the Reds of '76 and the '98 Braves played a schedule of 162 games, thus inflating the seasonal marks somewhat by the extra eight games. The '53 Dodgers, the '06 Cubs and the 1942 Cardinals played 154 games. Reiterating the subjectivity of such a discussion, it is worth repeating the opinion of Donald Honig. "One might say, arguably, the 1953 Dodgers were the strongest team in National League history."[38] With this I concur.

ELEVEN

Success and the
Road to Perdition

Preliminary diagnosis indicates that the cause of death was an acute case of greed.—Dick Young, *New York Daily News*

Every year was *next year* in Brooklyn until it finally came. The 1955 season opened with a bang. The Dodgers ripped off 10 straight wins, lost two of three to the Giants, and then strung another 11 victories together. With the 10th win they defeated the Phillies and Robin Roberts, 14–4, on April 21 and set a modern National League record for most consecutive wins at the start of the season. There was an oddity attached to the 22–2 opening record. Both losses were suffered by Johnny Podres, odd because the young left-hander would even that up with two World Series victories in October.

Of course, the Giants and Dodgers were still the Giants and Dodgers, and on April 23 they made sure there would be no lack of excitement for the new season. After getting hit with their first loss of the season the day before, Carl Erskine and Sal Maglie hooked up in a duel that Brooklyn iced with two in the eighth to break a 1–1 tie. They won, 3–1, for Erskine's third win against no losses. Both pitchers went the distance. The fireworks began in the second inning when the Barber cut loose with a fastball that passed behind Jackie Robinson's head. As the headhunting continued, Robinson squared off to bunt and then took the pitch, a sure sign to the pitcher under the circumstances. Sure enough, on the next pitch Jackie pushed a bunt toward first base. As the ball was fielded by first baseman Whitey Lockman, Robinson barreled down the line intent upon slamming into Maglie when the pitcher came over to cover the bag.

Only Sal never left the mound. It was the second baseman, Davy Williams, who covered the bag and was creamed by the charging Robinson.

Both teams swarmed the field with Alvin Dark charging Robinson, but the umpires were able to prevent any further physical contact between the players. The Giants weren't finished, however. In the fifth inning, Dark, their captain and shortstop, doubled to left, and though he had no chance for third, he continued anyway. When he arrived Robinson had the ball and tagged him hard on the side of the head, dropping the ball. Dark had come into third with a body block. Davy Williams was injured and out of the game, and afterwards Dark passed the word to Robinson through reporters that it was over.

After splitting a doubleheader with Cincinnati on the 15th of May, Brooklyn's record was 25–5. After a 2–1 loss to Gene Conley and the Braves, Carl Erskine still led National League hurlers with a 1.44 ERA. On June 8 Don Newcombe defeated the Reds, 3–1, for his 10th win in ten decisions so far this season. The big guy was waving a big stick as well. His triple against the Pirates drove home two on May 26 and he stole home on a potential suicide squeeze on a pitch that was too wide for the hitter to reach. In late June his three hits against Milwaukee put his average at .451. On June 17, as Don registered his 11th win against only one loss, another beanball incident surfaced, this time not involving the Giants.

It was in St. Louis and Cardinals right-hander Brooks Lawrence brushed Carl Furillo in the fourth inning. Furillo stomped towards the mound, bat in hand, while both benches cleared. But that was the extent of it. Furillo said later that Lawrence "said, 'Come out and fight,' so I did."[1]

On the first of June the Dodgers set a club record by banging out six home runs against the Braves at Ebbets Field; three came off the bat of Duke Snider. The Dodgers won, 11–8, and it was Erskine's seventh win. The next day they piled it on again, winning, 13–2, again against Milwaukee. Brooklyn scored 10 runs in the eighth. Reese walked, Snider and Campanella singled to score the first run. Sandy Amoros doubled for two more, and Hodges and Robinson walked to load the bases. Furillo drove in two with a base hit, Loes bunted, and Gilliam's triple sent two more in. Reese knocked him in with a single, followed by three more hits by Snider, Campanella and Amoros.

The next day the Cardinals used eight pitchers to try to stop the Dodgers' attack, but Brooklyn won, 12–5; Labine won his third in relief. The Dodgers ended the month of June with a record of 20–8. Newcombe was 13–1, Duke Snider had 12 home runs, 32 RBIs and a .327 batting average. Brooklyn was 52–19 and held a 13-game lead over the Braves.

In the nightcap of a July 6 doubleheader, Sandy Koufax, the bonus rookie from Brooklyn's Lafayette High School, received his first start. He lasted 4⅔ innings, giving up three hits and one earned run, but he walked six and threw

105 pitches against Pittsburgh. Two days later the Brooks beat Maglie, 12–8, after overcoming a 6–0 deficit. The winning pitcher was Labine in relief. The All-Star game was played on the 12th at Milwaukee County Stadium. In the last of the 12th inning Stan Musial hit a home run to break a 5–5 tie and win the game for the National League. Hodges, Snider and Newcombe played in the game. Campanella was chosen for the squad but an injury kept him from participating.

Newcombe ended July at 18–1, but a big surprise to the Dodgers' players came when they heard that Sal Maglie had been sold to the Cleveland Indians. It would have had a cataclysmic effect had they known that just about a year later Sal would be slipping into a Dodgers uniform. August began on a high note when Gil Hodges hit his 11th career grand slam on the third against the Braves. Gil added a two-run shot and Don Zimmer hit two.

The announcement came that the Dodgers would play seven games in Jersey City in 1956. The reasons became obvious—it was O'Malley's nudge to the city that if he didn't get his way, they would be gone. But it has never been satisfactorily explained what reason he gave the league and how they could possibly have allowed such a pointless action to take place.

Roberts beat Newcombe to get his 20th win, while Newk fell to 18–4. On August 27 Koufax received his second start and shut out the Cincinnati Reds, 7–0, on two hits while striking out 14. The next time out Sandy tossed a second consecutive shutout, this one over Pittsburgh, and gave up five hits. The beanball game continued to be played at Ebbets Field. On the 29th Podres hit Musial and the Cards' Tom Pohalsky threw one behind Robinson's head; nothing unusual about this game. Brooklyn ended August with a 12-game lead and an 84–46 record. They led the league in batting average (.275), runs (741), and home runs (181), and their pitchers led in ERA (3.69) and strikeouts (664).

Newcombe won his 20th and Erskine notched his 100th career victory. The Dodgers clinched the National League pennant on September 8, the earliest clinching in league history, breaking the record set by the 1953 Dodgers. The question of an American League opponent had not been settled but the mindset on the ball club seemed to be spoken by Carl Furillo.

"What difference does it make who we play?" he said. "If you're gonna win, you're gonna win, that's all. I think it's about time that we won."[2]

The Series opened in Yankee Stadium on September 28. Shortstops Phil Rizzuto and Pee Wee Reese were facing each other for the 31st time since 1941. In the first two games the Dodgers were opposed by left-handers Whitey Ford and Tommy Byrne and Brooklyn lost both contests. The fireworks started in the sixth inning of game one. After hitting a triple, Billy Martin attempted to steal home. He had made some earlier comments about Campanella tagging high because he was afraid of getting spiked. On this play Campy tagged Martin so hard he sent the second baseman sprawling. Martin took a couple of steps towards the catcher but then retreated to the dugout. Yankees first baseman Joe Collins hit two home runs off Don Newcombe in the first game before 63,869 fans, and in the top of the eighth, the Yankees led by a 6–3 score.

Furillo singled, Robinson hit a grounder off McDougald's glove at third, and as Furillo advanced all the way to third, Jackie pulled into second base. On Zimmer's sacrifice fly, Furillo scored and Robinson went to third. With the count 0–1 on pinch-hitter Frank Kellert, Robinson stole home. Umpire Bill Sommers made the safe call and Yogi Berra went wild. It was the third steal of home in World Series history, but the Dodgers came up short, 6–5. In game two Loes started for Brooklyn and gave up all four Yankee runs in the fourth inning. The final score was 4–2.

It looked like the same old story as the Bums limped home. There were 34,209 at Ebbets Field on a cloudy Friday. It was Johnny Podres' 23rd birthday, and Gladys Gooding played "Happy Birthday" as John was warming up. His 9–10 record for the year gave no indication of what lay ahead for the young southpaw. Mantle homered for the Yankees, but Campanella banged out three hits, including a home run, and Brooklyn won, 8–3. Podres was feted with a birthday cake in the clubhouse, but the best gift he received came from manager Walt Alston. He said to John after the game, "If we have a seventh game, you're my pitcher!"[3]

The Dodgers overwhelmed the Yankees in the fourth game with their power. Home runs from Campanella, Hodges, and Snider paced Brooklyn to an 8–5 victory and a Series tie at two games apiece. Clem Labine got the win in relief of Erskine and Don Bessent. He came in with the bases loaded and two out in the fifth and got Collins to ground out. With 36,796 at Ebbets Field, the Duke hit two more homers, giving him four for the Series, and Brooklyn edged ahead with the 5–3 win. Roger Craig started and went six, giving up two runs and recording the victory.

On the return to Yankee Stadium for games six and seven, the Dodgers ran up against Whitey Ford and were defeated in the initial contest, 5–1. Karl Spooner was manhandled by New York and gave up five first-inning runs. As Spooner was replaced after one-third of an inning, no one realized it would be his last major league game.

The stage was set for game seven. Brooklyn advanced this far twice, losing

Remembering the Dodgers of Brooklyn: Pee Wee Reese in a pepper game at Ebbets Field (author's collection).

in 1947 and again in '52. On this day the dream was fulfilled. The Dodgers were world champions. Johnny Podres gave up eight hits but not a single run. Gil Hodges drove in both Dodgers runs with a single and a sacrifice fly. Sandy Amoros ran like hell to haul in Yogi Berra's sixth-inning fly ball down the left field line with two on and turn it into a double play. It was the Dodgers' 12th double play in the Series. Podres threw a change to Elston Howard who grounded to Pee Wee at short for the final out.

Tommy Holmes, beat writer for the *Brooklyn Eagle*, had published a book in 1953 that concluded with the '52 World Series loss. Holmes final words were, "But one of these days, brother.... One of these fine days...." That day had come![4]

It was the most exciting day in Brooklyn baseball history and the borough responded as it hadn't done since V-J Day signaled the end of World War II. There was jubilation and an unparalleled sense of triumph at long last. Dave Anderson wrote in the *New York Times* 50 years later, "All over Brooklyn, the everyday people had tears in their eyes."[5]

There were tears in their eyes again, tears of sorrow and of anguish, two years later almost to the day when the Dodgers announced they would leave Brooklyn.

On October 9, 1957, a headline in the *New York Herald Tribune* placed a lingering fear into words that carried a dreaded finality. "It's Official—Dodgers Go to Los Angeles." Under the byline of Dodgers beat writer Tommy Holmes were the words, "The Dodgers yesterday took the irrevocable step from Ebbets Field to Los Angeles." And so it was over. The fat lady had sung; the song had ended; King Kong had fallen from the Empire State Building. For the fans of Brooklyn it was the beginning of the winter of our discontent. The Dodgers had left Brooklyn. It was with melancholy and sadness and depression, but not without rancor, that the Flatbush Faithful bid their Bums adieu.

The malice and resentment was directed at one man, and though New York City parks commissioner and "czar" Robert Moses has been implicated in the abduction, it was eminently clear to the populous of the borough that the man who carried the responsibility was one Walter Francis O'Malley. O'Malley, the president of the Dodgers, has been variously described as shrewd, congenial, and conversational to the point of manifesting a bit of the blarney. An astute businessman, he was outwardly candid, friendly and charming. Physically he was a bit portly, bespectacled, and perpetually armed with a cigar tucked into a long holder.

But he was often described in other ways. Red Barber described him as "the most devious man I've ever met," and Leo Durocher called him "Whale-belly" to his face.[6] Considered to be a superlative manipulator of people and events, the "Big Om" held court with convivial afternoons over drinks and poker at the Hotel Bossert. He grew to be a presence, *the* presence among his counterparts in the ownership circles of the National League. In engineering the exodus of major league baseball from the East Coast to the West, it appears to have been a plan he had been nurturing for years, all the while "negotiating" with the city of New York to keep the Dodgers in Brooklyn.

Walter Francis O'Malley was born in the Bronx on October 9, 1903. Most biographical information says that he received an engineering degree from the University of Pennsylvania. However, in his book, *After Many a Summer*, Robert E. Murphy disputes this fact, saying that "his (O'Malley's) transcript shows that he had trouble with math courses and took none in engineering."[7] He did enter Columbia Law School in 1926. He completed his law studies with evening classes at Fordham University and earned a law degree in 1930. It was during the Depression that O'Malley developed a law practice by specializing in bankruptcy law. It was in this regard that he came in contact with George V. McLaughlin, the president of the Brooklyn Trust Company, which held the mortgage for the Brooklyn Dodgers organization.

The ball club was nearly bankrupt and deeply in arrears in its mortgage loan payments to Brooklyn Trust. McLaughlin assigned O'Malley the job of monitoring the baseball organization's legal and business affairs. Thus, in 1943, O'Malley gave up his private practice to become vice president and general counsel for the Dodgers. On August 13, 1945, O'Malley, along with Branch Rickey and John L. Smith, then vice president of Pfizer Chemical, purchased 75 percent of the team stock, equally divided among them. O'Malley was now officially a part of the historic franchise whose roots can be traced to the late nineteenth century.

Pacific Coast League cities were considered to be on the fringes of major league since the 1930s when the league began petitioning for consideration as a third major league. Los Angeles began to be mentioned specifically as a site for expansion of the major leagues in 1941 when Don Barnes, the owner of the St. Louis Browns, requested that he be allowed to relocate his franchise to the California city. He believed that he had all the bases covered, including scheduling, and claimed to have the necessary votes from the other owners.

His request was on the agenda at the major league meetings and was to be addressed at 9 a.m. on Monday, December 8, 1941. Events of the previous day made the projected Browns move a moot point; the results of the Japanese attack on Pearl Harbor made the upcoming season anything but a certainty. Immediately following the dispatching of atomic bombs on Japanese cities Hiroshima and Nagasaki in August 1945, Los Angeles was back on track as a potential major league city.

Petitions by the PCL for greater consideration by the majors led to the minor league voting in 1945 to become a third major league. They were turned down by major league owners, but some concessions were garnered relating to the amount of compensation made to Pacific Coast League team owners for players drafted by the majors out of their league.

It became necessary for baseball to act, so in 1947 commissioner A. B. "Happy" Chandler presented a proposal that would allow four West Coast cities to become a part of the two existing major leagues. The intent was to increase both the National and American leagues from eight to 10 teams each. The additions would be four PCL cities—Los Angeles, Hollywood, San Francisco and Oakland. The National League approved the resolution, but the American League turned it down, failing approval by two votes.

In the July 7, 1948, issue of *The Sporting News*, it was reported that Los Angeles County supervisor Leonard Roach led a contingent of L.A. officials on a hunt for a big league ball club. They sought the St. Louis Browns and the Chicago Cubs. Although turned down at this juncture, California, and more specifically Los Angeles, was growing closer and closer. By the time O'Malley had forced Branch Rickey out of the Dodgers' picture and taken over total control of the organization after the 1950 season, it was no longer a question of *if* L.A. would become a major league city, but *when,* and who would be the one to nail it down.

While Los Angeles was talked about matter of factly as a potential major league city, rumors strong enough to be denied by league presidents Warren Giles and Will Harridge had the St. Louis Browns and Connie Mack's Philadelphia Athletics moving to Los Angeles and San Francisco. The Nationals wanted the Reds and Phils to relocate. As a result, it became a dispute over which league would get the rights to West Coast cities first.

By the spring of 1953 talk of relocating ball clubs had become a regular fact of life among the owners. Lou Perini of the Boston Braves requested permission to move his team to Milwaukee, citing desperate financial straits as the reason. Indeed, the Braves' home attendance for 1952 was a dismal 281,000. It was Walter O'Malley who put the motion on the floor at the league meeting, and without his considerable influence, there almost assuredly would not have been a unanimous positive vote. O'Malley undoubtedly saw the Braves' move as a test case for his own plan, and when the Braves topped their previous season's attendance in the first few weeks in Milwaukee, it seemed that all systems were a go for the Dodgers' president.

The move and the succeeding one that sent the Browns to Baltimore prompted the Pacific Coast League to feel a sense of relief that the threat of expansion had passed. *The Sporting News,* however, quoted the manager of the Chicago White Sox, Paul Richards, as saying, "The sooner the American

League makes a decision to incorporate Los Angeles and San Francisco in its circuit ... the better for the league and for baseball."[8] As it turns out, 1953 was somewhat of a turning point in the long history of baseball's move to the West Coast.

According to Browns owner Bill Veeck, George Weiss professed to have a syndicate ready to buy the Browns and move them to L.A. The American League turned down Veeck's request to transfer his ball club. Veeck was not a favorite of his fellow owners, and most would have loved a chance to get "Baseball's Barnum" out of the game completely. Predictably, his request was turned down, one executive even chastising him for suggesting such an audacious move so close to the start of a new season. Two days after the denial, permission was granted to Perini to move the Braves. Veeck was forced to sell the Browns, the new owners immediately getting permission to relocate the club to Baltimore. Frank Finch, writing in *The Sporting News*, said that while talk of a third major league was now "childish prattle," in view of current attendance figures, "Los Angeles is ripe for the plucking ala Milwaukee."[9] After being forced to sell his club, it was announced that Veeck had been hired by Chicago Cubs owner Philip K. Wrigley as special advisor "to spearhead the campaign to bring major league baseball to Los Angeles." In doing so, Veeck made a report that laid the groundwork for any future West Coast move, proclaiming expansion there to be inevitable and "reporting that the demand for baseball was great in both Los Angeles and San Francisco."[10]

Meanwhile, the saga of Walter O'Malley and Robert Moses was being played out in the mid-fifties. O'Malley had been hinting at the need for a new stadium to replace aging and decrepit Ebbets Field since the late forties. He was, however, making money in Brooklyn. In 1956 the Dodgers showed a net profit of $487,000; the Braves in Milwaukee netted $362,000. The Dodgers were recording a million-plus in attendance every season from 1941 until 1957, the last season in Brooklyn, a profitable number in the era, and were raking in $800,000 in television revenue. In those 17 seasons, they were first in National League attendance nine times and in four other years finished second. Still, with the changing dynamics of the neighborhood surrounding Ebbets Field and his ball players getting old, O'Malley wondered whether the revenues would be able to be maintained. In August 1955, the Dodgers announced they would play seven "home" games in Roosevelt Stadium in Jersey City, New Jersey. It was a subtle hint if he didn't get his way, the *Daily News* reported, that with the announcement the Dodgers "were inching their way westward."[11]

Owners are businessmen, and it has been pointed out that they have the right to seek the best profits for their enterprises. There is, however, a question of whether they should give consideration to the city and the fans who have provided them with the means to the profits that in O'Malley's case have been enjoyed by ownership in Brooklyn. Bill Veeck said, "Not only doesn't the city owe the operator of the franchise anything, but the ball club, as an organization which depends in many ways on the facilities of the city is totally dependent on the good will of its citizens, has *certain responsibilities toward the city*."[12]

O'Malley recognized no such responsibilities. Even as he complained about his ballpark, annual attendance at Ebbets Field remained above one million. From 1955 to 1956 there were 179,973 more fans in the seats. For O'Malley it was simply a matter of not making *enough* money. Between 1950 and 1957 "the attendance issue was the reddest of herrings. No team in baseball was more profitable."[13] Irving Rudd, Dodgers publicity director at the time, has said, "The Brooklyn ballclub was the richest club in baseball."[14] Between 1952 and 1956 the Dodgers showed a profit of $1,860,744, more than any club in baseball. All other franchise shifts before and since were motivated by poor attendance and diminishing revenues. Only Walter O'Malley left with his pockets full.

Through it all, one of baseball's finest ball clubs had blossomed. Beginning in 1941 when they won the first pennant for the franchise in 21 years, and excepting the war years of 1943, '44 and '45, the Brooklyn club was in the vanguard of National League pennant races virtually every season. With Jackie Robinson, Branch Rickey's "Great Experiment," spearheading the charge and Pee Wee Reese in the leadership role as team captain, a team developed that would dominate the National League over the last 11 years it resided in Brooklyn. Even in losing, they would provide thrills and unforgettable scenes.

In order to keep his array of stars—Carl Erskine, Duke Snider, Don Newcombe, Roy Campanella, Carl Furillo and all the rest—in Brooklyn, it was O'Malley's claim that he needed the city to turn over to him a parcel of land at Flatbush and Atlantic avenues in downtown Brooklyn where he would then build a new stadium. The authority being cited was Title I of the Federal Housing Act of 1949, allowing the city to condemn a piece of land to be replaced by a public project or to be sold to a developer whose construction would conform to a "public purpose." Robert Moses refused to allow the building of a ballpark on the site, as he considered it not to be in accord with the stated intent of the act. The entire question of blame hinges on whether or not the Dodgers' boss was sincere in his desire to obtain this piece of property and keep his team in Brooklyn.

Some thought not. Bill Veeck has written, "They couldn't have met his demand."[15] This same thought was echoed by writer Dave Anderson. "In my opinion," he said, O'Malley "would have found some reason to oppose any option at Atlantic-Flatbush."[16] O'Malley was then offered a site at Flushing Meadows in Queens, where the Mets eventually built Shea Stadium. He refused it, saying that Dodgers fans would know it wasn't in Brooklyn. Presumably, they wouldn't notice that Los Angeles was not in Brooklyn either. O'Malley's insistence upon being given the property that he would own was a precondition for building a ballpark anywhere, be it Brooklyn, Queens or California. Peter Golenbock has pointed out that it was O'Malley's insistence the city build and give him a ballpark at the Flushing Meadows site and Moses' refusal that doomed that particular project.[17] Following the Braves' shift to Milwaukee, Veeck maintains he made an offer to O'Malley to purchase the Dodgers with the idea of taking them to L.A. Veeck's offer was refused, but he came away with the distinct impression that "O'Malley wasn't going to sell the club to me because he had already mapped out Los Angeles for himself. And that was four years before he moved."[18]

There were two primary reasons for the Dodger president to want to build and own his own ballpark. One was parking, for which all proceeds would be his. At the downtown Brooklyn site, projections ranged from 2,000 to 5,000 parking spaces; in L.A. he got 16,000. Also many of the anticipated fans would be former Brooklynites who were part of the exodus to Long Island during this period. In all likelihood these people would travel by the Long Island Railroad whose terminal was likewise located at the Flatbush and Atlantic avenue site, rather than drive in, depriving the Dodgers' boss of the parking revenue. Another reason was television. Nobody would call O'Malley a fool. He was decidedly ahead of his time when he zeroed in on pay TV. With free television, he reasoned that the best approach was to air away games, thus whetting the fans' appetite for live baseball when the team came home. However, Brooklyn fans were already accustomed to 100 televised games—all of the home games plus select road games. With two teams in New York City televising National League games, O'Malley would not have exclusive control of the airways. His plan could not be effectively implemented in Brooklyn. Furthermore, he had made plans for the introduction of pay TV, another innovation that could not be realized in the Borough of Churches. The motivation of O'Malley's joust with the city was summed up by the mayor's executive secretary, William Peer, who said, "O'Malley knew all along he was going to Los Angeles. He just wanted to lay blame at the door of City Hall."[19]

A headline in the *Los Angeles Examiner* on August 19, 1953, boldly declared, "LA Major League Ball Plan Speeded Up ... Veeck's Big League Offer Studied." In 1953, four years before the actual move, L.A. was ready, baseball was ready, and so was O'Malley. The evidence is for the most part circumstantial, yet can we imagine this shrewd, calculating, manipulative, brilliant businessman standing in the anteroom of Robert Moses' office, hat in hand, begging for a piece of land so that he can keep his Dodgers in the bosom of their loving fans? It would seem rather that if Moses was the power broker he is accused of being, then he played into O'Malley's hands, and the borough of Brooklyn was merely a pawn in the charade.

It has been nearly 60 years since the Dodgers left Brooklyn and perhaps it no longer matters. Fans of the old Dodgers will live as they have for all this time with the mind's eye view of a Duke Snider home run majestically sailing over the right field screen and bouncing around on Bedford Avenue while a couple of dozen Brooklyn youths scramble for the prize. Or of Jackie Robinson glissading off third base and then running full out, stopping halfway to the plate and scurrying back to third without so much as drawing a throw, all the while the crowd yelling, "There he goes!" Or of Pee Wee Reese, number one, slapping one behind the runner.

It is the fans also that will not be forgotten. Hilda Chester and her cowbell and the Dodgers Sym-Phony Band banging out a tinny version of "Take Me Out to the Ballgame." O'Malley knew he had every opportunity of having it all on the gold coast. Brooklyn never had a chance! There is every reason to agree with writer Dave Anderson when he said, "O'Malley would have broken through a brick wall to get his team to L.A."[20] It wasn't quite that difficult.

On July 27, 2008, Walter Francis O'Malley was enshrined in the Baseball Hall of Fame in Cooperstown, New York, and it begs the question, *Why?* Listed in the Hall's by-laws for selection are the following criteria: record, ability, integrity, sportsmanship, character, and contribution to the game. Where exactly do O'Malley's qualifications take root in this list?

Perhaps the most significant category for an owner or executive to be considered would be his contribution to the game. Even his backers are wont to find anything more than his pioneering efforts in opening the West Coast to major league baseball. This implies that the California move was brokered by the Dodgers' boss and fostered by his efforts even to the point of indicating that the idea of an L.A. move came upon O'Malley like an epiphany at some point in 1956 or '57. This would belie the efforts of people like Don Barnes and A. B. "Happy" Chandler as well as relegating the record of related circumstances of the previous 16 years leading up to 1957 to the dust bin of history.

As noted above, the city of Los Angeles and the Pacific Coast League were clamoring for equal status with the majors as early as the 1930s. By 1953 when the first relocation took place, California was assured of a place in the big time of professional baseball with the assumption that it would go to an economically needy organization. Washington Senators owner Clark Griffith's prophetic statement during the discussion of the Browns' move of "I wouldn't be surprised if we move them to Los Angeles this year and follow up by moving another club to San Francisco in 1955" was made in '54, three years before the actual moves took place.[21] Said Arthur Daley in the *New York Times*, "That's the one ugly and inescapable fact that sets this deal apart from all other franchise transfers. Other teams were forced to move by apathy or incompetence. The only word that fits the Dodgers is greed."[22] And therein lies the genius of Walter Francis O'Malley. It was not in recognizing the gold in the California ravine; an economic neophyte could have done so, and many did. It was not in the disinterest of the Dodgers' fans. His inconsideration of the fans in Brooklyn who were supporting him regularly season after season did not hide the fact that he was cognizant of their loyalty. Kenneth Hahn, a member of the Los Angeles Board of Supervisors, recalled how in 1956 O'Malley passed the word that he was ready for L.A. "but, he said, 'I will deny it to the press.' He had another year to play in Ebbets Field and he told Hahn that the Dodger fans are rough fans. Literally [they] would kill him, he said."[23] While O'Malley complained about attendance in 1955, the figures would show a slight increase over the previous year. In 1957 there were 1,028,258 in Ebbets Field, guaranteeing the Dodgers would leave Brooklyn on top of the financial heap. His particular genius, by skullduggery, shrewdness or brilliance, lay in his ability to stay the course with a singleness of purpose and yet manage to create the necessary illusion of being the victim.

And so, Walter Francis O'Malley headed west, not as a crusading pioneer but as a carpet-bagging conquistador who merely had to say, "We'll come," to the salivating Los Angeles politicos. He played coy until they threw in everything but Grauman's Chinese Theater. His other manipulations, such as trading with Cubs owner Phil Wrigley for L.A.'s Wrigley Field and, incidentally, a block of Los Angeles real estate for the Dodgers' Fort Worth franchise for which Branch Rickey had paid $75,000 10 years before, and his concessions negotiations with Los Angeles, tend to make one wonder whether O'Malley was that shrewd or his adversaries that dense. It is, however, to be noted that Phil Wrigley willingly made the trade with O'Malley out of his desire to see the National League reach California first and in the choice spot, which was L.A.

O'Malley, however, nearly outsmarted himself at one point. As Irving Rudd said, "There were a few people in LA who didn't have orange juice for brains."[24] They squawked loudly about O'Malley taking over Chavez Ravine and its 300 valuable acres, which included the oil rights should any of the black gold be found beneath the land. The result was a referendum to vote whether to give him the land or not. O'Malley ran a telethon on the Sunday before the vote, pulling out all the stops. He won, of course, by a slim margin, but a 1–0 game is a win as much as one that ends up 10–0. For this he is rewarded with a plaque in what was at one time a hallowed institution. Brooklynites know better.

As time marches on, there are less of them to fight the good fight. Writers Pete Hamill and Dave Anderson, Brooklyn boys, are still swinging. It was Anderson who wrote, "There was no reason except Walter O'Malley's greed that the Dodgers left Brooklyn and went to California."[25] Walter O'Malley died on August 9, 1979. To be honest, there were not a lot of tears shed in Brooklyn for the Dodger boss. The next day Pete Hamill wrote in the *Daily News*, "The flags will not fly at half-mast in Brooklyn today. My father will not go up to Holy Name Church on Prospect Ave. and light a candle. Brooklyn remembers. Brooklyn does not easily forgive."[26] Pete said it for all of the Flatbush faithful!

But the pleas for the truth are getting less meaningful every year. Saddest of all is that one day as a dad leads his son through the hall of plaques at Cooperstown, he will point to O'Malley's and say, "That's the guy who opened up the West Coast to the majors." And he will not get a whimper of protest. It will be too late. Everybody who knows will be gone.

TWELVE

Redux: Brooklyn
Without the Dodgers

And flights of angels sing thee to thy rest!"—William Shakespeare, *Hamlet*

The borough of my youth no longer exists. It was the end of a time, certainly in Brooklyn, and it coincided with the Dodgers abandoning their home for the western gold coast. In January 1955 the borough newspaper, *The Brooklyn Eagle*, folded. By October '56 the picturesque trolley cars, the vehicles that had given the name to the ball club, were replaced by buses, the last line to go was at Church and MacDonald avenues, though it would be some years before the street asphalt completely covered the iron tracks on the Brooklyn streets. The great Brooklyn Navy Yard closed in 1964.

Changes also affected the once-thriving amusement areas of Coney Island. Old owners began to sell out and the quality of the food deteriorated as prices escalated. The city did not maintain the area adequately; it became appallingly run down. On September 20, 1964, at 7:35 p.m. Steeplechase officially closed down permanently. Another great Brooklyn institution had yielded to the end of an era.

Theaters that were thriving in 1953 passed from the scene. The Fox at 10 Flatbush Avenue opened its doors in 1928 and in 1971 became an addition to the Con Edison Company. The fabulous Brooklyn Paramount had seen munificent days since it began operation in 1928. Known for movies and live rock 'n' roll shows in the fifties, it is little remembered for its extensive showcase of jazz. Duke Ellington first appeared at the Paramount in 1931, followed over the years by Dizzy Gillespie, Ella Fitzgerald and Miles Davis. It is now the Arnold and Marie Schwartz Athletic Center of Long Island University (LIU) and has been since 1962. The Loew's Kings on Flatbush Avenue, long one of the largest of Brooklyn's movie theaters with 3,200 seats, remains at its perch, broken and derelict, long since closed up, nothing more than a dismal reminder of another time.

Once the largest hotel in New York City when it boasted 2,632 rooms, the St. George dates to 1885. Located at 100 Henry Street in the Brooklyn Heights district, the historic edifice is now used as student housing for surrounding colleges. The view from the rooftop restaurant illuminated by 12,000 lights and called Colorama was glorious. The hotel's most enduring feature, however, was the 40 × 120-foot salt water pool that attracted over the years such luminaries as Johnny Weissmuller, Buster Crabbe and Eleanor Holm. A mere memory now.

The memories fade, but not without a struggle. The Prospect Park Zoo is still a great place to visit, if you like your zoo without lions, tigers, elephants or bears. You can pick up a great-tasting piece of Entenmann's cake at any supermarket, good, but not Ebinger's. There are no live chicken markets or local movie houses like the Beverly or the Bushwick or the Boro Park that showed early Saturday morning "kiddie" shows with flashlight-wielding matrons running up and down the aisles keeping order throughout the entire three films, 10 cartoons and movie serial showing.

The horse path on Ocean Parkway that ran from Church Avenue to Coney Island is gone. No more will the ground shake as galloping equines rumble past. The trolley tunnel that ran under Ocean Parkway between East Fourth and East Fifth streets is long since filled in. The original F.W.I.L. Lundy Brothers of Sheepshead Bay closed its picturesque doors in 1979, the victim of labor problems and family disagreements. You can still get a great hot dog at Nathan's in Coney Island, but the chow mein on a bun has gone the way of the seven-cent egg cream. Coney Island may be the most altered of all the Brooklyn communities. The famous Carolina Restaurant on Stillwell and Mermaid is long gone. The freak shows on Surf Avenue and Eddie's Fascination, which was across the street from Nathan's, and where you would roll little balls at holes in a table that corresponded to playing cards and thus play a hand of poker, are gone. There was steaming corn-on-the-cob in a tub of boiling water that was brushed with butter before being turned over to the customer.

The wild thunderbolt ride on West Fifteenth Street and Surf was closed in 1982 and torn down in 2000 to make way for a stadium for the brand-new minor league Brooklyn Cyclones. The bumper cars still exist in a smaller, less turbulent version, but some things thankfully don't change. Both the carousel, also known as the merry-go-round, and the cyclone ride are still flourishing. The famous parachute jump, reaching 250 feet straight upwards and burnished with brightly colored lights at night, is now immobile. It remains, however, on the boardwalk towering above the right field fence of the stadium, Municipal Credit Union Stadium; the name, one more reminder of the deterioration of a way of life, remains as a monument to what used to be.

It was clearly a way of life when the Dodgers and Brooklyn came together and it was never more true than in the fifties. Your mom wanted to know how the Dodgers did because if they lost, your dad would be in no mood for supper. The great Dodgers broadcaster, Red Barber, was fond of noting that if the Dodgers lost an afternoon game, "There'd be a lot of cold suppers in Brooklyn."[1]

All of this is the legacy the Brooklyn Dodgers left for the borough and its people. They are also left with a cavernous void that has been impossible to fill. But Brooklyn is still a great place and many luminary locales from the Dodgers era are still operating full tilt. The main library at Grand Army Plaza is now one of 60 branches borough-wide. The museum, the Botanical Gardens and the Academy of Music (BAM) are thriving. The first professional sports team to come to Brooklyn since the Dodgers left arrived in 2001. The minor league Brooklyn Cyclones play their New York–Penn League games at a beautiful facility in Coney Island 'neath the silent parachute jump. The Cyclones are an affiliate of the New York Mets, whose owner, Fred Wilpon, a Brooklyn guy from Lafayette High, was once a pretty good left-handed pitcher on the Brooklyn sandlots. Wilpon remembers his roots. And Carl Erskine remembers the Brooklyn of his Dodger days. In 2000 the old pitcher brought his family to revisit the place of his baseball glory days. At the site of Ebbets Field rose a 30-story apartment complex. "It just didn't look right," he thought. "Then we drove to Coney Island. Thank God that Nathan's was still there. I don't know if I could have controlled myself if they had torn down Nathan's."[2]

The majestic Loew's Kings Theater on Flatbush Avenue was renovated and in February 2015, opened with a sold-out performance by Diana Ross.

In 2012 the new Brooklyn Nets made their NBA debut at Barclays Center in downtown Brooklyn, the site that O'Malley would have you believe would have kept him in Brooklyn had only Robert Moses given the land free and clear. In revisiting the old home grounds, there are so many more notable absentees. As one passes the Botanical Gardens, there is no longer the aroma of fresh-baked bread from the Bond Bread Company. Built in 1925, it sits opposite the Gardens at 495 Flatbush Avenue off Empire Boulevard. In 1997 the building was sold to the owners of Phat Albert and it is now utilized as a warehouse; the watch tower still rises over Flatbush Avenue. With just a short stretch of memory one can visualize the banners and bunting draped from the windows on October 4, 1955.

Professional baseball returns to Brooklyn in 2001. The minor league Brooklyn Cyclones play in Coney Island, towered over by a 1950s remnant. The famed 250-foot Parachute Jump is no longer operational but has achieved landmark status in Brooklyn's post–Dodgers era (courtesy Christine Love).

Just a block or so from Ebbets Field, the delectable aroma of the fresh bread was a prologue to the hot dogs and roasted peanuts outside the ballpark. Once inside the park, the color and excitement was overwhelming. There was barely a spot on the walls in left and right fields that were not covered with huge commercial ads. The center field wall was blank so as to make a better background for the hitters. On the left side fans were encouraged to eat at the Brass Rail Restaurant, to bank at the Manufacturers Trust Company, to buy their gas from Tydol Flying Gasoline, and were reminded that "Luckies Taste Better."

The right field wall lauds the values of Van Heusen shirts, Mobilgas, and Gem Razors. The "h" and the "e" in the Schaefer Beer sign on top of the scoreboard lit up to let the fans know how a play had been scored. When the huge Bulova clock was installed over the scoreboard, the company offered a free watch to any player who hit one against the timepiece. On May 30, 1946, an incident occurred that writer Bob McGee called "another of those only in

Ebbets Field moments."[3] A Braves outfielder, Bama Rowell of Citronelle, Alabama, hit a ball that smashed the clock. It was ruled a ground-rule double. An hour later the clock stopped. The scene was recreated in the film, *The Natural*, based on the novel by Bernard Malamud. Malamud was a Brooklyn boy, and it has been suggested that the incident inspired the scene. Rowell never got his watch. In 1987, while doing a magazine article, writer Bert Sugar came across the film incident and the Rowell connection. He contacted Rowell and learned that he was not given the Bulova watch. So he arranged for Bulova to present the gift to the 71-year-old Bama Rowell in a ceremony in his hometown, just 41 years after the fact.

The ads on the wall worked as an unintended method of expression for some Brooklyn fans. There used to be one for a product called Lifebuoy Soap. The ad proclaimed, "The Dodgers Use Lifebuoy Soap." This was in the era of the sixth-place Daffiness Boys, and some fan motivated more by his dissatisfaction with the team and less with his own safety somehow reached high enough to scribble in red paint his admonition," … and they still stink!"

The most famous of the Ebbets Field signs was the one under the scoreboard for Abe Stark clothes. It read, "Hit Sign, Win Suit." Then, "Abe Stark—1514 Pitkin Avenue." At three feet high and thirty feet long and with Dixie Walker and then Carl Furillo guarding it, Abe didn't give away many suits. He did, however, ride the notoriety into local politics and the job as Brooklyn borough president. In the right field corner the Esquire Boot Polish sign looked down upon the bullpen and the pre-game show, *Happy Felton's Knot Hole Gang.*

It was here that the Dodgers bonded best with the youth of the borough and Brooklyn's young ballplayers got to live a dream, if only for 30 minutes or so. Born in Bellevue, Pennsylvania, and a violin soloist with the Pittsburgh Symphony at the age of seven, Felton was a fixture at Ebbets Field from 1950 to 1957. He met Walter O'Malley on a fishing trip and sold the Dodgers' boss on the idea of a TV show dedicated to the youth. Airing 30 minutes before each Dodger home game, three local young players would compete, with the winner being selected by a Dodger player. He would then be invited back the next day to visit with the Dodger of his choice in the dugout.

George Lopac was a 15-year-old shortstop playing for the 73rd precinct PAL team in Brownsville when he got the opportunity to appear on the Felton show, where he and two other boys would be judged by Junior Gilliam. As it turned out the Dodgers' second baseman selected Georgie as the winner. His choice to speak to Pee Wee Reese the next day, unfortunately, was cancelled because the game was rained out. The three boys were given gifts, and Lopac came away with a bat, a new glove and a bank account with 10 dollars in it from the Greenpoint Savings Bank, one of the show's sponsors.

An unexpected highlight for the excited youngster came after the game when he was escorted into the Dodgers' locker room. He met the players and got their autographs. "I was so excited," he recalled, "I didn't know what was going on. They were all there. I met Hodges and Campy and Labine. There was Erskine on the massage table and Ralph Branca just stepping out of the shower."[4]

But the memorable evening was not yet over. When George got back home to 1801 Park Place off Saratoga Avenue, "All my friends were outside cheering when they saw me," he said. "What a night and what a time to be alive and living in Brooklyn."[5] The show created immeasurable goodwill between the ticket-buying public and the ball club.

There was seldom a dull day at Ebbets Field. There was the day Babe Herman doubled into a double play as three Dodgers wound up on third base. Incidentally, Brooklyn's Babe, who owns the highest lifetime batting mark outside of Cooperstown, drove in the winning run during the fiasco. Mickey Owen's infamous passed ball in the fourth game of the '41 Series happened there. Night baseball was the inspiration of Larry MacPhail, first in Cincinnati, then Brooklyn in 1938, the night Johnny Vander Meer pitched his second consecutive no-hitter.

Here also Cookie Lavagetto slammed one off the right field wall to drive in the tying and winning runs to deprive the Yankees' Bill Bevens of a World Series no-hitter and victory in the '47 Series. It was in 1947 and the Dodgers faced the Yankees in Brooklyn's first World Series since 1941. Though not the prettiest, it was one of the most exciting Series ever. New York won the first two at Yankee Stadium and Brooklyn took the third game by a 9–8 score. It was game four, however, that prompted Dick Young to write in the *New York Daily News*, "Out of the mockery and ridicule of the worst World Series in history, the greatest game ever played was born yesterday."[6]

Said Peter Golenbock, "Game four of the 1947 World Series was perhaps the most exciting single game ever played at Ebbets Field."[7] What made the game subject to such plaudits was the half-inning that *LIFE* magazine called "the most exciting two minutes in the history of the World Series."[8]

Harry Taylor, 10–5 on the year, started the game for Brooklyn but didn't get past the first inning. The Yankee starter was a right-hander named Floyd "Bill" Bevens, just 7–13 for the season. Bevens walked two Dodgers in the first inning but neither scored. He issued another walk in the second, another in the third, and two more in the fifth. In that inning Spider Jorgensen scored

George Lopac (second from left) is chosen the winner by Junior Gilliam (right) on Happy Felton's *Knot-Hole Gang* show. Felton is second from right; others are unidentified (courtesy George Lopac).

the Dodgers' first run on a fielder's choice. The Bronx Bombers scored one in the first off Taylor and another in the fourth off Hal Gregg when Billy Johnson tripled and Johnny Lindell doubled; they took that 2–1 lead into the ninth inning.

In eight complete innings Bevens had walked eight but had not yet given up a base hit. So with the game and the first-ever World Series no-hitter on the line, the 6'3," 210-pound right hander faced Bruce Edwards leading off the ninth. The Dodgers catcher flied deep to left where Lindell hauled it in at the base of the wall. Carl Furillo drew a walk, the ninth given up by Bevens. Jorgensen popped to first baseman George McQuinn in foul ground for the second out. With pitcher Hugh Casey due up, manager Burt Shotton sent Pete Reiser up to hit. He also sent reserve outfielder Al Gionfriddo to run for Furillo.

And now the wheels started to spin. In the previous game, Reiser was injured in a play at second base when he collided with shortstop Phil Rizzuto. His ankle was bandaged against what would turn out to be a fracture. Even knowing that, Shotton still wanted his best available hitter in there in such a spot. With a count of two balls and a strike on Reiser, Gionfriddo stole second. The pitch was ball three. Yankee manager Bucky Harris went against the book and put Reiser on intentionally with the potential winning run; it was Bevens' 10th walk. Eddie Miksis was promptly sent in to run for the hobbled Reiser. Eddie Stanky was due up but Shotton pulled a surprise move and ordered Cookie Lavagetto in as a pinch-hitter.

Harry Lavagetto was from the California Bay area, born on December 1, 1912. He attended Oakland Technical High School and played semi-pro ball in the Oakland area. When asked if the Bevens hit was the most important of his career, surprisingly, Cookie said no. He explained that in a 1933 semi-pro game with the bases loaded he faced a pitcher named Pudgy Gould, who had had a "cup of coffee" in the big Leagues and threw a spitball. Lavagetto's hit to left-center cleared the bases. It was that hit that got him some pro offers. Harry's parents emigrated from the Lagoria Province near Genoa in Italy as did the parents of his wife, Mary. Cookie liked to tell about how he learned to hit—by swatting at flies with a broomstick in his granddad's room where he made homemade wine. This helped him, he said, "to hit Carl Hubbell's famous screwball."[9]

Lavagetto began his professional career in the Pacific Coast League with his hometown Oakland Oaks in 1933. He hit .312, earned the nickname "Cookie" after one of the team owners, and was purchased by the Pittsburgh Pirates. After three seasons with the Pirates, Lavagetto was traded to Brooklyn, where he was a four-time All-Star at third base and hit .300 in 1939.

It was following the pennant year of 1941 and the Japanese attack on Pearl Harbor a couple of months later that prompted Lavagetto to be one of the first major leaguers to join the military. He enlisted in the navy in February 1942. Part of his motivation, however, was the result of anti–Italian fervor that was prevalent in the early months of the war, the result of the stand taken by Italian dictator Benito Mussolini. A promotional deal he had was canceled because of his Italian heritage and Cookie felt obligated to prove his patriotism. Like so many others in his profession, he lost valuable playing years of his prime. In Lavagetto's case it was four years before he returned to baseball. He hit just .236 in '46 while playing in 88 games. He appeared in just 41 games and was used mostly as a pinch-hitter and hit .261 in 1947.

According to pitcher Rex Barney, when Shotton called for Lavagetto,

Cookie was drowsing in the corner of the dugout, belt unbuckled, shoes off and shirt out of his pants. His son, Ernie, explained that due to a slight allergy to the woolen uniforms that were worn then, Cookie often loosened his clothes while on the bench to get some relief. Barney and Ralph Branca hurried him. "Come on, Cookie, you're gonna hit." They tucked in his shirt, got his spikes on and got him to the plate.[10]

Lavagetto swung and missed at the first pitch and then sent the next one, a fastball away, off the scoreboard in right field. As right fielder Tommy Henrich had some trouble with the rebound, both Gionfriddo and Miksis scored the tying and winning runs. Bevens lost both the ballgame and the no-hitter on that one swing. Mary Katherine Lavagetto, Cookie's wife, had given birth to the couple's first son just two weeks before and was listening to the game on the radio. "When Harry hit that double that won the game," she said, "I just sat down and had a good cry."[11]

The very next day, again in the ninth inning, again with the score 2–1 and the tying run in scoring position, again with two out, Lavagetto was called on again to pinch-hit. Against the Yanks' Frank "Spec" Shea, he ran the count to 3–2, and then Cookie struck out. The next day the *Brooklyn Eagle* had it right. "The Gods of baseball can be pushed just so far."[12]

On May 21, 1952, the Dodgers hosted the Cincinnati Reds and faced Ewell Blackwell, the side-arming right-hander they called "The Whip." It took exactly one hour and three minutes to complete the first inning and by that time the Dodgers had a 15–0 lead. Brooklyn scored 12 of the 15 runs after two were out. Billy Cox grounded out and Reese walked before Snider homered. Robinson doubled to left-center field, Andy Pafko drew a walk, and George Shuba singled to right, scoring Robinson. Pafko was out trying to steal third and Shuba took second. Then with two out, Hodges walked, Rube Walker singled, and Chris Van Cuyk, the pitcher, got a base hit to score Hodges. Cox singled to left, Reese singled, Snider walked, loading the bases. Robinson was hit by a pitch, Pafko singled to left, driving in two, and Shuba walked, loading them up again. Hodges walked, Walker got a base hit, and Van Cuyk singled again. After Cox was hit by a pitch and Pee Wee walked, Snider struck out for the final out to end the Reds' misery.

Twenty-two men came to bat, producing ten hits and drawing seven walks. Nineteen consecutive batters reached base safely. Two batters were hit by a pitch. The carnage tied one record and broke six others. The final score was 19–1; Chris Van Cuyk was the winning pitcher.

In spring training 1934, Dizzy Dean of the zany St. Louis Cardinals' "Gas House Gang" introduced his brother, Paul, to the assembled scribes with the outlandish prediction, "Me and Paul'll win 45 games between us, and if we have six more pitchers who can win about 50 other games, that will put us in the World Series."[13] According to the brash Dizzy, it wasn't bragging if you could do it, and he and Paul certainly did. They won 49, Diz was 30–7 while Paul in his rookie season won 19 games and lost 11. But it was on September 21 in a doubleheader at Ebbets Field that Diz dotted the "i's." Dizzy started the first game, throwing seven no-hit innings and giving up three hits as he shut out the Dodgers, 1–0. In the nightcap Paul pitched the first no-hitter in the National League since 1920, shutting down the Dodgers, 3–0. "How do you feel?" asked Brooklyn's manager Casey Stengel, repeating a reporter's question. "You get three itsy-bitsy hits off the big brother in the first game, and then there's the little brother with biscuits from the same table to throw at you."[14]

As usual, Old Diz had the last word. "If'n I'd knowed Paul was gonna throw a no-hitter," he said, "well, I'd a throwed one too."[15]

Red Barber had brought the word "rhubarb" to Brooklyn and on September 16, 1940, he got to describe one of the many that occurred on the Ebbets Field turf. In a September 16 game during the 1940 pennant race with Cincinnati, the Dodgers lost a tough one to the Reds, 4–3, in 10 innings. But as usual in Brooklyn, there was a lot more on tap for the fans. In that 10th inning Cincinnati had runners on first and second with one out when Frank McCormick hit a ground ball to Johnny Hudson at short. Pete Coscarart took the relay at second, held it, and then dropped the ball. The umpire was Bill Stewart, and he called the runner out and whirled to make the call at first. He didn't see Coscarart drop the ball. Umpire George Magerkurth overruled Stewart and called the runner safe.

Durocher bolted from the dugout and raged at Magerkurth. After Leo was bounced, a sacrifice fly scored the winning run. As the game ended, a fan jumped out of the stands and leaped on the back of the 6'3," 230-pound umpire. The photo that appeared in the *New York Daily News* showed the man, Frank Germano, on top of Magerkurth with his fists cocked. Germano was arrested, and as it turned out, he was an ex-convict out on parole. His specialty was pick-pocketing. In an exchange with a judge, Germano admitted that he was pretty sore over the umpire's decision, but added, "To tell the truth, judge, I had a partner working the stands that day."[16]

Sometimes the players just took after each other. A memorable donnybrook took place at Ebbets Field on June 12, 1957, in a game between the Dodgers and the Milwaukee Braves. Now taking over from the great Cardinal rivalries and the early-fifties Giants, the Braves became contenders and competitors in the beanball wars. On this day the Dodgers' hard-throwing right-hander, Don Drysdale, who had been learning his trade at the feet of his Socrates, Sal Maglie, slammed Braves shortstop Johnny Logan in the back with a fastball after Billy Bruton had hit a home run.

Logan yelled something to Drysdale, and a couple of pitches later Drysdale threw over to first and hit Logan again. The angered Braves player charged the mound, expecting his teammate, Eddie Mathews, another hard nose, to join in. Logan took a punch in the eye from the pitcher before Mathews arrived and jumped on Drysdale. There was a pileup on the mound, but the peacemaker, the Paul Bunyan of the National League, Gil Hodges, was there to intervene. Gil, Drysdale's roommate, pulled Mathews out of the fray by grabbing him by the leg and dragging him off the field.

Braves catcher Carl Sawatski jumped on Drysdale while swinging his fists until Don Newcombe pulled him off and then got Drysdale off the field. The Braves won the game, 8–5, and moved into first place.

The great rivalry in the forties was between Brooklyn and the Cardinals, as both clubs dominated the non-war years. In the fifth inning of a May 15, 1945, game, Brooklyn's Lew Webber dusted off Enos "Country" Slaughter. The outfielder responded by pushing a bunt up the first base line and running over Webber as the pitcher attempted to field the ball. Both benches emptied, and it was another one of Red Barber's famed Ebbets Field "rhubarbs." Howie Pollet bested Webber in the game by a 1–0 score. But Brooklyn didn't limit such brawls to the Cardinals and Giants.

In a game the following season, the Dodgers and the Chicago Cubs went into the 10th inning tied at Ebbets Field. The Cubs' Lennie Merullo slid with spikes high into Dodgers second baseman Eddie Stanky. The two came up swinging, and according to the script, both teams joined in. Pee Wee Reese slugged Merullo, giving him a black eye, and Cubs pitcher Claude Passeau ripped the shirt off Leo Durocher. The Dodgers won the game in the 13th inning. But it wasn't over. These kinds of brawls don't usually spill over to the next day, but this one did.

During batting practice the next afternoon, Merullo complained to Reese that the shortstop had hit him from behind and challenged him to a fight. Dixie Walker then whacked Merullo from the rear and the two grappled, Dixie losing a tooth in the struggle. The police responded and Chicago's Phil Cavaretta took on several of the cops as well as any Dodger player he could reach. Calm was restored and the game was played, but five policemen were positioned in each dugout to keep the peace. There were a number of ejections before the game started and Reese, Walker, Cavaretta and Merullo received fines. Just another day at the old ballpark!

In early June of 1940 the Dodgers' Larry MacPhail closed a deal with the Cardinals that brought a future Hall-of-Famer, Joe Medwick, to Brooklyn. It cost the Dodgers four players and $125,000, but they also received pitcher Curt Davis, who would make a valuable contribution to Dodgers' pennant drives. Medwick was in his ninth season in the big leagues, all of them spent with St. Louis. He had hit over .300 in the previous eight, winning the batting title in 1937 with a .374 average. The deal was hailed all over Brooklyn, but on June 9, the first time playing against his old team, Medwick was hit in the head with a pitch thrown by Bob Bowman. There had been an exchange of words between Medwick and Bowman in the hotel prior to the game and the Dodgers felt the pitch had been intentional.

Manager Leo Durocher stormed out of the Dodgers dugout and took wild swings at Bowman. McPhail climbed out of the owner's box next to the dugout and challenged the entire St. Louis team. The outrage was such that Bowman had to be escorted from the field by policemen. MacPhail called Ford Frick, the president of the National League, and accused Bowman of intentionally beaning Medwick. He wanted to have the pitcher arrested and talked of going to the district attorney for an indictment. As Medwick improved and returned to the lineup a week later, MacPhail cooled down. The outfielder played another eight years and hit over .300 five times, finishing at .317, although he never hit quite as well as before and lost some of the aggressiveness that had made him such a feared hitter.

The Dodgers and Cardinals wound down the '46 season in a dead heat, which prompted the first playoff in National League history. Game one was played in St. Louis and the Cardinals won, 4–2. The next two of the best-of-three series were scheduled for Ebbets Field. On Thursday, October 3, it was sunny and 65 degrees as 31,437 fans filled the little ballpark hoping to see their Dodgers even up the series and then pull out a pennant. It was not to be. The opposing pitchers were the Cardinals' dependable right-hander, Murray Dickson, 15–6 on the year, and Joe Hatten, the Dodgers' lefty who had won 14 and lost 11. After Slaughter tripled in two runs in the fifth inning, St. Louis led, 4–1. An array of Dodgers relievers, five in all, gave up four more runs, and in the last of the ninth the score stood at 8–1. Brooklyn's hopes seemed dismal at best.

But Augie Galan led off with a double, which was followed by a triple, a single, a wild pitch and a walk. Out came Dickson and in came Harry "The Cat" Brecheen. Bruce Edwards singled and drove in two. With the score now 8–4, a walk to Lavagetto loaded the bases for "The Steeple." Howie Schultz, the 6'6" first baseman who had hit a homer the day before, stepped in and energized the crowd. Schultz drove the first pitch down the left field line, but the ball was foul by inches. On a three-and-two count, Brecheen threw a screwball to strike out the towering first baseman and end the Dodgers' hopes for a pennant. The Dodgers did, however, set a National league attendance record in 1946 with 1,746,824 paying customers.

The most memorable Ebbets Field moments were not always provided by the home team. There were at times members of the loyal opposition who were pretty destructive at the Dodgers' expense. "He murdered us, killed us," moaned a fan on July 31, 1954. "One of those shots cleared the roof."[17] The terminator was the Braves' Joe Adcock, who that day hit four home runs and a double in Brooklyn. He spread the wealth by hitting them off four Dodger pitchers—Don Newcombe, Erv Palica, Pete Wojey, and Johnny Podres. He drove in seven runs, and his 18 total bases set a record as the Braves romped over the Dodgers, 15–7.

One of Brooklyn's saddest days at Ebbets Field was the 1947 afternoon when fans witnessed what proved to be the final demise of one of the greatest talents ever to reach the big time, Pete Reiser. Reiser could do everything on a ball field except stop a few inches short of a concrete outfield wall. When the Dodgers finally added padding to the walls, it was too late to save "Pistol" Pete. Before the '47 season began there were 850 box seats added to the left and center field stands, bringing the walls 40 feet closer in left and 30 feet closer in center. On Wednesday, June 4, the Dodgers were leading the Pirates, 7–2, in the sixth inning. Ralph Branca was heading for his sixth victory of the 21 he would record that year. A Pirate outfielder, Cully Rikard, sent a fly ball deep towards the wall in left-center field. "'Hell, this is an easy out,'" Reiser remembered thinking. "I'm going full speed ... and oh, my God, I'd completely forgotten about the 40 feet that wasn't there any more. When I woke up, I couldn't move."[18] He crashed into the wall and was unconscious when he hit the ground, still holding onto the ball. The umpire, Butch Henline, ran out to the fallen outfielder and signaled an out when he saw the ball in Pete's glove.

A priest was summoned to give the ballplayer the last rites of the Catholic Church. Reiser was out for five weeks. Then, after bumping heads with a teammate during batting practice, a noticeable lump sent him to Johns Hopkins Hospital in Baltimore where he was operated on for a blood clot. An oddity to the story is that Gene Hermanski had come over from left field and says he saw the ball on the ground just beside Reiser's glove. "The first thing I did," said Hermanski, "was to put the ball in his glove. The umpire came out and saw the ball in the glove and said, 'You're out!'"[19]

There was never a more glorious time at the old ballpark than July 22, 1955, a night given to a birthday party for captain Pee Wee Reese. Reese was one of the most popular and respected of the Brooklyn Dodgers, and more than 33,000 of the faithful turned out to wish Pee Wee a happy 37th birthday. Irving Rudd, the Dodgers' publicist, wanted to make sure that on his night Pee Wee got his due, so he reached out to local businesses for gifts. Chock Full O' Nuts baked a 250-pound cake and gave the Reeses a lifetime supply of coffee. Paul Grossinger of the Catskill resort hotel presented the Dodger captain with a lifetime pass to the hotel and threw in a set of golf clubs. There were trips to Europe and new clothes for Pee Wee as well as his wife, Dotty, and daughter, Barbara, and, of course, a new car.

Red Barber and Vin Scully dutifully and enthusiastically promoted the event on the air. During the presentations telegrams were read from President Eisenhower, Vice President Nixon and General Douglas MacArthur. A teary moment came when the cars were driven onto the field, and to his surprise, Pee Wee's mom stepped out of one of them. The car gimmick was to have Barbara Reese select a key from a fishbowl and Pee Wee would get whichever car the key fit. She picked the Chevy, though most folks were rooting for the Chrysler.

The lights were turned out and the crowd was asked to light matches and sing "Happy Birthday" to Pee Wee. It was a beautiful experience and a sight to behold. According to Rudd, the only problem was that Pee Wee was afraid "he'll stink out the joint once the game starts."[20] He didn't. He hit two doubles off the Milwaukee Braves' Gene Conley and the Dodgers won, 8–5. The only downside for Rudd came when Campanella let him have it about the car, saying, "You could have arranged for her to pick the Imperial."[21]

He was the voice of the Dodgers, or "the Verce," as would be said around any corner candy store in the borough in the fifties. Walter Lanier Barber seemed a highly unlikely selection to be the direct conduit between the action on the field and the Brooklyn fan listening. After all, Brooklyn had its own language and the refined Mr. Barber could never mistake "erl" for oil. Born in Columbia, Mississippi, and raised in Sanford, Florida, Barber landing in Brooklyn would seem to be the ultimate faux pas. Yet the truth was just the opposite. Brooklyn fans took to Red Barber ever since Larry MacPhail brought him to Brooklyn in 1938. His highly professional reporter's approach to his job mingled with the southern colloquialisms he introduced to Brooklyn made Barber an extremely popular and necessary commodity of the Dodger experience.

He introduced such phrases as "sittin' in the catbird seat," "tearin' up the pea patch," and "Oh, doctor!," to Brooklyn radio and television audiences. He once said as a Dodgers pitcher looked as if he might need some help, "There's no action in the Dodger bullpen yet, but they're beginning to wiggle their toes a little."[22]

Red, a southerner, was one of the first people Branch Rickey let in on his plan to bring Jackie Robinson to the Dodgers. In March 1945 at a Brooklyn eatery called Joe's, the two had lunch and after a lengthy buildup, Rickey spilled the beans. "I'm going to tell you something only the Brooklyn board of directors and my family knows," he told the broadcaster. "I'm going to bring a Negro to the Brooklyn Dodgers."[23] Barber was troubled by the news. He was white, southern, and the product of his upbringing. His first reaction was to quit, but his wife, Lylah, convinced him to give it a while before making such a rash decision. He did. He dwelt on it, reasoned about it, and in the end decided that the only right thing to do would be to abide by Rickey's decision with no opposition from him.

Brooklyn native Larry King referred to Barber as "an indelible part of my life. He was the best sports announcer I ever heard." He remembered how Red was a "poet in the broadcast booth."[24] A general consensus among the fans of Brooklyn was that Red Barber was indeed a class act.

Gladys Gooding was the soul of Ebbets Field. She came to New York from Missouri where she was born in Macon and raised in St. Louis. This was in 1923 and she worked as an organist in both the Loew's and RKO theaters. Hired to play at Madison Square Garden, Gooding became the answer to a trivia question: Who is the only person to play for the Dodgers, the Knicks, and the Rangers? She rode the subway each day from her room at a hotel near the Garden to Ebbets Field, often accompanied by her fox terrier, who sat beside her at the organ.

A 70-year-old retired music teacher named J. Reid Spencer, who lived near the Dodgers' ballpark, complained that Gladys' music disturbed his afternoon nap. He went so far as to take the Dodgers to court over the issue. According to Richard Goldstein, "Even a legal genius would be unlikely to win a suit against the Dodgers in a Brooklyn court. The complaint was thrown out on a technicality."[25] It's anyone's guess how Mr. Spencer would have reacted to the Dodgers' Music Appreciation Night held on August 13, 1951.

The genesis of the evening stems from the Brooklyn Dodgers Sym-Phony band, a group of amateur musicians from Greenpoint who made themselves fixtures at Ebbets Field. It began with a picnic in Queens canceled by rain. The boys had their instruments, and when the skies cleared they made their way to Ebbets Field. Prevented from bringing the instruments into the park,

The Brooklyn Dodgers Sym-Phony Band keeps the "Flatbush Faithful" in high spirits (Brooklyn Public Library—Brooklyn Collection).

their ingenuity took over. One of the boys went in, climbed a ramp and lowered some rope down to the street. The instruments were hoisted up and a gig was born. It took a few years but considering the popularity of the group among the fans, the Dodgers sanctioned them and they were given permanent seats in Section 8, behind first base. Some pundits claimed that the selection of the section was intentional, relating to the army mental discharge.

The group consisted of Shorty Laurice, with Pat Palma on cymbals, Jerry Martin on snare drum, Lou Soriano played trombone, Marty Pecora blew trumpet and Jo-Jo Delio banged the bass drum. They serenaded the denizens of the ballpark with their inimitable sound and zany antics. A huge fan favorite was the practice of following an opposing player to the bench after he had made an out with a rhythmic *da-dum-dee-dum* until the player hit the seat at the exact time that Jo-Jo would bang the bass drum. The fans loved it when players would try to fool the boys. Ralph Kiner of the Pirates was one of them. Kiner would delay the inevitable by going to the water cooler or standing around for a while. At times it would be two or three pitches into the next batter that the drum would pound. Nobody could fool the Sym-Phony.

In July 1951 Local 802 of the American Federation of Musicians threatened to put up a picket line around Ebbets Field because they felt the boys ought to be carrying union cards. The Dodgers counted the ploy with one of their own. They staged a Musical Unappreciation Night on August 13. Anyone attending the game with a musical instrument would enter free of charge. More than 2,000 fellow musicians showed up with instruments ranging from a glockenspiel to two fellows who wheeled in a piano. New York City mayor Vincent Impellitteri took part in the festivities. "Today," wrote Dodger publicist Irving Rudd, "baseball belongs to marketing consultants who have hearts like cash registers. They don't understand the Sym-Phony and they never will, which really tells you all you need to know about what they really meant to me and Brooklyn."[26]

But Ebbets Field belonged to the fans as much as it did to the players and they made themselves heard. Many were well known to the team. Hilda Chester was a lady who rang a big cow bell, usually sat in the center field bleachers, and announced, "Hilda is here," to anyone within earshot. Fan effect was not limited to cheers as Hilda proved one afternoon. She hollered to Pete Reiser playing center field, "Hey, Pete, give this to Leo," and tossed a crumpled note onto the field. Reiser put it into his back pocket, and when the inning ended he headed for the dugout. Larry MacPhail sat in a box next to the bench and when Pete passed him, the two exchanged a few words.

"I gave Hilda's note to Leo and sat down," Reiser explained. "Next thing I know he's getting somebody hot in the bullpen. In the next inning Wyatt, who was pitching a good game, gave up a hit and Leo yanked him and brought in Casey. Casey got rocked a few times and we just did win the game." Durocher was hot in the locker room and told Pete never to give him another note from MacPhail. "MacPhail?" Reiser said. "That note was from Hilda." The note said, "Get Casey ready. Wyatt's losing it." A fan in the center field bleachers made a pitching change for the Dodgers. They say it could only happen in Brooklyn; they're probably right.[27]

The first and only time an All-Star game was played at Ebbets Field was on July 12, 1949. It was baseball's 16th mid-summer classic, and it was represented for another historic first. For the first time ever there were four African American players taking part. The Dodgers' trio of Jackie Robinson, Don Newcombe and Roy Campanella were joined by Larry Doby of the Cleveland Indians. A crowd of 32,577 sat through two rain showers and saw the American League win for the 12th time, 11–7, behind the hitting of Joe DiMaggio. The

Yankee Clipper was chosen as a reserve but he singled, doubled and drove home three runs. Stan Musial and Ralph Kiner hit home runs for the Nationals.

The little ballpark in Brooklyn, the chapel in the valley, also stood godfather to the christening of one of baseball's most enduring nicknames. Brooklyn fans were known around the league for their knowledge of the game as well as the appreciation they showed for quality play, even when it involved an opposing player. It is not surprising, therefore, when those same fans lauded the greatest Dodger killer of them all, the St. Louis Cardinals' Stan Musial. Nor should it be a surprise that he was dubbed "The Man" within the confines of the Dodgers' home park.

On June 21, 1946, the Redbirds came into Ebbets Field having won five of seven road games, trailing Brooklyn by a game and a half. The Dodgers won two of three, but Musial had eight hits in 12 at-bats. As he came to the plate for the first time in the third game, St. Louis sportswriter Bob Broeg thought he heard the Brooklyn crowd chanting, "Here comes that man." He asked traveling secretary Leo Ward, but Ward said it sounded more like, "Here comes *the* man."[28] Broeg wrote the anecdote in his column in the *St. Louis Post Dispatch,* and a great nickname was born out of respect by the rivals he devastated every time he entered the ballpark.

"We loved the Brooklyn fans but had only one thing against them. They *cheered* Musial," Dodger pitcher Carl Erskine said incredulously. "And all the time he's killing us, they're cheering him!"[29]

It was more than 60 years ago that these Dodgers glorified the game and our lives, and it was yesterday, though another world completely. Who cannot be nostalgic for a 10-ounce package of frozen asparagus spears for 43 cents at Grand Union Supermarkets or 14 ounces of Seabrook Farms chopped spinach at 19 cents? Or spend an evening out at the Avalon on Kings Highway and East 18th Street where *The Jazz Singer* stars Danny Thomas or the Tuxedo on Ocean Parkway and Brighton Beach Avenue screening *The Bad and the Beautiful,* which stars Kirk Douglas?

At Sears you can pick up an area rug for $4.44, a sale, down from $5.29. Alexander's is offering famous maker's pure wool worsted suits for women for $39, and the men get a topcoat for $36 at S. Klein. For the ladies Klein's has handbags of imported French calfskin for $9. And, hey, get right over to Macy's for that 36-piece china service for six on sale for $9.94. Weisman Furniture on Utica Avenue just off McDonald Avenue has loads of furniture buys, such as a roll arm sofa and loveseat set for $599 and free delivery.

Times change, sometimes for the better and at times, unfortunately, for the worst. So for better or worse my generation will have memories to savor that will serve to blot out any that were not as worthy to recall. Certainly the Brooklyn Dodgers remain a potent and indelible force in our eidetic imagery, and the quality of the 1953 club is not to be denied. Carl Erskine remembers the '52 and '53 clubs as the best he ever played on. "It gets forgotten," he said, "because we didn't win the World Series. But the numbers were so big in '53, and think about it, we had to do it without Newcombe."[30]

The Brooklyn Dodgers mystique continues to grow with each passing year for a number of reasons. A great team in a great era, yes, but perhaps the diminishing returns from the game since have served to make the memories all the more potent. The expanding major leagues have produced 30 teams with nary enough talent to stock them all. Pitchers work every fifth day instead of four and a complete game is cause for celebration. Erskine says the greatest changes in the game have been in the reconstructed strike zone. It is lower and the high strike is gone. "The strike zone is no higher than the plate is wide," said the Dodger star. "I don't think hitters today would be successful against the hard high strike." He is quick to add that the good hitters will always hit but "the more marginal ones would, I think, have had a lot of trouble."[31] The little right-hander may be thinking of the 164 times he had to face Stan Musial in his career and wondered how "The Man" would fare today by laying off pitches that would now be called balls.

Erskine still receives mail from Brooklyn fans that arrives from all over the country and he stays in touch with old Brooklyn neighbors like the Rossis—Joe was the Bay Ridge butcher the Dodgers who lived in the area frequented. And Brooklyn remembers the Dodgers. Driving along the Belt Parkway past Sheepshead Bay and before JFK airport, there is an exit sign that reads "Erskine Street," named for the Dodger pitcher. "What an honor," he said. "A guy from Indiana with a street named for him in Brooklyn, New York."[32]

During the Dodgers heyday, Brooklyn was Johnny pumps and spauldeens, double-feature movies, ring-o-livio and kick-the-can, singing doo-wop on the corner under a lamppost, or seeing a rock 'n' roll show downtown at the Brooklyn Paramount. There was Joyva Halva, the chocolate covered "sweetmeat" made at Varick Avenue in Williamsburg, Junior's cheesecake and Walter's egg creams. There were stickball games, the Bat-A-Way batting range in Coney Island, and the Dodgers.

A way of life, certainly; a religious experience, maybe; but life in Brooklyn without the Dodgers in the middle of the twentieth century was unthinkable. Hopes, dreams, and expectations were placed in the able hands of guys named

Oisk, Pee Wee, Jackie, Campy, Skooonj, and the Dook, and they didn't let us down. Even in defeat they taught us humility, courage and perseverance. So allow us to never forget where we came from, and let Dan Parker's words be a dictum for our reveries: "*Leave us go root for the Dodgers, Rodgers, that's the team for me!*"[33]

Appendix

Player Records: Brooklyn Dodgers 1953

Individual Batting

Name	GP	AB	H	HR	RBI	Pct.
Pee Wee Reese	140	524	142	13	61	.271
Jackie Robinson	136	484	159	12	95	.329
Duke Snider	153	590	198	42	126	.336
Roy Campanella	144	519	162	41	142	.312
Billy Cox	100	327	95	10	44	.291
Carl Furillo	132	479	165	21	92	.344
Jim Gilliam	151	605	168	6	63	.278
Gil Hodges	141	520	157	31	122	.302
Wayne Belardi	69	163	39	11	34	.239
Bobby Morgan	69	196	51	7	33	.260
George Shuba	74	169	43	5	23	.254
Rube Walker	43	95	23	3	9	.242
Bill Antonello	40	43	7	1	4	.252
Don Thompson	96	153	37	1	12	.242
Dick Williams	30	55	12	2	5	.271

Individual Pitching

Name	G	IP	GS	CG	W	L	Pct.
Clem Labine	37	110.1	7	0	11	6	.647
Bob Milliken	37	117.2	10	3	8	4	.667
Ray Moore	1	8	1	1	0	1	.000
Jim Hughes	48	85.2	0	0	4	3	.571
Carl Erskine	39	246.2	33	16	20	6	.769
Ben Wade	32	90.1	0	0	7	5	.583
Johnny Podres	33	115	18	3	9	4	.692
Preacher Roe	25	157	24	9	11	3	.786
Billy Loes	32	162.2	25	9	14	8	.636

Name	G	IP	GS	CG	W	L	Pct.
Russ Meyer	34	191.1	32	10	15	5	.750
Joe Black	34	72.2	3	0	6	3	.667
Ralph Branca	7	11	0	0	0	0	.000
Glen Mickens	4	6.1	2	0	0	1	.000
Erv Palica	4	6	0	0	0	0	.000

Chapter Notes

Preface

1. Monte Irvin with James A. Riley, *Nice Guys Finish First* (New York: Carroll & Graf, 1996), p. 144.
2. Peter Golenbock, *Bums* (New York: G. P. Putnam's Sons, 1984), p. 360.
3. Richard Goldstein, *Superstars and Screwballs* (New York: Plume, 1992), p. 329.
4. Carl Erskine, telephone interview, Anderson, Indiana, March 2014.

Chapter One

1. Donald Honig, *Baseball's 10 Greatest Teams* (New York: Macmillan, 1982), p. 117.
2. Donald Honig, telephone interview, 2014.
3. Dave Anderson, *Pennant Races* (New York: Galahad, 1994), p. 244.
4. Ibid.
5. Ibid.
6. Robert Creamer, "Subject: Don Newcombe," *Sports Illustrated* (August 22, 1955).
7. Ibid.
8. Joshua Prager, *The Echoing Green* (New York: Parthenon, 2006), p. 316.
9. Ibid., p. 317.
10. Donald Honig, *Baseball When the Grass Was Real* (New York: Simon & Schuster, 1975), p. 56.
11. Roger Kahn, *The Boys of Summer* (New York: Harper & Row, 1971), p. xii.
12. David Fury, *Chuck Connors: The Man Behind the Rifle* (New York: Artist Press, 1997), p. 45.
13. Golenbock, *Bums*, p. 304.
14. Ibid., p. 307.

15. Donald Honig, *Baseball's Ten Greatest Teams* (New York: Macmillan, 1982), p. 10.
16. Golenbock, *Bums*, p. 305.
17. Erskine, telephone interview, March 2014.
18. Al Stump, "Did the Series Make the Duke?" *Sport* (March 1953).
19. Roscoe McGowen, "Gilliam Glitters in Field," *The Sporting News* (April 8, 1953).
20. Roscoe McGowen, "If Campy Merits Orchids, How About Roses for Loes," *The Sporting News* (May 20, 1953).
21. Roscoe McGowen, "If Campy Merits Orchids, How About Roses for Loes," *The Sporting News* (May 20, 1953).
22. Golenbock, *Bums*, p. 62.
23. Roger Kahn, *The Boys of Summer* (New York: Harper & Row, 1971), p. 310.
24. Jackie Robinson as told to Alfred Duckett, *I Never Had It Made* (New York: G. P. Putnam's Sons, 1972), p. 63.
25. Gene Schoor, *The Pee Wee Reese Story* (New York: Julian Messner, 1956), p. 46.
26. Golenbock, *Bums*, p. 161.
27. Kahn, *The Boys of Summer*, p. 449.
28. Erskine, telephone interview, 2014.
29. Golenbock, *Bums*, p. 359.
30. Ibid., p. 342.

Chapter Two

1. Robert Creamer, *Baseball and Other Matters in 1941* (Lincoln: University of Nebraska Press, 1991), p. 7.
2. Elliot Willensky, *When Brooklyn Was the World* (New York: Harmony Books, 1986), p. 61.
3. Frank Graham, *The Brooklyn Dodgers*

(Carbondale: Southern Illinois University Press, 1945), p. 13.

4. Tommy Holmes, *Dodger Daze and Knights* (New York: David McKay, 1953), Foreword, p. v.

5. Andrew Paul Mele, *The Boys of Brooklyn* (Bloomington, IN: AuthorHouse, 2005), p. 10.

6. James L. Terry, *Long Before the Dodgers* (Jefferson, NC: McFarland, 2002), p. 9.

7. Ibid., p. 106.

8. Tom Clavin and Danny Peary, *Gil Hodges* (New York: New American Library, 2012), p. 3.

9. Ibid., p. 17.

10. Ibid., p. 20.

11. Ibid., p. 40.

12. Ibid., p. 134.

13. Erskine, *Tales from the Dodgers Dugout*, p. 42.

14. Gabe Verde, telephone interview, 2012.

15. Clavin and Peary, *Gil Hodges*, p. 154.

16. Marino Amoruso, *Gil Hodges: The Quiet Man* (Middlebury, VT: Paul S. Erikson, 1991), p. 58.

17. Ibid., p. 179.

18. Art Shamsky, personal interview, 2007.

19. Joe Pignatano, personal interview, 2010.

20. Ibid.

21. Ibid.

22. Erskine, telephone interview, March 2014.

10. Milton Gross, "Trouble on the Dodgers," *New York Post* (March 23, 1953).

11. Bob Luke, Bob, *The Baltimore Elite Giants* (Baltimore, MD: Johns Hopkins University Press, 2009), p. 125.

12. Gross, "Trouble on the Dodgers," *New York Post*.

13. Roger Kahn, *The Boys of Summer*, p. 176.

14. Arnold Rampersad, *Jackie Robinson: A Biography* (New York: Ballantine, 1997), p. 256.

15. Tot Holmes, *Brooklyn's Best* (Gothenburg, NE: Holmes, 1988), p. 92.

16. Ibid.

17. Erskine, telephone interview, March 2014.

18. Gross, "Trouble on the Dodgers," *New York Post*, March 23, 1953.

19. Rampersad, *Jackie Robinson*, p. 253.

20. Roscoe McGowen, "Gilliam Shifts into Second," *The Sporting News* (March 25, 1953).

21. Harold Burr, "Milliken, Podres, Mickens Keep Dressen Happy," *Brooklyn Eagle* (March 17, 1953).

22. Steven Michael Selzer, *Meet the Real Joe Black* (Bloomington, IN: NiUniverse, 2010), p. 45.

23. Ibid.

24. Dan Daniel, "Stengel Pins Five-Straight Hope on Pitching," *The Sporting News* (April 8, 1953).

25. Ibid.

Chapter Three

1. Charles Dexter, "Pennants Are Won in the Spring," *Sport* (April 1953).

2. Harvey Frommer, *Rickey and Robinson* (New York: Taylor, 1982), p. 42.

3. Carl Erskine, telephone interview, Anderson, Indiana, June 23, 2014.

4. Kahn, *The Boys of Summer*, p. 235.

5. Roscoe McGowen, "Another Starter First in Chuck's Man-Wanted List," *The Sporting News* (February 18, 1953).

6. Roscoe McGowen, "Brooks Land Extra Starter, Russ Meyer," *The Sporting News* (February 25, 1953).

7. Golenbock, *Bums*, p. 339.

8. Ibid., p. 340.

9. Ibid., p. 432.

Chapter Four

1. Joseph McCauley, *Ebbets Field: Brooklyn's Baseball Shrine* (Bloomington, IN: AuthorHouse, 2004), p. 36.

2. Bob McGee, *The Greatest Ballpark Ever* (New Brunswick, NJ: Rutgers University Press, 2005), Preface, p. ix.

3. Ibid., p. 85.

4. McCauley, *Ebbets Field*, p. 7.

5. Golenbock, *Bums*, p. 401.

6. James D. Szalontai, *Close Shave* (Jefferson, NC: McFarland, 2002), p. 311.

7. Ibid., p. 24.

8. Larry Freundlich, ed., *Reaching for the Stars* (New York: Ballantine, 2003), p. 118.

9. Ted Reed, *Carl Furillo: Brooklyn Dodgers All-Star* (Jefferson, NC: McFarland, 2011), p. 95.

10. Freundlich, *Reaching for the Stars*, p. 189.
11. Golenbock, *Bums*, p. 415.
12. Carl Furillo, Jr., telephone interview, Stoney Creek Mills, PA, 2010.
13. Reed, *Carl Furillo*, p. 10.
14. Ibid., p. 12.
15. Freudlich, *Reaching for the Stars*, p. 113.
16. Reed, *Carl Furillo*, p. 19.
17. Kahn, *The Boys of Summer*, p. 339.
18. Carl Furillo, Jr., telephone interview, Stoney Creek Mills, PA, 2011.
19. Clavin and Peary, *Gil Hodges*, p. 94.
20. Reed, *Carl Furillo*, p. 56.
21. Goldstein, *Superstars and Screwballs*, p. 359.
22. Reed, *Carl Furillo*, p. 48.
23. Carl Furillo, Jr., telephone interview, 2010.
24. Ibid.
25. Ibid.
26. Ibid.
27. Charles Dickens, *A Tale of Two Cities* (London: Heron Books, 1967), p. 1.
28. Golenbock, *Bums*, p. 284.
29. Gerald Eskenazi, *The Lip* (New York: William Morrow), p. 188.
30. Golenbock, *Bums*, p. 283.
31. Carl Furillo, Jr., telephone interview, 2011.
32. Reed, *Carl Furillo*, p. 174.
33. Ibid., p. 164.
34. Erskine, *Tales from the Dodgers Dugout*, p. 201.
35. Kahn, Views of Sport; Carl Furillo, 1922–1989 obituary, *New York Times* (January 29, 1989).

Chapter Five

1. Roscoe McGowen, "Dodgers Dashing to Big Theft Lead," *The Sporting News* (May 13, 1953).
2. Bill Veeck with Ed Linn, *Veeck as in Wreck* (New York: Simon & Schuster, 1962), p. 285.
3. Ibid., p. 296.
4. Ibid., p. 297.
5. Roscoe McGowen, "Jackie May Join in Parade of Dodgers' Left Fielders," *The Sporting News* (May 27, 1953).
6. Carl Erskine, telephone interview, March 2014.
7. Ibid.
8. Milton Gross, "The Emancipation of Jackie Robinson," *Sport* (October 1951).

9. Robinson and Duckett, *I Never Had It Made*, p. 5.
10. Ibid., p. 10.
11. Lee Lowenfish, *Branch Rickey: Baseball's Ferocious Gentleman* (Lincoln: University of Nebraska Press, 2007), p. 359.
12. Rampersad, *Jackie Robinson*, p. 120.
13. Lowenfish, *Branch Rickey*, p. 388.
14. Honig, *Baseball When the Grass Was Real*, p. 149.
15. Lowenfish, *Branch Rickey*, p. 373.
16. Frommer, *Rickey and Robinson*, p. 14.
17. Honig, *Baseball When the Grass Was Real*, p. 151.
18. Oscar Ruhl, "From the Ruhl Book," *The Sporting News* (May 6, 1953).
19. Joseph F. Drury, Jr., "The Hell It Don't Curve," *The American Mercury Magazine* (1953).
20. Ibid.
21. Ibid.
22. Ibid.
23. Erskine, telephone interview, March 2014.
24. Ibid.
25. Erskine, *Tales from the Dodgers Dugout*, p. 29.
26. Erskine, telephone interview, March 2014.
27. Glenn Stout, *The Dodgers: 120 Years of Dodgers' Baseball* (New York: Houghton Mifflin, 2004), p. 213.
28. Ibid., p. 214.
29. Dave Anderson, telephone interview, July 2014.
30. Al Hirshberg, "Restless on Bench, Dom DiMag Quits," *The Sporting News* (May 20, 1953).

Chapter Six

1. Al Hirshberg, "Milwaukee's Mister Strikeout," *Sport* (August 1953).
2. Duke Snider with Bill Gilbert, *The Duke of Flatbush* (New York: Zebra, 1988), p. 56.
3. Frank Graham, "Why Don't They Stop Knocking the Duke?" *Sport* (September 1957).
4. Al Stump, "Duke Snider's Story," *Sport* (September 1955).
5. Ibid.
6. Snider with Gilbert, *The Duke of Flatbush*, p. 70.
7. Henry D'Amato, telephone interview, Brooklyn, New York, April, 2014.

8. Aidan Gardiner, www.dnainfo.com, April 1, 2014.

9. Stump, "Duke Snider's Story."

10. Dave Anderson, "Snider's Catch Called Greatest," *Brooklyn Eagle* (June 1, 1954).

11. Ibid.

12. Ibid.

13. Snider with Gilbert, *The Duke of Flatbush*, p. 198.

14. Ibid., p. 255.

15. Ted Schrieber, personal interview, Brooklyn, New York, 2013.

16. Lee Congdon, *Baseball and Memory* (South Bend, IN: St. Augustine's Press, 2011), p. 7.

17. Snider with Gilbert, *The Duke of Flatbush*, p. 283.

18. Ibid., p. 13.

19. Milton Gross, "How Kluszewski Became a Hitter," *Sport* (August 1953).

20. Ibid.

21. Ibid.

22. Carl Prince, *Brooklyn's Dodgers* (New York: Oxford University Press, 1996), Introduction, p. xi.

23. Leroy "Satchel" Paige as told to David Lipman, *Maybe I'll Pitch Forever* (Lincoln: University of Nebraska, 1993), p. 172.

24. Veeck with Linn, *Veeck as in Wreck*, p. 183.

25. Paige as told to Lipman, *Maybe I'll Pitch Forever*, p. 183.

26. Veeck with Linn, *Veeck as in Wreck*, p. 183.

27. Ibid., p. 251.

Chapter Seven

1. Preacher Roe and Sarah Preslar, *When Baseball Was Still a Game* (Hardy, AR: Catalyst Apex, 2005), p. 102.

2. Snider with Gilbert, *The Duke of Flatbush*, p. 141.

3. Roe and Preslar, *When Baseball Was Still a Game*, p. 91.

4. Ibid, p. 19.

5. Ibid., p. 82.

6. Ibid., p. 60.

7. Ibid., p. 95.

8. Erskine, *Tales from the Dodgers Dugout*, p. 105.

9. Faust Sofo, personal interview, Staten Island, New York, 2009.

10. Ibid.

11. Ralph Branca with David Ritz, *A Moment in Time* (New York: Scribner, 2011), p. 63.

12. Holmes, *Brooklyn's Best*, p. 83.

13. Ibid., p. 84.

14. Ibid.

15. Roe and Preslar, *When Baseball Was Still a Game*, p. 64.

16. Kahn, *The Boys of Summer*, p. 421.

17. Golenbock, *Bums*, p. 335.

18. Ibid.

19. Ibid.

20. Kahn, *The Era*, p. 313.

21. Golenbock, *Bums*, p. XXX.

22. Ibid., p. 278.

23. Kahn, *The Boys of Summer*, p. XXX.

24. Ibid., p. 48.

25. Ibid., p. 88.

26. Ibid., p. XX.

27. Erskine, personal interview, 2010.

Chapter Eight

1. Golenbock, *Bums*, p. 298.

2. Ibid., p. 301.

3. Ibid., p. 301.

4. Kahn, *The Era*, p. 218.

5. Golenbock, *Bums*, p. 301.

6. Neil Lanctot, *Campy* (New York: Simon & Schuster, 2011), p. 292.

7. Bob Luke, *The Baltimore Elite Giants* (Baltimore: Johns Hopkins University Press, 2009), p. 44.

8. Roy Campanella, *Good to Be Alive* (New York: New American Library, 1959), p. 52.

9. Lanctot, *Campy*, p. 392.

10. Ibid., p. 423.

11. Ibid., p. 426.

12. Snider with Gilbert, *The Duke of Flatbush*, p. 155.

13. Rudy Marzano, *The Last Years of the Brooklyn Dodgers* (Jefferson, NC: McFarland, 2008), p. 111.

14. Ben Bradlee, Jr., *The Kid* (New York: Little, Brown, 2013), p. 366.

15. Snider with Gilbert, *The Duke of Flatbush*, p. 145.

16. Roscoe McGowen, "Too Many Hurlers? Dressen Will Find a Way to Use 'Em All," *The Sporting News* (August 5, 1953).

17. "Grammarian Rules Giants Is Dead," *Brooklyn Eagle* editorial (August 21, 1953).

18. Prince, *Brooklyn's Dodgers*, p. 12.

19. Marzano, *The Last Years of the Brooklyn Dodgers*, p. 112.

20. *Brooklyn Eagle* (August 31, 1953), photograph caption.
21. Tommy Holmes, "Makes Mistake in Unloading on Robinson," *Brooklyn Eagle* (August 31, 1953).
22. Ibid.

Chapter Nine

1. Dave Anderson, "Dressen—He Made the Second-Guessers Shut Up," *Brooklyn Eagle* (September 13, 1953).
2. Kahn, *The Boys of Summer*, p. 181.
3. Dave Anderson, *Brooklyn Eagle* (September 13, 1953).
4. Roscoe McGowen, "It's Hold Hats Everybody When Dodgers Celebrate," *The Sporting News* (September 23, 1953)..
5. Snider with Gilbert, *The Duke of* Flatbush, p. 137.
6. Ibid.
7. Graham, *The Brooklyn Dodgers*, p. 167.
8. Lee Allen, *The Giants and the Dodgers* (New York: G.P. Putnam's Sons, 1964), p. 11.
9. Ibid., p. 124.
10. Ibid., p. 125.
11. Ibid., p. 126.
12. Graham, *The Brooklyn Dodgers*, p. 155.
13. Allen, *The Giants and the Dodgers*, p. 164.
14. Eskenazi, *The Lip*, p. 229.
15. McGee, *The Greatest Ballpark Ever*, p. 229.
16. Rampersad, *Jackie Robinson*, p. 194.
17. Golenbock, *Bums*, p. 96.
18. Monte Irvin with James A. Riley, *Nice Guys Finish First* (New York: Carroll & Graf, 1996), p. 147.
19. Harvey Frommer, *New York City Baseball—The Golden Age* (New York: Taylor Trade Publishing, 1980), p. 160.
20. Eskenazi, *The Lip*, p. 252.
21. Dave Anderson, *Pennant Races* (New York: Galahad Books, 1994), p. 235.
22. Monte Irvin with James A. Riley, *Nice Guys Finish First* (New York: Carroll & Graf, 1996), p. 144.
23. Marzano, *The Last Years of the Brooklyn Dodgers*, p. 114.
24. Irvin with Riley, *Nice Guys Finish First*, p. 24.
25. Ibid., p. 144
26. Ibid.
27. Ibid.

28. Ibid., p. 145.
29. Dan Daniel, "Caseyt Clamoring for Clincher and Two-Week Coast," *The Sporting News* (September 2, 1953).
30. Dan Daniel, "Brooklyn and Not Browns Sought by L.A.—O'Malley," *The Sporting News*, September 2, 1953.
31. Roger Kahn, "Dodgers Win 100th Game," *New York Herald Tribune* (September 18, 1953).
32. Roscoe McGowen, Letter signed "Dodger Hater," *The Sporting News* (September 23, 1953).
33. Martin Gorst, *Measuring Eternity* (New York: Broadway Books, 2001), p. 239.
34. Robert W. Creamer, *Stengel: His Life and Times* (New York: Simon & Schuster, 1984), p. 54.

Chapter Ten

1. Harold Parrott, "Dynamic Larry Has Dodgers Smiling," *Brooklyn Eagle* (October 6, 1941).
2. Creamer, *Baseball and Other Matters in 1941*, p. 310.
3. Goldstein, *Superstars and Screwballs*, p. 276.
4. Andrew P. Mele, ed., *A Brooklyn Dodgers Reader* (Jefferson, NC: McFarland, 2005), p. 126.
5. Arthur Daley, "Sports of the Times," *New York Times* (October 1, 1953).
6. *Brooklyn Eagle* (October 3, 1947).
7. Goldstein, *Superstars and Screwballs*, p. xv.
8. Carl Erskine with Burton Rocks, *What I Learned from Jackie Robinson* (New York: McGraw-Hill, 2005), p. 8.
9. Erskine, telephone Interview, March 2014.
10. Ibid.
11. Erskine with Rocks, *What I Learned from Jackie Robinson*, p. 8.
12. Ibid., p. 20.
13. Erskine, telephone interview, March 2014.
14. Ibid.
15. Ibid.
16. Ibid.
17. Ibid.
18. Erskine, *Tales from the Dodgers Dugout*, p. 80.
19. Erskine, telephone interview, March 2014.

20. Erskine with Rocks, *What I Learned from Jackie Robinson*, p. 120.
21. Ibid.
22. Erskine, personal interview, 2010.
23. Ibid.
24. Red Smith, "Howard Ehmke," *New York Herald Tribune* (March 19, 1959).
25. Ibid.
26. Erskine, telephone interview, March 2014.
27. Smith, "Howard Ehmke."
28. Erskine, telephone interview, March 2014.
29. Smith, "Howard Ehmke."
30. Erskine, telephone interview, March 2014.
31. Editorial, "Dressen Used Wrong Judgment," *The Sporting News* (October 21, 1953).
32. Joe King, "The Deluge of Reese Mail Floods O'Malley," *The Sporting News* (October 28, 1953).
33. Scott Simon, *Jackie Robinson and the Integration of Baseball* (Hoboken, NJ: John Wiley & Sons, 2002), p. 42.
34. Golenbock, *Bums*, p. 367.
35. Red Barber and Robert W. Creamer, *Rhubarb in the Catbird Seat* (Lincoln: University of Nebraska Press, 1968), p. 289.
36. Bob Quinn, "Mayor for Day Tops Anderson's Salute to Erskine," *The Sporting News* (October 21, 1953).
37. Ibid.
38. Honig, *Baseball's Ten Greatest Teams*, p. 117.

Chapter Eleven

1. Tot Holmes, *This Is Next Year* (Gothenburg, NE: Holmes, 1995), p. 33.
2. Ibid., p. 106.
3. Maury Allen, *Brooklyn Remembered* (Champaign, IL: Sports Publishing, 2005), p. 182.
4. Holmes, *Dodger Daze and Knights*, p. 175.
5. Dave Anderson, "Remembering the Day That Next Year Arrived," *New York Times* (October 4, 2005).
6. Robert E. Murphy, *After Many a Summer* (New York: Union Square Press, 2009), p. 49.
7. Ibid., p. 44.
8. Russel J. Birch, "Veeck Now Ogling 'Frisco for Browns' Shift, Coast Hears," *The Sporting News* (September 2, 1953).

9. Frank Finch, "Veeck's Westward Ho! Project Stirs Fans," *The Sporting News* (September 2, 1953).
10. Veeck with Linn, *Veeck as in Wreck*, p. 371.
11. Dick Young, "Young Ideas," *New York Daily News* (April 23, 1957).
12. Veeck with Linn, *Veeck as in Wreck*, p. 371.
13. Irving Rudd and Stan Fischler, *The Sporting Life* (New York: St. Martin's, 1990), p. 140.
14. Ibid., p. 140.
15. Veeck with Linn, *Veeck as in Wreck*, p. 371.
16. Ibid.
17. Golenbock, *Bums*, p. 439.
18. Veeck with Linn, *Veeck as in Wreck*, p. 371.
19. Robert E. Murphy, *After Many a Summer* (New York: Union Square Press), p. 288.
20. Golenbock, *Bums*, p. 407.
21. Veeck with Linn, *Veeck as in Wreck*, p. 358.
22. Golenbock, *Bums*, p. 447.
23. Dick Young, "Young Ideas," *New York Daily News* (September 22, 1957).
24. Golenbock, *Bums*, p. 443.
25. Anderson, "Remembering the Day That Next Year Arrived."
26. Pete Hamill, "Brooklyn Still Can't Forgive Man Who Stole Their Dodgers," *New York Daily News* (August 10, 1979).

Chapter Twelve

1. Red Barber hosted by Marty Brennaman, *From the Catbird Seat* (The VXYou Network, 1993).
2. Erskine with Rocks, *What I Learned from Jackie Robinson*, p. 135.
3. McGee, *The Greatest Ballpark Ever*, p. 184.
4. George Lopac, personal interview, March 2014.
5. Ibid.
6. Dick Young, "Young Ideas," *New York Daily News* (October 4, 1947).
7. Golenbock, *Bums*, p. 175.
8. Lyle Spatz, ed., *The Team That Forever Changed Baseball and America* (Lincoln: University of Nebraska Press, 2012), p. 310.
9. Ernest Lavagetto, telephone interview, Walnut Creek, California, 2010.
10. Rex Barney with Norman L. Macht,

Rex Barney's Thank Youuuu (Centreville, MD: Tidewater, 1993), p. 107.

11. William Marshall, *Baseball's Pivotal Era, 1945–1951* (Lexington: University Press of Kentucky, 1999), p. 163.

12. Tommy Holmes, "Yankees Nip Dodgers 2–1, as Shea Stars," *The Brooklyn Eagle* (October 5, 1947).

13. John Heidenry, *The Gashouse Gang* (New York: Public Affairs, 2007), p. 68.

14. Ibid., p. 189.

15. Ibid.

16. McGee, *The Greatest Ballpark Ever*, p. 148.

17. Marzano, *The Last Days of the Brooklyn Dodgers*, p. 145.

18. Honig, *Baseball When the Grass Was Real*, p. 241.

19. Marzano, *The Last Days of the Brooklyn Dodgers*, p. 83.

20. Rudd and Fischler, *The Sporting Life*, p. 95.

21. Ibid.

22. Golenbock, *Bums*, p. 186.

23. Red Barber, *1947: When All Hell Broke Loose in Baseball* (New York: Da Capo Press, 1982), p. 50.

24. Golenbock, *Bums*, p. 187.

25. Goldstein, *Superstars and Screwballs*, p. 309.

26. Rudd and Fischler, *The Sporting Life*, p. 86.

27. Honig, *Baseball When the Grass Was Real*, p. 230.

28. Robert Weintraub, *The Victory Season* (New York: Little, Brown, 2013), p. 196.

29. Erskine, personal interview, 2009.

30. Erskine, telephone interview, March 2014.

31. Ibid.

32. Ibid.

33. Charles Einstein, ed., *Third Fireside Book of Baseball* (New York: Simon & Schuster, 1968), p. 374.

Bibliography

Books

Allen, Lee. *The Giants and the Dodgers.* New York: G.P. Putnam's Sons, 1964.

Allen, Maury. *Brooklyn Memories.* Champaign, IL: Sports Publishers, 2005.

Amoruso, Marino. *Gil Hodges: The Quiet Man.* Middlebury, VT: Paul S. Eriksson, 1991.

Barber, Red, and Robert Creamer. *Rhubarb in the Catbird Seat.* Lincoln: University of Nebraska Press, 1968.

Branca, Ralph, with David Ritz. *A Moment in Time.* New York: Scribner, 2011.

Brown, William. *Baseball's Fabulous Montreal Royals.* Montreal: Robert Davies, 1996.

Campanella, Roy. *It's Good to Be Alive.* New York: New American Library, 1959.

Clavin, Tom, and Danny Peary. *Gil Hodges.* New York: New American Library, 2012.

Congdon, Lee. *Baseball and Memory.* South Bend, IN: St. Augustine's Press, 2011.

Creamer, Robert W. *Baseball and Other Matters in 1941.* Lincoln: University of Nebraska Press, Lincoln, NE. 1991

_____. *Stengel: His Life and Times.* New York: Simon & Schuster, 1984.

D'Agostino, Dennis, and Bonnie Crosby. *Through a Blue Lens.* Chicago: Triumph, 2007.

Dickens, Charles. *A Tale of Two Cities.* London: Herons, 1967.

Durocher, Leo, with Ed Linn. *Nice Guys Finish Last.* New York: Simon & Schuster, 1975.

Eliot, Marc. *Song of Brooklyn.* New York: Broadway, 2008.

Erskine, Carl. *Tales from the Dodgers Dugout.* Champaign, IL: Sports Publishing, 2004.

_____, and Burton Rocks. *What I Learned from Jackie Robinson.* New York: McGraw-Hill, 2005.

Eskenazi, Gerald. *The Lip: A Biography of Leo Durocher.* New York: Morrow, 1993.

Freundlich, Larry, ed. *Reaching for the Stars.* New York: Ballantine Books, 2003.

Frommer, Harvey. *Rickey and Robinson.* New York: Taylor, 1982.

Goldstein, Richard. *Superstars and Screwballs.* New York: Plume, 1992.

Golenbock, Peter. *Bums.* New York: G. P. Putnam's Sons, 1984.

Gorst, Martin. *Measuring Eternity.* New York: Broadway, 2001.

Gould, Stephen Jay. *Triumph and Tragedy in Mudville.* New York: Norton, 2003.

Graham, Frank. *The Brooklyn Dodgers.* Carbondale: Southern Illinois University Press, 1945.

Heidenry, John. *The Gas House Gang.* New York: Public Affairs, 2007.

Holmes, Tommy. *Dodger Daze and Knights.* New York: David McKay, 1953.

Holmes, Tot. *Brooklyn's Best.* Gothenburg, NE: Holmes, 1988.

_____. *This Is Next Year.* Gothenburg, NE: Holmes, 1995.

Honig, Donald. *Baseball's Ten Greatest Teams.* New York: Macmillan, 1982.

_____. *Baseball When the Grass Was Real.* New York: Simon & Schuster, 1975.

Irvin, Monte, with James A. Riley. *Nice Guys Finish First.* New York: Carroll & Graf, 1996.

Jacobson, Sidney. *Pete Reiser: The Rough-and-Tumble Career of the Perfect Ballplayer.* Jefferson, NC: McFarland, 2004.

Kahn, Roger. *The Boys of Summer.* New York: Harper & Row, 1971.

_____. *The Era.* New York: Ticknor & Fields, 1993.

Lanctot, Neil. *Campy.* New York: Simon & Schuster, 2011.

Leavy, Jane. *Sandy Koufax: A Lefty's Legacy.* New York: Harper Collins, 2002.

Lowenfish, Lee. *Branch Rickey: Baseball's Ferocious Gentleman.* Lincoln: University of Nebraska Press, 2007.

Luke, Bob. *The Baltimore Elite Giants.* Baltimore: Johns Hopkins University Press, 2009.

Marshall, William. *Baseball's Pivotal Era, 1945–1951.* Lexington: University Press of Kentucky, 1999.

Marzano, Rudy. *The Last Years of the Brooklyn Dodgers.* Jefferson, NC: McFarland, 2008.

McCauley, Joseph. *Ebbets Field: Brooklyn's Baseball Shrine.* Bloomington, IN: AuthorHouse, 2004.

McGee, Bob. *The Greatest Ballpark Ever.* New Brunswick, NJ: Rutgers University Press, 2005.

Mele, Andrew Paul. *The Boys of Brooklyn.* Bloomington, IN: AuthorHouse, 2008.

_____. *A Brooklyn Dodgers Reader.* Jefferson, NC: McFarland, 2005.

Moore, Marianne. *Hometown Piece for Messrs. Alston and Reese.* 1956.

Murphy, Robert E. *After Many a Summer.* New York: Union Square Press, 2009.

Ninfo, Bill. *Carl Furillo: Forgotten Dodger.* Bloomington, IN: 1st Books Library, 2002.

Oakley, J. Ronald. *Baseball's Last Golden Age, 1946–1960.* Jefferson, NC: McFarland, 1994.

Paige, Leroy "Satchel," as told to David Lipman. *Maybe I'll Pitch Forever.* Lincoln: University of Nebraska Press, 1993.

Parrott, Harold. *The Lords of Baseball.* Atlanta: Longstreet, 2001.

Prager, Joshua. *The Echoing Green.* New York: Parthenon, 2006.

Prince, Carl E. *Brooklyn's Dodgers.* New York: Oxford University Press, 1996.

Rampersad, Arnold. *Jackie Robinson: A Biography.* New York: Ballantine, 1997.

Reed, Ted. *Carl Furillo: Brooklyn Dodgers All-Star.* Jefferson, NC: McFarland, 2011.

Robinson, Jackie, as told to Alfred Duckett. *I Never Had It Made.* New York: G. P. Putnam's Sons, 1972.

Robinson, Ray. *The Home Run Heard 'Round the World.* New York: Harper Collins, 1991.

Roe, Preacher, and Sarah Preslar. *When Baseball Was Still a Game.* Hardy, AR: Catalyst Apex Publishing, 2005.

Rudd, Irving, and Stan Fischler. *The Sporting Life.* New York: St. Martin's Press, 1990.

Schoor, Gene. *The Pee Wee Reese Story.* New York: Julian Messner, 1956.

Simon, Scott. *Jackie Robinson and the Integration of Baseball.* Hoboken, NJ: Wiley & Sons, 2002.

Snider, Duke, with Bill Gilbert. *The Duke of Flatbush.* New York: Zebra, 1988.

Spatz, Lyle, ed. *The Team That Forever Changed Baseball and America.* Lincoln: University of Nebraska Press, 2012.

Stout, Glenn. *The Dodgers: 120 Years of Dodgers Baseball.* New York: Houghton Mifflin, 2004.

Szalontai, James D. *Close Shave: The Life and Times of Baseball's Sal Maglie.* Jefferson, NC: McFarland, 2002.

Veeck, Bill, with Ed Linn. *Veeck as in Wreck.* New York: Simon & Schuster, 1962.

Weintraub, Robert. *The Victory Season.* New York: Little, Brown, 2013.

Newspapers and Periodicals

Brooklyn Eagle
New York Daily Mirror
New York Daily News
New York Herald Tribune
New York Post
New York Times
New York World Telegram and Sun
Sport
Sporting News
Sports Illustrated

Index